Library of
Davidson College

A BANGLADESH VILLAGE

Political conflict and cohesion

A.K.M. Aminul Islam

A BANGLADESH VILLAGE
POLITICAL CONFLICT AND COHESION

A BANGLADESH VILLAGE
POLITICAL CONFLICT AND COHESION

A.K.M. Aminul Islam

Prospect Heights, Illinois

For information about this book, write or call:
Waveland Press, Inc.
P.O. Box 400
Prospect Heights, Illinois 60070
(312) 634-0081

Copyright © 1974 by A.K.M. Aminul Islam
1987 reissued with changes by Waveland Press, Inc.

ISBN 0-88133-297-6

All rights reserved. No part of this book may be reproduced, stored in a retrieval system, or transmitted in any form or by any means without permission in writing from the publisher.

Printed in the United States of America

To
Shahan and Salim

Foreword

Anthropology makes a major contribution, so the teachers of anthropology say, in allowing students to understand societies and cultures that are not their own in relatively detached and objective terms; once they learn the objective analysis of behaviour they can then use the same viewpoint in looking at behaviour in their own society. In practice the second step is a hard one to take. Few researchers even have produced significant anthropological studies of their own societies, and most of them, as for example Whyte's study of Italians in Boston have been of sub-cultures other than the authors'.

Dr. Islam's study of a Bangladesh village which he has known all his life is thus all the more remarkable. It is a deliberate attempt to use the concepts of anthropology to interpret and make explicit the structure of a society familiar to the author. In so doing he gives the outsider a deeper awareness of everyday life in rural Bangladesh, and also makes a significant contribution to anthropological theory.

In anthropology the earlier tradition of analysing political behaviour in terms of groupings, offices and roles was rejected by many workers in the early 1960's. They felt that such analyses were too static, based as they were on Radcliffe-Brown's definition of the political as involving "social control" and "the maintenance of social order." Instead, workers looked at conflict, and at the ways in which disputants combined or recruited followings to form factions. Yet the study of such processes has tended, in its turn, to become a static one, viewing conflict as continuous motion, going nowhere, with factions constantly changing their personnel but persisting in form.

Dr. Islam, with his longer perspective of history and knowledge of the people of Badarpur, has been able to combine both approaches. He has recorded the changes in the formal political organization of the village under the British raj, as part of East Pakistan, and as political consciousness built up towards the creation of Bangladesh. He has analysed the conflicts at each stage and the processes of village factionalism and decision-making. The result is that one can now see the relationship between changes in the formal organization and changes in the processes of political action. Increasing wealth and increasing flows

Foreword

of communication to villages, like changes in the procedures for election of parliamentary representatives, alter the process of discussion and conflict and modify the formal organization. Modification of the formal organization changes the nature of the political "game" and its processes. In this way national politics appears as the "formal organization" or frame, within which the dynamic of local politics is worked out. Neither analysis is static, with neither domain "determining" the other since both influence each other.

From Dr. Islam's personal history it is possible to see how he arrived at this recognition of the linking of national and local politics and how he came to phrase it in anthropological terms. By 1947 when Partition came to the subcontinent, he was a literate Bengali, fluent also in English and Urdu. His personal awareness of the association between Urdu-speaking and power in the new state of Pakistan, led him to participate in the struggle to establish Bengali as an official language, and to the deeper study of Bengali literature and history. The emergence of written Bengali literature in the nineteenth century, produced by a new educated class, and in opposition to the Urdu-oriented aristocratic class provided a parallel to the pre-1971 unease at the dominance of West over East Pakistan. Work on the early archaeology of Bengal then acquainted Dr. Islam with anthropology, and he proposed, as a student at McGill, to look at the nineteenth century movements and their modern rural counterparts as revitalisation movements. But back in Bangladesh and in the village the political processes assumed wider importance, reflecting in action and in the realities of land ownership and power the ideologies of the urban educated. His focus changed to the study of those processes, but he was able to retain the vision of the village as being in dialogue with the national political structure. Although all the fieldwork was completed well before the independence of Bangladesh, the study has needed only a postscript, as it clearly anticipated the nature of the fight for independence.

Dr. Islam's study shows how "relevant" a detached anthropological viewpoint can be, when informed by historical knowledge. It has been a rewarding experience to have been associated with the study's development.

RICHARD F. SALISBURY
McGill University

Preface

This is a study of the political processes in a Bangladesh village prior to the independence of the country which came on December 16, 1971. As early as the beginning of 1960, it was apparent that Bangladesh would separate from Pakistan; it was only a question of time. Village politics, at a micro level, reflect the national or macro-politics. Therefore, although most of the field material was collected before 1969, this study may be of interest today as illustrating trends which resulted in the independence of Bangladesh.

My research has dealt with contemporary social processes, and I have encountered several problems as a result. Many of my informants value secrecy, and often I had difficulty in getting data. I was in Badarpur more than a dozen times, and spent a total of more than three years there between 1954 and 1966. Because much of the material I have covered was current, I often felt the pressure of the legitimate demand that I show discretion and compassion. If this demand has not been satisfied to the extent desired, despite the use of fictitious names, I truly regret it. I did have the advantage, though, of having been able to interview personally the villagers involved, and also had the satisfaction of gathering materials which are not recorded elsewhere.

The village of Badarpur, which is, of course, not its real name, has interested me for a number of years. I express my sincere gratitude to the villagers; they were extremely cooperative and many helped me get accommodations and other services in the village. Special mention goes to the village doctor, because of the experience gathered in his dispensary, and to the student community of the village because of their assistance in collecting and collating data. Very special thanks go to my niece, Miss Saeqa Dil, who spent hours typing the entire manuscript from the scribble of notes, and to Miss J'Neanne Gregoire who typed most of the final manuscript.

It is not possible to mention all of the persons to whom the author of this volume is indebted. At Dacca, the capital city, I was helped by Mr. Kamruddin Ahmad, former Ambassador of Pakistan to Burma, who spent much of his valuable time discussing my problems; he gave me many valuable suggestions. I should like also to acknowledge

Preface

the assistance of Mr. Zahirul Alam, presently Senior Sub-Editor of the *Daily People,* who accompanied me during my field trip of 1966 and helped me while I was taking the photographs used in this book.

While at McGill University, Montreal, I worked closely with Dr. Richard F. Salisbury; his untiring advice and counsel is gratefully acknowledged. As a methodical and tireless field worker, his example inspired his students to emulate him. Much of the merit of this work is due to Dr. Salisbury's friendly, critical expostulation; errors of interpretation, however, are entirely my own responsibility.

I wish to thank also Professor Frances Henry at McGill University and George Spindler at Stanford University for their reading of an early draft of the manuscript and for drawing my attention to a number of points. They both helped me further develop my thinking and reshape the manuscript. I am also indebted to Dr. F. W. Voget who in 1962 initiated me into the field of Anthropology and who has helped and encouraged me all along. I am most grateful to my present colleague, Dr. Lawrence J. Cross of the Sociology and Anthropology Department of Wright State University, for all sorts of help while I was preparing this manuscript. Other colleagues in my department were also helpful.

Funds for much of the research described here came in the form of a research fellowship for 1966-1967 from the Center for Developing-Area Studies of McGill University. The Liberal Arts Research Fund of Wright State University enabled me to give this work its present form. Certain funds for expenses were also available from my publisher, even prior to submission of the manuscript; his enthusiastic support has been invaluable. For all of the above noted assitance, both financial and nonfinancial, I am grateful.

A.K.M. Aminul Islam

Preface, 1987

The first version of this book, entitled *A Bangladesh Village — Conflict and Cohesion: An Anthropological Study of Politics,* was published more than a decade ago in early 1974. Both scholars of South Asia and students of South Asian cultures have given me reason to believe that the work is informative, as well as comprehensive, in its theoretical orientation. Soon after its original publication, all the copies were sold out. Now I am gratified that Waveland Press, Inc. has made it available once again.

A Bangladesh Village is an ethnographic case study representing a portion of non-Western, specifically South Asian, cultures. The village has changed since the ethnographic data were collected. In the late 1970s, a sequel to this book was published under the title *Victorious Victims: Political Transformation in an Indigenous Society* (1978). *A Bangladesh Village* is written in terms of "ethnological present," a standard anthropological technique used by anthropologists for describing "other" cultures; hence I did not feel it necessary to detail the changes.

A Bangladesh Village gives the reader a basis for understanding South Asian and, more generally, non-Western cultures. In particular, it provides a glimpse of a Bangladesh village where the "social structure, cultural values and other universal categories of human behaviour" change, but very slowly.

For students of non-Western cultures, as well as for others who might ponder about the "present" situation in Bangladesh, a short postscript has been added, despite the knowledge that such postscripts have the tendency to become dated very quickly.

A.K.M. Aminul Islam

Table of Contents

Chapter 1—Introduction 3
   The setting 3
   Problems studied in this book 3
   Relevant literature 8
   Context of field work and the sources of information 12

Chapter 2—Locality and the Historical Background 16
   Socio-cultural history of Bengal 19

Chapter 3—Badarpur in the National Setting 31
   Demographic features 34
   Language and literacy 37
   Land in Badarpur 44
   Agriculture in the village 46
   Seasons 50
   Fishing 52
   Property ownership 55
   Religion and festivals 61
   Summary 63

Chapter 4—Social Organization 66
   Gushthis of Badarpur 69
   Marriage and selection of mate 78
   Religious groupings 83
   Occupational groupings 89

Chapter 5—Political History of Badarpur 96
   Pre-partition village politics in Badarpur 96
   Post-partition village politics (1947–61) 101
   Basic democracies systems 105

Chapter 6—Political Processes 113
   Situation of straightforward confrontation 113

Table of Contents

Situation of conflict using cross-cutting ties 124
Situation of conflict and outside links 136
Discussion 139

Chapter 7 — Village Politics and National Issues 142
1965 election from East Bangali National standpoint 142
Intermediaries between villagers and national parties 145
Reinterpretation of National Issues by the village 146

Chapter 8 — Summary and Conclusion 155

Appendix
A — *Note on Non-English Words Used in the Study* 165
B — *Glossary of Non-English Words* 165

Notes 171

References Cited 179

General Bibliography 183

Epilogue, 1987 193

List of Photographs and Sketches

	Page
1. Narayanganj is the largest river-port of the country	4
2. All items must be carried by head loads	33
3. Village School	38
4. A village girl husking paddy by having the cattle walk on the grain until it is separated from the husks	40
5. During the harvest time even little boys help their elders	41
6. Hindus have a cremation ground which is on the other side of the river	47
7. Farmers work from sunrise to sunset	49
8. A village lad carrying a head load of rice (crops)	51
9. Flood is a constant threat	51
10. Fishing for a living is not an honourable profession, but fishing for domestic consumption is quite acceptable	53
11. A village man fishing for domestic consumption	54
12. Fisherman's net drying in the sun	54
13. A typical village home, consisting of kitchen (center), living room (left), and bedroom (right)	56
14. Cattle at Kabir's house are either busy munching hay or remain standing with a sorrowful expression as they wait for Kabir's nine year old son Wadud to come and take them to the field to graze	57
15. During Idd-ul-Azha Muslim villagers will sacrifice a cow or goat and distribute meat among the poor	58
16. Every morning villagers cross the river to go to the market place	60
17. Traders gossip in a *hat* (market) before shoppers come	60
18. Villagers are poor, but happy	62
19. After having delivered goods, the boat returns with a hoisted sail	64
20. Rivers serve as the main highways. A loaded boat on to its destination	64
21. Idris Kabiraj (the traditional healer) believes that only the pungent odor of his medicine can control the supernatural powers that visit the village occasionally	87
22. Farmer clears his field, removing the dry straw by hand	91

List of Charts

		Page
Chart 1.	Seasonal Cycle of Agricultural Activities of Badarpur	52
Chart 2.	Gushthi *A* consisting of Three Paribars, Four Baris and Twelve Ghars	72
Chart 3.	Gushthi *B* Consisting of Three Paribars, Sixteen Baris and Thirty-one Ghars	74
Chart 4.	Gushthi *C* Consisting of Three Paribars, Nine Baris and Fourteen Ghars	76
Chart 5.	Farmer Paribar	77
Chart 6.	One Type of Marriage in Badarpur	80
Chart 7.	Change of Structure of Village Administration in Jampur Union	108
Chart 8.	Election: Participants and Elected Members	110

List of Maps

	Page
1. India After Partition (As of Aug. 15, 1947)	1
2. Bangladesh and Her Divisional Boundaries	1
3. Dacca Division and District Boundaries	30
4. Dacca District, Narayanganj Subdivision	30
5. Village Badarpur and Its Surroundings	35
6. Para and Constitutional Boundaries of Badarpur	95

List of Cases

		Page
Case 1.	Awal and the Trader	114
Case 2.	Grazing Rights in the School Yard	115
Case 3.	Case of the Flood Victims	116
Case 4.	Hafez Abul Basir vs. Karim	117
Case 5.	Man Without Gushthi Support	119
Case 6.	Conflict and Cohesion in the Gushthi	124
Case 7.	Majhab Conflict	129
Case 8.	Case of the School Renovation	130
Case 9.	Case of Two Bhairas	130
Case 10.	Case of the Political Marriage	131
Case 11.	Karim and His Several Wives	133
Case 12.	Story of Four Friends	134
Case 13.	Hadudu Game	136
Case 14.	The Emergence of Gafur	138
Case 15.	Fence Around the River	152

List of Tables

		Page
Table 1.	University Graduates in India (1857–1882, by Province)	25
Table 2.	Village Badarpur in the National Administrative Structure	32
Table 3.	Badarpur in Relation to a Few Other Villages of Jampur Union	36
Table 4.	Occupational Groups Living in Badarpur with Numbers of Household Heads and Size of the Domestic Groups	36
Table 5.	Level of Schooling in Badarpur and the Number of Literates per Household	39
Table 6.	Percentage of Literacy in the District of Dacca, According to Various Census	43
Table 7.	Percentage of Literacy Among Communities, Total Population of Each Community 100%	43
Table 8.	Languages Commonly Spoken in Pakistan	43
Table 9.	Population of Badarpur and Its Landholding Composition and Occupation	45
Table 10.	Acreage and Production of Principal Crops in East Pakistan	49
Table 11.	Locations of Marital Ties of Badarpur	79
Table 12.	Plural Marriages in Badarpur	80
Table 13.	Seven Marriages of Badarpur During the Years 1965–1966	81
Table 14.	Occupation and Social Organization in Badarpur	92

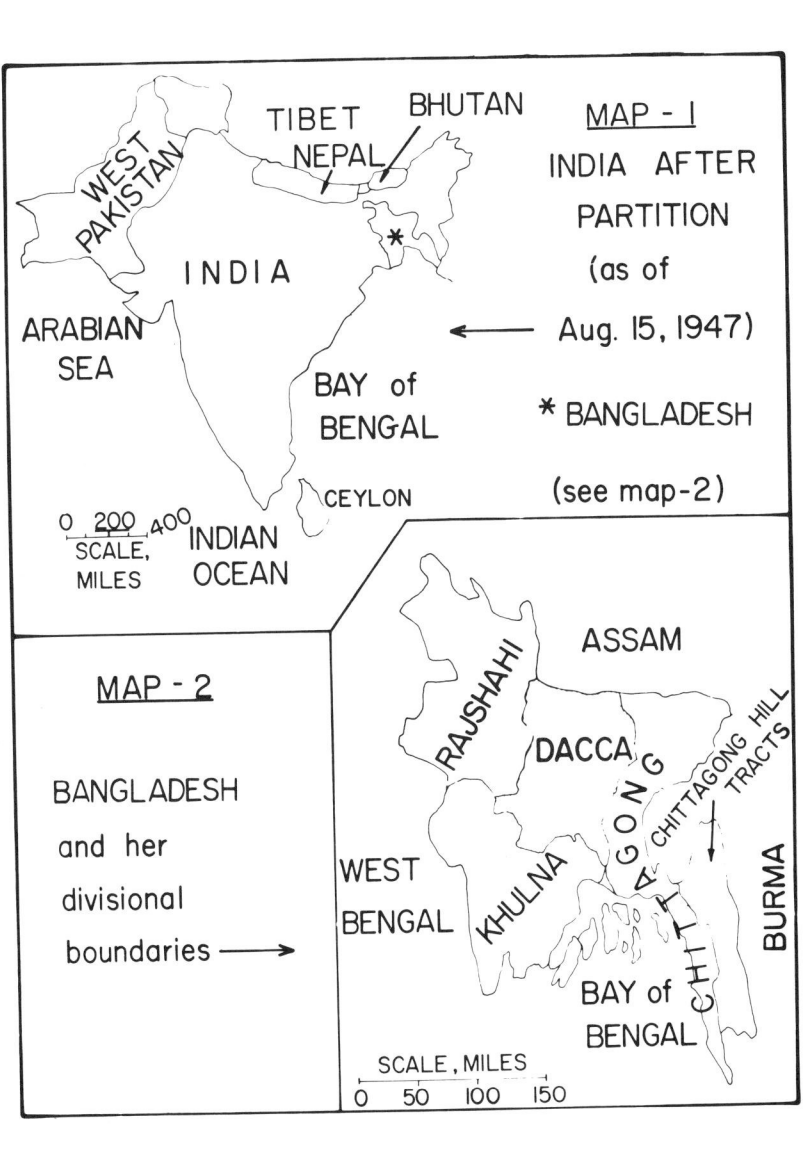

CHAPTER ONE

Introduction

The purpose of this study is to analyse the process of change in a particular East Bengali village and the manner in which it relates to the process of change in the wider community and in the country as a whole. The study will also attempt to show how the "national ideology" is reflected in the political behaviour of village people. More concretely, the study will show how and why political loyalties in the village vary from one situation to another, and the effect of governmental or nation-directed policy on the local polity.

The Setting

Badarpur, the village selected, is situated within sixteen miles of the capital city of Bangladesh, Dacca, and only six miles from Narayanganj, the largest riverport of the country (photo no. 1). I have been familiar with this village for years, speak the villagers' language, and understand their dialect. My reasons for selecting this village for study can be stated thus: The society's retention of traditional organization, even though it lives in close proximity to an urban center; the society's characteristic role of intermediary with its underlying conflict between nation-directed policy and village parochialism; the society's acute rural and urban gap, accompanied by a distinct conflict between emergent and traditional leadership; the society's ability to be taken as typical of Bengali villages, showing a continuum of socio-political changes that are taking place in rural Bangladesh.

Still more important than the reasons mentioned above, on various occasions in the past, even when I had not yet been introduced to anthropological methods and techniques, I wrote on the life and practices of these village people in Bengali periodicals. My anthropological training only added impetus to my enthusiasm about the people of Badarpur.

Problems Studied In This Book

Shifting loyalties of individuals have been studied in the past by scholars who have shown effectively that each individual is some-

4 A Bangladesh Village

Photo no. 1. Narayanganj is the largest river-port of the country.

what unique; his pattern of group affiliation is never exactly the same as that of any other individual. Merton and others have successfully shown in their "reference group theory" (1964) that the individual defines his situation in reference to groups of social categories, and in so doing distinguishes himself from the other individuals, even though in actuality he may belong to the same groups. This is the situation which Simmel notes as the individual "standing at the intersection of social circles" (Wolff and Bendix, 1964).

Group affiliation in Badarpur, as well as the pattern of shifting loyalties resulting from changes in the political structure of the country, is the subject matter of this book. It has been argued that the individual villagers, as well as kin groups, with their existing cognitive structure of kinship, religion and affiliation to village factions, select individuals of whom they approve and so help to restructure the village factions. It is also argued that on the national level there are political parties manifestly trying either to capitalize on religious feelings or to keep religion out of government and politics. On the village level there is continuous tension between "groups" clinging to tradition and between groups aiming at modernization. Both splits involve villagers in politicking between and within groups. Not only is traditional authority now being challenged by the new emerging leaders, but the shift of loyalties is also significantly related to family and other primary bonds, all of which are instrumental in changing the power structure of Badarpur.

Now, to deal with such a problem, it is necessary to define a few concepts which have been used throughout this book. We turn first to the term "politics," since the political processes of a single village form the foundation of this study. Swartz, Turner and Tuden (1966:4) may be quoted here: "Politics, *as a concept* [italics are mine], is almost as difficult to define as it is easy to use as a description of occurrences within societies and their constituent parts." Similarly, Easton (1953: 94) remarked, quoting Bentley (1949:199): "Who likes may snip verbal definitions (like paper dolls) in his old age, when his world has gone crackly and dry." Yet, politics has been defined a number of times, by a number of social scientists. Harold Lasswell's aphoristic definition of politics as *Who gets what, when, how* (1958) approaches the crux of the matter and casually takes in all of economics on the way. According to the dictionary, politics refers to "the organization or action of individuals, parties, or interests that seek to control the appointment or action of those who manage the affairs of a state" (Webster, 1961:654). But in this definition, the assumption of the existence of a state makes it rather difficult for anthropologists to carry it to a further use at a micro-level.

Swartz, Turner and Tuden (1966:4) note three generally accepted features of politics: that it is public rather than private, that it always involves public goals, and that it involves the use of power. Power has been defined by Bailey (1960:10) as command over resources and control over men. Consistent with these definitions, Nicholas (1965:28) has regarded politics as "organized conflict about the use of public power." In a study of factions, however, it is not always clear how much of the leader's power is public and how much is private. In fact, to quote Lasswell again (1931:51), "A faction seems to subordinate the public goal to private gain." Swartz, Turner and Tuden also state "individual, private goals will always be importantly involved" (p. 4). Private power, more specifically, refers to control over kinsmen, members of the same sect, etc. Since this private power becomes public power when it controls voting behaviour, it is public power that is most significant even in factional politics. Thus politics in this book will be regarded as a "struggle for power," as a process by which men set the conditions of their common alliances, thus helping to create a stable and enduring system.

Secondly, the word "conflict" has been used in this book as it is defined by Coser and by Beals and Siegel. Coser (1956:201) pointed out that conflict takes place due to the existence of scarce goods and that ". . . if within any social structure, there exists an excess of claimants over opportunities for adequate reward, there arises strain and conflict." Beals and Siegel (1966:18), going beyond Coser, insisted that scarce goods are responsible not only for the development of conflict but also for the development of cooperation. In fact, these two authors have divided conflict into a number of types and sub-types and have concluded that "actually, regressive mechanisms are brought into play at every stage as escalation in scope occurs." Turner wrote (1957:91):

> On a number of occasions during my field work I became aware of marked disturbances in the social life of the particular group I happened to be studying at the time. The whole group might be radically cloven into two conflicting functions; the quarreling parties might compromise some but not all of its members, or disputes might be merely interpersonal in character. Disturbance in short had a variable range of social inclusiveness.

How conflict occurs in the village and how decisions are reached despite the conflict is depicted in chapter six in a series of case studies.

Political conflict in the village was not the only thing studied. The overall trends of change which took place at various institutional levels of the village as a result of the struggle for power were also examined.[1] This work is not restricted to the classification of structure, but extends to show how existing structures are continually changing as a result of the inter-group and intra-group village factions, and conversely, how these factions grew as a result of social change. Hence, it is necessary at this stage to elaborate on and define the third concept used in this study, the concept of faction in political change.

Factions are characterized by Nicholas (1965) in terms of five distinctive features: (1) they are conflict groups; (2) they are political groups; (3) they are not corporate groups; (4) the members are recruited by a leader; (5) the members are recruited on the basis of diverse principles. Factions emerging out of social conflict, which is their *raison d'être,* are political groups in the sense that they organize conflict over the use of public power in certain kinds of society and institutions. Factions are different from other kinds of political conflict groups: they are not corporate groups. Nicholas maintains that membership in a faction can be obtained only through a leader, since the faction is not a corporate group and does not have an obvious single principle of recruitment. The diversity of principles on which recruitment of faction members is based is clearly noted by Nicholas. As examples of these principles he suggests kinship, patron-client relations, and religious or politico-economic ties. To this list could be added spreading rumors against one's opponent and political marriage, both of which are depicted in chapters of this book.

Students of factional politics have generally been interested in one of two aspects of factions: the organization of factions, or the nature of factional conflict. Some students have counted the number of factions, and have examined the way in which hostilities between factions are expressed. This text will study both organizational and conflict aspects of factions, and show how the factions emerge as a result of social change, how divisions are made between factions, and how factions organize conflict to facilitate social change.

This type of factional politics has also been studied by Bailey, who, in his *Caste and Economic Frontier: a Village in Highland Orissa* (1957) spelled out the significance of the village and the complex interaction of its people in different spheres of activities, all of which are interdependent. This complex interaction of village people in different spheres of activities constitutes a major theme of my study. Bailey in his later (1963) article "Politics and Society in Contemporary Orissa" showed also that there is a strong link between the traditional village panchayat and its modern successors. To understand the way in which the latter works, we have to know something of the former. Bailey's hypothesis is that "the energies of traditional panchayat members go largely into factional disputes, especially in villages where the dominant caste is numerically large in relation to other castes" (Bailey, 1965:15). In this study Nicholas's proposition and Bailey's hypothesis will be developed further by applying them to the situation of a Bangladesh village where there are no such caste groupings. It will be argued that, in the Badarpur situation, while the numerically dominant group is involved in factional politics, a numerically smaller group dominates the political "field," first because factional disputes within this smaller group do not have the effect of weakening its cohesion, and second because members of the group can manipulate other relatively smaller factional groups to their support while the dominant group is split due to their interfactional conflicts.

Bailey further states: "These factional disputes often cause total paralysis, and such panchayats appear as arenas where there is an endless disputation about decisions which are seldom taken, and, if taken rarely implemented" (Bailey, 1965:15). This study differs from Bailey by proposing that the factional conflicts of Badarpur do result in an effective implementation or rejection of decision. Also, these factional politics tend to polarize around the political parties of the country through a number of "brokers" who connect the parochial factionalism to national political groupings. Hence, it is essential to elaborate on two more concepts, political parties and brokers.

The definition of political party is as difficult as the definition of politics. It is somewhat easier to describe the processes of formation of political parties, particularly in a situation where national politics are playing an increasingly important role alongside the purely parochial ones, as has been described by Boissevain. Boissevain in his *Saints and Fireworks: Religion and Politics in Rural Malta* (1965) has shown that in Malta national political disputes swiftly become issues which divide the village, whereas in Badarpur (because they are not yet homogeneous), the social groupings are unable to coalesce with the national political parties. In Badarpur the "politicians" are still involved in factional politics, trying to utilize their own factional groupings to bring them into alliance with different national political parties at different times. In the Maltese village described by Boissevain issues have already become identified with political groupings. This shifting of loyalties to national political parties in Badarpur is only now beginning to follow along the lines of income, residence, occupation and religious belief. In other words, the national political parties do not have any definite followers in the village situation as there are no specific groups of followers to any particular faction at all times. Yet the villagers do tend to ally with some individual who brokers the two systems and recruits support from the villagers for the national political party that he supports in specific issues and times. These intermediaries who work as "reliable bridges" between the city and the country are the "brokers."

The concept of "broker" has been used to refer to individuals who occupy linkage roles between sectors of a society. These are labelled as "henchmen" by Fallers (1958), as "patronage" by Salisbury (1964), and as "brokers" by Boissevain (1965). Wolf (1956) suggested that this kind of articulatory role could be seen operating in individuals who related social elements which are unequal, where the elements linked were on different levels of society, and thus stood in relatively different positions of power. This extension of the concept has facilitated the conceptualization of the linkages between local levels of a society and the larger system. As important steps toward this conceptualization, chapter three describes the place of the village in the national setting, and chapter four shows the village social organization.

Relevant Literature

Contemporary literature on micro-politics organizes around "traditional" corporate groupings and relates factions and political processes.

For example, Gluckman (1955), when studying African tribal societies, pointed out that there exist some basic mechanisms of social control which regulate the affairs of the tribe and resolve conflicts that arise continuously among its component groups. He generalized that every social system contains forces which bring about equilibrium. In his own words, the most important among these mechanisms are "the inherent tendencies of groups to segment and then to become bound together by cross-cutting alliances." This he terms a "multiplex" relationship. The data collected on Badarpur also clearly shows the same splitting and binding together by cross-cutting alliances in the *gushthi*.[2] But the peasant community studied here, notwithstanding its multifunctional characteristics, differs from Gluckman's "multiplex" relationship, and the idea of multiplex relationship as a means of keeping "conflict and rebellion within bounds," does not properly apply. In the community of Badarpur, the village headman (if the Union Council Chairman can be counted a village headman), cannot be considered its religious as well as socio-political "head" by any stretch of imagination. Nonetheless, whether religious, economic, political or otherwise —disputes arising within the village are resolved by different leaders in different situations. In Badarpur, although there are groupings which constitute "fields" from which these various leaders recruit support, yet, since each villager has membership in more than one field resolution of conflicts does show Gluckman's "multiplex" relationship, thus making Gluckman's paradigm relevant to this study.

As a result of having multiple decision-makers for different problems in this village, frequently conflicts create schisms which help the villagers achieve the desired unity and continuity of the village. In this respect there is more resemblance to Turner's (1957) village than to Gluckman's. Turner studied a series of crises in a village over a period of twenty-two years. He recognized four stages in the development of social crisis in that village, where the successive breach of norms widened the village cleavages but where at the same time adjustive and regressive mechanisms still worked and the villagers continued the attempt to reintegrate the schism. Stability and continuity were perpetuated in the village life through conflict between traditional vs. modern and regional vs. national trends of change.

Orenstein (1965), following Gluckman, has also shown how cross-cutting ties bring about equilibrium in conflict situations. In a study of *Conflict and Cohesion in an Indian Village: Gaon,* he puts forth the hypothesis that conflict under certain conditions may function to maintain cohesion. Although Badarpur differs from Gaon in many respects, such as the absence of castes, the data from Badarpur would seem to support Orenstein's hypothesis. The difference lies in the fact that there is less closeness of fit between *gushthi* and faction in Badarpur than there is between caste and conflict groups in Gaon, since the factions are much more cross-cutting than in Orenstein's village conflict groups. Since each *gushthi* in Badarpur is sub-divided on many bases, such as sect, and since boundaries of kinship groups, sect groups and other groups do not coincide, factions in Badarpur do not help to strengthen lineage divisions in the way that conflict groups strengthen caste divisions in Gaon. Rather, factions put lineage divisions under tremendous strain.

The politics within kinship which may affect spheres beyond the kinship line on which this study centers has been studied by scholars in places outside the Subcontinent. These studies are rich in content and theoretical orientation. For example, Van Velsen (1964) in his *The Politics of Kinship* showed the whole complex of social life and how it was maintained and generated through the social network. Since kinship does not take care of friendship, he developed the concept of network which presented to him a multi-dimensional outlook. In the present study, the intricate arrangement between kin and non-kin is of particular importance. The disputes between these must be seen and interpreted not in isolation, but as part of the political and social process in the village. In fact, in Badarpur, in some conflicts, factions are based on the lineage structure (*paribar*) of the village. Each of the factions is composed of a nucleus lineage allied with certain other lineages or with important individuals who act as the spokesmen for the lineage. Even though these lineages are corporate groups, sometimes they utilize different constellations to create new factions.

Scholars of political science assert that political change comes from the national level, and they label the process political modernization. I wish to question this particular proposition since, as this case study will show, the people who in fact bring knowledge of the political institutions of the city to the country are the brokers who are involved and committed both in urban as well as in village life. Thus, we can classify three different types of brokers.

The first type of brokers are the ones described by Fallers (1956) in his *Bantu Bureaucracy*. Fallers shows that in the traditional system authority was organized by corporate lineage and centralized state structure. The two were antagonistic in that norms and expectations governing role behaviour and the exercise of authority differed for lineage and state organization. Fallers' brokers had political positions. This meant they were in tremendous conflict, since the villagers demanded "patronage" and the administration demanded efficiency. The application of the same individuals of incompatible but equally legitimate sets of expectations was associated with personal and institutional strain and instability. In Bangladesh, however, the men who have held administrative positions and from whom villagers expected patronage have managed to maintain local support as well as the confidence of the administration.

The second type of brokers, who closely resemble those described by Geertz (1963), are the traders and educated people of the village who may be considered as the cultural representatives of the national system working in a culture different from that within which they are used to operating. While these brokers may serve to make national traits available, they usually have no power themselves. They can offer the support of the local population to regional and national political figures only if they can then be sure that these figures will respond to their calls of need. Their actual control over either sphere depends upon their success in dealing with the other; their control on one level of articulation provides a basis for control on another; and to achieve their objectives they utilize cross-cutting alliances and disputes between various factional groups.

The third type of brokers, as we find in Frankenberg's (1957) *Village on the Border,* are the political party agents, students from the city, mass organization leaders etc. Frankenberg's material is particularly relevant as it shows how these outside brokers tend to become regarded as "outsiders," even though they play an important role in village politics. I hope to point out that these third type brokers are the agents through whose efforts the village conflicts that arise out of village parochialism and interpersonal politics might in the future become integrated with the ideological politics of the nation.

Finally, this study will discuss how in fact change is produced in the socio-political structure of the village and how different types of brokers are effective in the various situations I have described. The hypothesis to be examined can be stated as follows:

> First, Bailey's hypothesis regarding the numerically dominant caste group in faction disputes: The political field in Badarpur is dominated not by the numerically dominant kinship group, but by a numerically smaller group. This is because the cohesion of this group is less affected by intra-factional dispute than is the larger group, and also because relatively smaller factions can be brought to its support.
>
> Secondly, Nicholas's proposition that factions are not corporate groups: Since there are multiple decision makers for different prob-

lems, conflict creates schism which tends to maintain unity and continuity in Badarpur. In some cases in which the core of a conflict group is a *gushthi,* the faction is essentially a corporate group.

Thirdly, the effectiveness of the three different types of brokers in producing political change in the village: In making use of cross-cutting ties which maintain intra-group cohesion, they strengthen political factions which implement change.

Finally, Bailey's hypothesis states that factional disputes often result in situations where decisions are seldom taken, and, if taken, rarely implemented. This will be disputed, for when political decisions are made in Badarpur, factional conflict is not a hindrance, but rather a vehicle through which decisions are implemented or rejected.

Context of Field-work and the Sources of Information

Before leaving for Badarpur, I called on the District Magistrate at Dacca and the Sub-Divisional Officer at Narayanganj. From them I obtained two letters of introduction to the C.O. (Circle Officer) of the Baidyar Bazar Thana (Police Station). Although these were never used, they gave me a feeling of protection, for I knew that they could be of immense help if ever I were in any trouble.

On arriving in the village, my first visit was with the Bhuiyans, the only relatively rich family in the village. It so happens, that the house of Abdul Karim, the head of the Bhuiyan family, is situated in the southeast corner of the village where I had to leave my *kosha* (country boat). As I had already visited the village several times in the past without giving any indication as to when I would next be coming, Karim was not particularly surprised to see me. I told him that this time I would live in the village for several months and he seemed a bit curious, but did not question me.

After a brief chat and exchange of greetings, Karim offered me a room in his own home. There were several reasons for not wanting to stay there. First of all, I had planned to take a room in the center of the village, close to the mosque (where the maximum number of villagers congregate for prayers), from where I could easily get to the village *Hat* (market) (see map no. 5 on p. 35).

Secondly, previous experience in the village gave me the impression that many of the villagers would not feel free to talk (even amongst themselves) in the presence of Karim or in his house.

Yet, I did not refuse Karim's offer flatly; instead I explained that since I intended to stay in the village for some time, I would try to rent a place rather than inconvenience him by accepting his gracious offer. I assured him that it would be a privilege to live at his home if I failed to rent any other place.

Karim seemed to like my answer. He immediately invited me to come for supper that night, and I gratefully accepted. During the supper Karim introduced me to several other villagers (most of these I had already met) who were also invited, together with his assistant (clerk of the Union Council) who later became one of my steady informants.

The first night at the village was spent at Karim's home, but the following day I was able to rent a room in a Hindu home from which most of the family members had migrated to India. I was fortunate to be able to get this room since the house was situated almost at the center of the village, facing the *hat* on the other side of the river. I spent then almost a full day to get organized (to set up my improvised table and chair) and find a servant who could look after my things, cook for me, and work as a messenger. For this he received thirty rupees (almost six dollars) a month plus room and board.

Most people in Badarpur already knew me personally, and those who did not, knew me at least by name; hence I did not have to introduce myself. The first thing I decided to do was to take a census of the village. In this I was assisted by four village students and the Union Council clerk, together with a village schoolteacher.

The first difficulty I faced appeared while I was taking the census. Somehow several villagers had gotten the idea that my figures would help the government impose more tax on them in the future. Further, on one occasion an elderly villager challenged me, complaining that one of my assistants was asking the age of his daughter. Now it happened that this assistant was a prospective candidate for his daughter's hand and that a marriage proposal had already been sent to the bride's father from the groom's side. In Badarpur, as in all other villages of Bangladesh, a girl's age is not normally disclosed except to very close relatives. I had a hard time convincing the old gentleman that my assistant did not mean any harm. Eventually, however, I had to abandon the idea of getting the ages of the female population of the village.

I managed to gather some information by helping the village doctor. Every morning for two hours, 7:00 to 9:00 a.m., I used to work with Doctor Gafur, giving villagers treatment for minor wounds and occasionally administering injections. I was qualified to do this, and the villagers knew that in the past I had come to this village several times with medical missions during floods and epidemics. When I volunteered to help, Doctor Gafur gladly accepted my offer since he had been without an assistant for the previous three months. I carefully prepared a form where every visitor was to write his name, age, sex, father's name and number of persons in the family. Information collected through Doctor Gafur's dispensary later on helped me verify a good percentage of data collected by my informants while taking the census.

In addition to my seven assistants (four village students, one schoolteacher, Union Council clerk, and my own servant) I had other sources of information in the villagers themselves. Whenever and wherever I talked to them I tried to remember what was said and immediately on returning to my den tried to record it in my notebook. When people came to visit me at my place I always had a tape recorder on to record the conversation. Afterwards one of my assistants would write out the entire conversation from the tape. I used to go to every possible village gathering—social, religious or otherwise, and the specific methodology and techniques I used were as follows:

The first and the most important technique adopted in collecting information was participant observation. By participating in family, work, play, religious and various other activities, the information received was more reliable than that I was able to assemble through descriptions of the activities in question. There were occasions, however, when I had to rely on informants, since I could not make myself present in more than one place at a time; it simply was not possible for me to participate in each and every activity of the village.

Second was familiarity with the language and local dialects of the neighboring villages. This was a tremendous help; I was able to use it in getting at covert and implicit social patterns without the risk of misinterpretation or any kind of misunderstanding.

Third was the direct observation of behaviour. I distinguish this technique from the technique of participant observation because through it I was able to observe many ordinary and everyday routines of the people and their activities such as play, family life and ritual occasions where I was not necessarily a participant observer. In this technique of direct observation I was able to use my camera and tape recorder. Sometimes I found viewing of pictures and listening to tapes of actual speeches more valuable and informative than the field notes collected by my informants. Most of the time the tapes and notes were complementary.

The fourth technique used was interviews. I secured information by talking to people in various situations and by listening to and participating in conversations. Many a time this technique coincided with the technique of participant observation; but for my purposes this interview technique was of vital importance, particularly when I interviewed older people in the village to collect their memoirs. There were people in this village seventy-five years of age. By interviewing them and getting their life histories I was able to reconstruct their statuses and roles and see the process of change within the society described from the standpoint of an individual assuming them, learning them, and finally rejecting them.

As for the analysis of the data collected by these several techniques preference was given to the "Situational Method" in "Conflict Analysis" as applied by some of the Africanists. This was found to be the most suitable for the data. In this connection I quote from Van Velsen 1967 (140–143):

> By this method the ethnographer not only presents the reader with abstractions and inferences from his field material but also provides some of the material itself . . . when several or most of the actors in the author's case material appear again and again in different situations, the inclusion of such data should reduce the chance of cases becoming merely apt illustrations . . . a situational analysis pays more attention to the integration of case material in order to facilitate the description of processes.
>
> . . . situational analysis may prove very useful in dealing with this process of optation, that is, selection by the individual in any one situation from a variety of possible relationships—which may themselves be governed by different norms . . . relationships which they consider will serve their aims better. The particular relationships and norms selected are likely to vary in regard to the same individuals from one situation to another in regard to similar situations from one individual to another.

Since practically every one of the individuals in the case material appear in several case studies (Karim appears in fourteen cases, Gafur in at least seven, Latif in four, Zaman in three out of a total of fifteen cases) the possibility of biased data selection has been reduced; integration of the case material has been attempted in order to make the underlying political processes apparent.

CHAPTER TWO

Locality and Historical Background

Although the subject matter of this book concentrates on the search for power and the control of decisions within a single village, this power-seeking can only be understood against the historical and cultural background of a wider society which, from 1947 to 1971, was that of Pakistan as the unit composed of East Pakistan (previously East Bengal; now the independent country of Bangladesh) and West Pakistan (the union of the Punjab, Sind, Baluchistan, and North West Frontier Province, which retains the name of "Pakistan").

This union of East and West Pakistan gave rise to numerous difficulties. To begin with, the two regions were separated by over 1000 miles of foreign territory. This distance was not only responsible for obvious inconveniences in communications; it also symbolized fundamental differences in the origin of customs, outlook, economic conditions and political tendencies. Lack of a common language was also an extremely disturbing factor. Finally, inequality between the two sections in administrative power produced a tension which forced the eastern region to proclaim itself and emerge as the independent nation of Bangladesh.

The shape and function of Bangladesh (55,126 square miles in area) have been compared to an inverted funnel (Wilber, 1964:17). The major rivers, the Ganges and the Brahmaputra, flow in from the north and merge; they then fan out across the flat, alluvial country to form a delta with a complex network of branches emptying into the Bay of Bengal which marks the southern border of the country.

In the southeast, Bangladesh shares her border with the Union of Burma. The Bay of Bengal is on the south; and on all other sides she faces Indian territory. At the time of the division of British India in 1947, East Pakistan was carved out of the Province of Bengal. Hence, she is also known as East Bengal. Incidentally, a division of the Province into East Bengal and West Bengal was unsuccessfully tried out by the British between 1905 and 1912 "for administrative purposes."[3]

Present day Bangladesh also includes the Sylhet District of Assam, although the major part of Assam which is drained by the Meghna river is part of India. These areas include tea plantations and tropical rain forests inhabited by tribal people and wild animals such as tigers, boa constrictors and elephants. The Sylhet and Chittagong districts of Bangladesh are covered with forests, and make up a tenth of the land area of the country; the rest of Bangladesh is an unbroken plain. This plain has more than eighty inches of rain annually and is hot and humid throughout most of the year, December and January the coolest months. Early spring brings hot winds and dust storms, while from mid June until October the monsoons, blowing from the ocean, bring torrents of rain.

Apart from its peculiar geographical position Bangladesh as a whole is "homogeneous." When it was East Pakistan, it had 56% of Pakistan's total population of 120 million and used only one language. West Pakistan, on the other hand, with its 44% of the 120 million people, is "multi-national" and heterogeneous.

Due to differences in climate and other ecological conditions,* the life of the people of East Pakistan was completely different from that of West Pakistan in all its social aspects. Both the regions had their own distinct foods, habits, dress, housing, as well as racial consciousness and bigotry. To some extent the difference in topography between the monsoon plain of the East and the arid tract of the West is accountable for the development of different mental qualities and outlooks.[4]

Immediately before the division of India in 1947, East Bengal was a developing agricultural country in the process of industrialization, whereas West Pakistan had only a pastoral economy and a developing agricultural system. The agricultural products of East Pakistan were mainly jute, rice, and tea; until recently it was the only exporter of jute in the world.[5] West Pakistan had cotton, wheat, and maize. In foreign relations and trade, the natural affinity for East Pakistan was with India, Burma, Malaya, Thailand, Cambodia, Philippines, China, and Japan. West Pakistan traditionally traded with India, Iran, Afghanistan, Turkey, and the Arab countries. This difference in economic organization and products was bound to create special economic problems. The solution of these by the development of a common-based economic organization was the most important task shared by these two regions when they formed one country.

As to the social background of the two regions, there was also a

---

* In Pakistan, the temperature is extreme, varying between a high of 120° in summer and a low of 28° on winter nights. In Bangladesh the temperature varies from 102° in summer to 45° in the winter.

marked difference. The economic organization of the western region was based on a medieval semi-feudal system, whereas in the eastern region, the attempt by the colonial power in 1793 to impose a semi-feudal system through Permanent Settlement was resisted by the Muslim middle class from the very outset; East Pakistan, with its developed middle class was always socially far ahead of West Pakistan (where a middle class was just beginning to evolve). And the striving in East Pakistan for a more equitable distribution of wealth contrasted sharply with the rigid social system in West Pakistan which led to monopoly controls by the elite. The Bengali system of land tenure has thus always been in advance of that of the west.

Before the partition in 1947, West Pakistan, as well as other parts of northern India, supplied armed forces to the British Raj for about a century. Almost every family, poor or rich, derived some kind of benefit from the armed forces in the form of salary, pension, or other kind of reward. The West Pakistanis' pride in their strength developed into an illusion that they were the people in charge of defending the entire British empire. On the other hand, the Bengalis accuse the West Pakistanis in general and Punjabies in particular of being responsible for the delay of Indian independence; they feel it could have been achieved earlier.

Differences in religious organization are also important. While of all non-Hindu areas East Pakistan had the highest number of Hindus and of all non-Buddhist areas had the highest number of Buddhists, there was hardly any religious minority in West Pakistan. Islam, the religious faith for the majority of the people in both regions, was also treated quite differently. In the West, Islam came as a by-product of Middle Eastern Islamic expansion or, in other words, it was incorporated into the social fabric of West Pakistan by the sword. For East Pakistan, however, religious and spiritual leaders came directly from Arabia through the sea route; the conversion of the local people was a social and organizational effort that worked gradually through peaceful means. Consequently, the social aspects of Islam were more flexible and secular in East than in West Pakistan. The people of East Pakistan were devout Muslims, but they believed in religious toleration and peaceful co-existence of different religions in the same country. In West Pakistan, the social system, principally because of the feudal land system, was extremely rigid and most of the people were embedded in religious chauvinism.

With such sharp differences in the backgrounds of East and West Pakistan, the attempt to yoke together the two peoples inevitably led to growing discontent. The history of Pakistan since the partition of

Locality and Historical Background   19

1947 is a long, drawn out tension between the East and West which Khalid-bin-Sayeed (1960) has portrayed clearly in his book *Pakistan: the Formative Phase*. Many other writers have written on the subject. The more important amongst them include Smith, 1947; Symonds, 1950; Callard, 1957; Gopal, 1959; Campbell, 1963; Stephens, 1963, 1964; Tinker, 1963; Wilber, 1966; Wilcox, 1963, 1968. Instead of recapitulating what these scholars have already said I will describe briefly the socio-cultural history of Bengal which has not been sufficiently dealt with in English. I believe this will increase our understanding of the village we are going to study, and will help us in the following chapter to place the village in its national setting.

Socio-cultural History of Bengal

The early history of Bengal is extremely obscure.* There is hardly any archeological evidence to be used in reconstructing its past. It is only through the literary history of the country and through her mythology and folk-tales that we actually do know something about it.

> The earliest history of Bengal is shrouded in mystery. It is mentioned in the Mahabharata, *the Hindu religious epic, probably written or compiled 1000 years B.C. by a mythical Veda Vyas*, and already appears as a land comparatively free from social and religious orthodoxy. From the mass of legends, fables, and traditions which have come down through the ages, it is clear that Bengal was one of the regions last affected by the Aryan invasion.
>
> The Aryan attitude toward this borderland in the far eastern region of India is expressed in their description of it as the *Pandava Vargita Desha*—the land beyond the pale of Pandava (or Aryan) rule (Kabir, 1958:2–3). *(Italicized portion added.)*

Again, through the efforts of the literary historian we know that the Aryan penetration into this border land may have taken place circa 400 B.C.[6]

> The dialects of East Pakistan indicate the Tibeto-Burman influence in their pronunciation of the Aryan [gh], [dh], [bh], as stressed [g], [d], [b], *i.e. the aspirated voiced plosives lose their aspiration* and the palato-dental pronunciation of the Aryan pure palatal (Shahidullah, 1964:2–3). *(Italicized portion added.)*

---

* The word Bengal comes from *Bang,* the name of a people of Dravidian stock who were probably pushed out of their original homeland by the Aryan expansionists and migrated southeast to settle in the delta region of the Ganges and Brahmaputra. The Aryans used the word *Banga* to mean a territory where the Bang tribe used to live in the Vedic Era. (The "desh" in Bengali signifies country.) (Ahmad, 1970.)

After Chandra Gupta Maurya established his capital at Patna, soon after Alexander's invasion (300 B.C.), Bengal may have come under its influence. From the end of the rule of Chandra Gupta's able son Asoka the Great, until the middle of the eleventh century, Bengal was ruled by the Sena kings (who were Hindus) from the south.

Abul Fazal, a great historian of the Mughal Court of the Emperor Akbar, mentions one king, Sukh Sena (A.D. 1063), and from this time on there is recorded chronological history of Bengal. The last Hindu king of Bengal was Laksman Sena, who in A.D. 1203 was overthrown by Ikhtiar Uddin Muhammad Bin Baktier, a general of Muhammad Ghori.[7] For over five hundred years after that, Bengal was ruled by Muslims who always owed allegiance to the Pathan emperor of Delhi. In 1765 treaties entered into by the British and the emperor of Delhi placed Bengal under the administration of the British East India Company.

As is to be expected, during the five hundred years before the British came, rulers and ruled came into close contact and, through interaction, made acculturation an ongoing process. This period in the history of Bengal is also of vital importance because the seeds of the Bengali language and literature (in the modern sense) were sown under Pathan rule. Before the Muslim conquest, Sanskrit was the language of the court as well as of the scholars, even though Bengali was the language of the bulk of the population. (But for outsiders, as the Pathans were, familiarity with the local language made local people and cultural patterns more understandable than did Sanskrit, a classical language; perhaps this was the main reason for the Pathans' patronizing of Bengali writers, and, thus patronized by the kings and courts, writers started pouring out their creations in the Bengali language.)

The Bengalis maintained the Bengali identity in spite of the conquerors and the Sanskrit introduced by the Aryan invasion. Towards the end of the sixteenth century, with the coming of the Europeans a new phase began in the history of Bengal. Until the middle of the eighteenth century, these Europeans in Bengal were primarily traders and lived there (as well as in other parts of India) mainly due to the patronage and favour of the emperor or the local rulers.[8] It was not until 1757, the year of the Battle of Plassey, that the traders became the rulers, and Bengal, Behar, and Orissa came under the direct control of the British. The last independent Bengali Muslim *Nawab,* Siraj-ud-Duallah, was defeated when his general Mir Zafar, and some powerful Hindu landlords (Jagat Seth, Umi Chand, Roy Durlav) betrayed him by siding with Clive. Even today, everywhere in Bangladesh and in West Bengal, if anyone shows any dishonesty and betrayal of faith, he is called Mir Zafar, the name having become synonymous with "treacherous."[9]

After the Battle of Plassey, the entire country gradually came under British subjugation. The efforts of the British were completed by a declaration of Queen Victoria in 1858, bringing the entire country under the British crown immediately after the "crisis" of 1857, which some people of the subcontinent call the First War of Independence.[10]

Although the impact of British administration in this country was always that of an external power with its main base and source thousands of miles away, this external influence did prove, paradoxically, much more far-reaching and effective than did many of the earlier large-scale immigrations by invaders. In the case of the early invaders, Bengal had always been the area last to come under authority and first to get out from under it (Kabir, 1958:23), whereas, with the British in this country, Bengal became the first victim, and thus became the centre for all socio-political and economic activities. No other part of the subcontinent was more deeply affected by the Western impact than Bengal.

A common saying even these days is that what Bengal thinks today, the rest of the subcontinent thinks tomorrow. The basis for this saying lies in the history of Bengal, particularly in her nineteenth century history. The Sree Rampore Mission College, established in Calcutta in 1789, was renamed Fort William College in 1801 and was the school where many of the renowned literary figures of nineteenth century Bengal received their initial training. As the intended function of the college was to train British civil servants in the languages, history, law and customs of the country the college's curriculum included the study of Bengali. This official recognition eventually influenced the progressive element among educated Bengalis, and encouraged the cultivation of the vernacular language.

Aristocratic Muslims of Bengal, however, did not yet attempt to take advantage of this new seat of learning. They were not only apathetic towards it, a group of them were even hostile towards learning Bengali, to say nothing of English. In other words, aristocratic Muslims, particularly the Urdu-speaking descendants of the former rulers, continued to use Urdu and rejected modernization and schooling. Yet, nineteenth century Bengal did evolve as the leader of the entire subcontinent both spiritually and politically. Since Bengal was the first to come under the British rule, it was first to think of ways out from under British domination. Ram Mohan Roy, as early as the first decade of the nineteenth century, started talking about liberty, equality and fraternity as political goals to be realized by the people. The "crisis" of 1857 started in Barrackpore, a few miles from Calcutta. The first president of the All-India National Congress Party, W. C. Bannerjee, was a lawyer from Calcutta. In short, until the emergence of Gandhi on his return from South Africa (in the nineteen twenties), Bengal supplied the intellectual leadership for the entire subcontinent (Islam, 1955:7).

The seeds of Bengali language and literature started germinating during the patronage of the Muslim Nawabs, rulers of Bengal; however, those Muslim Nawabs were subordinate to the Pathan-Mughal emperors of Delhi and so had to carry on their own correspondence in Persian and later in Urdu. Hence at an All-India level there was a tendency to down-grade Bengali in favor of Urdu, and later during the early part of British rule, in favor of Hindi. But despite all this, the Bengalis developed a sense of local identity and pride in local traditions and language to be observed in few other areas that have come under foreign control. Voget (1956) applied the term "nativism" to this local identity and pride, and distinguished three specific types, depending upon the degree of the incorporation of foreign cultural elements in the local cultural traditions.

Professor Voget was concerned with American Indians, who for a long time had been in the process of acculturation through contact with outsiders. Conditions in Bengal or in India have obviously not been the same as those of the American Indians, yet there are similarities because of political dependency. Voget suggests that people who, under alien control, take an attitude of critical appraisal towards the past may be labelled as Dynamic Nativists (Voget, 1956:250). After making critical appraisals, some of the members of such a group became social innovators. These "reformers" are identified as Reformative Nativists, and are often people who synthesize elements of the past with new elements. Finally, there are those who attain "a personal and social reintegration through a selective rejection, modification, and synthesis of the traditional and alien cultural components" (*ibid.*, p. 249) and they are dominated by feelings of deprivation and frustration, being essentially a *passive* group which Voget named as "Passive Nativists." These three classes of nativists are to be seen in many Bengali activities. Accordingly, Voget's terminology may also be used to differentiate three prominent literary movements.

For example, some Bengalis not only changed the tune of Bengali literature; they also tried as social reformers to direct individuals toward a new path, attempting to synthesize Western and Eastern thought. Thus they can be called Reformative Nativists (Voget, 1956).

Due to Western and specifically to English impact, Bengalis, particularly non-aristocratic intellectuals, for the first time became acquainted with the literature of different parts of the world and got to know of the world before the rest of India did. Bengali poets and essayists sought to give new shape to their traditional patterns which had been mainly stories and tales of gods, kings or kingly people; the new literary trend emphasized equality, liberty and fraternity. Ram Mohan Roy, the first to adopt the new approach, was followed by Modhusudan Datta,[11] and many others came forward to break the chain of bondage that had inhibited Bengali Literature.

The defeated Bengali Muslim aristocrats on the other hand, as they did not like the newcomers, were active and violent against any kind of westernization (the attitudes expressed by recent political parties toward national ideologies are similar to those of the nineteenth century literary groups toward westernization), and were also fanatics in religion. Using Voget's terminology, they may be conveniently classified as the Dynamic Nativists. These were the traditionalists in outlook and way of expression, more politically oriented than the Reformative Nativists. None stood out as literary artists probably because their objective was not to create literature but rather to express political views. They were well-versed in Arabic and/or Persian literature and had received their education mostly from private tutors, trained in theology. Their inherited money and property enabled them to devote their time and energy to the politics of the country with the hope that they would regain their political supremacy through revivalism.

As for the majority of the people, the villagers never came directly in contact with western ideas and thought since they were under constant pressure from the ruling class. They developed a passive attitude towards authority and merely accepted life. They became indifferent to a world which to them was a symbol of anxiety and incurable helplessness. Yet they loved their country, and would not leave the soil for all the riches of the world. To them, land (soil) was valuable; "you do not possess any land, but land possesses you, you belong to your land."[12] There was a group of writers in whose writings this attitude toward the life, hopes and joys, pathos and sufferings of the people was of particular prominence. But due to their lack of education and unfamiliarity with the changing world, these writers were not successful either in creating lasting literature or in spelling out a coherent philosophy. Turning again to Voget's terminology, this attitude can be labelled one of "passive nativism." The religious tales and lores emphasizing helplessness, misery and fatalism were absolutely contrary to the patterns of educated Bengali prose and poetry. As for the social background of these authors, they came from rural areas and never had any formal education beyond their village-level, traditional religious teachings. Within their own horizon they were respected as poets, and their writings fall under the category of folklore, if judged by ordinary literary canons. Even today, writers of this type cannot afford to live on their literary works and are working people, such as farmers, barbers, and grocers of the village.*

As can be expected, the far-reaching revolutionary changes that took place in the nineteenth century involved a number of social reform movements; they sincerely aimed at removing many social evils. It was a time of intellectual and social ferment and renaissance. "Reason and scientific judgment took the place of superstition and blind faith. Liberty and independent thinking overpowered rigidity and conservatism" (Bose, 1960:61).

The Britishers established a number of liberal arts colleges in the subcontinent which created a large number of educated people. In addition, this establishment of liberal arts colleges in India meant more poets and writers for the provinces. And between 1857–1882, a total of 3,248 B.A.s and 536 M.A.s were graduated in the whole of India. Table 1 shows the number of colleges in the subcontinent was sixty-five (twenty-two of which were in Bengal province).

With this cultural background, one might well ask why the Bengalis agreed to join the western Muslims in the creation of Pakistan. In order to answer this question we must return to the final collapse of Muslim rule and the gradual eclipse of Muslim modes of government which left the Muslim-educated people baffled, vexed and outraged. The Hindu literary castes who had at one time easily adapted themselves to the Persian language of the Mughals (Shahidullah, 1953:74), were able to adapt themselves readily enough to the English used by the British administration. But to the Muslims, Persian and Arabic were not merely a means of communication; these languages represent their religious and literary heritage.[13] For half a century Muslims largely remained outside the new western institutions of higher learning and to an increasing extent were unable to enter the higher grades of the administration. Gradually, however, it became clear to the more forward-looking members of the community that, as a consequence of their withdrawal, the Muslims had placed themselves at a crippling disadvantage, and that the formerly plain, submissive Hindus of the literary castes were well on their way towards controlling the new

* Although the working classes then, as now, included ninety-seven percent of the total population of the country, Bengal has long been able to claim the largest number of educated people of the entire subcontinent (See Table 1).

TABLE 1*

University Graduates in India (1857–1882, by provinces)

Provinces	B.A.	M.A.	Number of Arts Colleges
Madras	1,042	29	25
Bombay	456	62	6
N.W.F. and Oudh	156	38	9
Bengal	1,585	396	22
Punjab	45	11	2
Central Province	..	..	1
Total:	3,248	536	65

(Source: Gopal, 1959:22)

* The table indicates that Bengal had more than half of the total M.A.s of all India. Although Madras province exceeded Bengal in the number of arts colleges (twenty-five), Bengal with only twenty-two colleges produced over 500 more graduates than Madras. Bengal with the largest number of educated people was ahead of all other provinces in literary and all other academic activities, as well as in social and political life.

institution of government. It became recognized too that even if they made a determined effort to recapture lost ground, the Muslims would be at least half a century behind their Hindu counterparts in their ability to manipulate the British machine to their own advantage.[14] This led to the development of the All India Muslim League in 1906 under the leadership of the Aga Khan.[15]

The League itself did not grow into a mass organization immediately, and for all practical purposes, the Muslims of India remained without a political organization of their own. But whenever political settlements were made, Muslim leaders in the limelight made use of the League as representatives of the Muslims. The Muslims' interest in politics, at this time, however, was due less to desires for internal reform than to concern over the fate of Turkey during the War, and the Muslim community adopted an anti-government attitude over the Khelafat question[16] (Islam, 1955:21), which concerned the temporal power of the Caliph, the spiritual leader of Islam, as well as the Sultan of Turkey. Foremost in drawing the attention of Muslims to the dangers related to the fate of Turkey were the Ali brothers, Muhammed and Sawakat, whose fiery speeches helped crystallize Muslim community interests down to the village level.[17] Muhammed Ali even went in person to England to protest the Greek attack on Turkey as a direct violation of England's pledge, but was politely ignored. Jinnah, on the other hand, the leader of the Muslim league, was not interested in getting involved with Turkish affairs because they did not directly concern Indian Muslims. On his return to India Muhammed Ali preached that the Government of India, as a party to the peace treatises,[18] had trampled the Law of Islam underfoot and was an infidel government no longer to be obeyed. His influence was so powerful that thousands of Muslims in Sindh and Frontier shook the hated dust of India from their feet and migrated to Afghanistan. History records that there they were turned back and many of them perished on the way home (Islam, 1959:103). But all this agitation had been in vain; even the Turks, after their republic was established, repudiated the Khelafat movement (Islam, 1959:139). It had petered out because, in the words of W. C. Smith (1947:236), "it was a wrong ideology, romantic and out of touch with actualities."

After the nineteen twenties, when the Muslims of India began to polarize around the Muslim League and Islamic ideology began to crystallize in their minds, another political party became active in Bengal under its charismatic leader A. K. Fazlul Huq. In coalition with independent members, he formed a Muslim Ministry in Bengal with himself as the Chief Minister. This party was known as Krisak Praja Samiti (Peasants and Workers' Party),[19] which although active at a provincial level, was not very active in all-India politics. Fazlul Huq, most popularly known as Sher-e-Bangla (Tiger of Bengal) always showed a passive attitude towards any national issue (presumably because of his personality clash with Jinnah) after the Round Table Conference in which the Muslim League was involved. But as a humanist he perhaps did more for the welfare of the Bengali Muslims than any other single individual.

From the very beginning of this Muslim nationalist movement, the Muslims of the subcontinent had emphasized two main complementary points: that they were Muslims and not Hindus (Indians) and that they believed in Islam, which is not compatible with Hinduism. It is thus Islam, the religion, which overshadowed all the other cultural elements of Bengal and caused Bengali Muslims to group with the Muslims of the subcontinent in the demand for "Pakistan," while more Hindu Bengalis migrated to India. The prospect of majority Hindu domination in undivided India acted as the unifying factor for the Muslims under the banner of Islamic Ideology, and the result was Pakistan. Redfield said:

> A sense of common cause brings them together on a mutual platform to share each other's sorrow and sufferings, joy and happiness. The very pain of deprivation is the birth pang of new thought, a fresh teaching (Redfield, 1953:57).

This "common cause" was the fear of a Hindu majority and under the leadership of Jinnah it caused Indian Muslims to forget or to put aside all other regional problems to become integrated in the fight for independence.

The partition of 1947, however, arrived too suddenly; the people had not yet had time to consider the possibility of having a viable arrangement with the Hindus of the subcontinent. Similarly, they had not given sufficient thought to the tremendous problems of co-existence liable to erupt as a result of such a union.

It was only after embarking upon this union that so many of the regional problems which previously had not claimed attention gradually began to emerge. The Muslims of Bengal realized that the threat from the neighboring Hindu majority country had not been as pressing as they had thought. In considering the assets and liabilities of the new arrangement, East Pakistan felt that, as usual, it was the losing side: the lion's share was being reserved for the development of West Pakistan. Despite the fact that East Pakistan earned the foreign exchange, more jobs, factories, and industries were developed in West Pakistan, and despite the fact that East Pakistan constituted the majority not only with respect to population but also with respect to literates, West Pakistan had the greater control of the government.

Still harder to bear for the East Pakistanis, however, was the attempt to keep their Bengali from attaining the status of a state language of Pakistan.

In March 1948 when Quaid-i-Azam[20] first visited East Pakistan and pleaded for one state language,[21] Bengalis did not say a word; after all it was said by their beloved Quaid-i-Azam. But in 1952 after the death of Liaquat Ali Khan,[22] when Khwaja Nazimuddin became Prime Minister of Pakistan and repeated what Mr. Jinnah had said as to Urdu becoming the only state language of Pakistan, Bengalis could no longer remain silent and riots broke out.

Chaos and panic ruled the country for some time. Finally in October, 1958, Field Marshal Muhammad Ayub Khan took over the government with the help of his army. President Ayub Khan attempted to minimize the existing disparity between these two sectors. He increased the financial assistance for East Pakistan and tried to remove a number of the grievances of the East Bengalis. Although, at least from the time of the Ayub Regime, financial assistance was apparently equal for both East and West Pakistan, there were still a number of factors to trouble the Bengalis:[23] Equal assistance could not bring the Bengali standard of living up to the West Pakistani standard. Bengalis earned most of Pakistan's foreign exchange (by exporting jute).

East Bengal constituted the majority of the population. And West Pakistanis had far greater representation in the army and other governmental services. These grievances simmered in East Bengal and finally influenced election results defeating Muslim League in every election.[24]

In 1964 there was the first Presidential election on the basis of the Basic Democracies System,[25] and Miss Fatimah Jinnah, sister of Muhammad Ali Jinnah, having been persuaded by the Combined Opposition Parties,[26] ran against Ayub Khan. Although this campaign was unsuccessful, the message of the opposition party, mostly organized by Bengali leaders, was brought to the doors of all their countrymen.

The lives of the people and their ideas about Pakistani national ideology were changed. The new developments meant the end of the Muslim League in East Pakistan and the virtual death of the "national ideology" for the East Bengalis. The majority of the members of the Constituent Assembly from East Pakistan became critical of the disparities noted above as early as 1951.

By 1954 the Muslim League, the founding organization of Pakistan and the main preacher of the "national ideology," was little more than a corpse. Its nominees in the central and provincial legislatures were defeated. The newly-formed Awami Muslim League together with the Niazm-E-Islam and Krisak Sramik Party formed a ministry in East Pakistan. The Republican Party formed a ministry in West Pakistan, and a coalition of the Awami League and the Republican Party ousted the Muslim League from the Central Cabinet. Yet, this coalition in the central ministry could not heal the conflict between East and West Pakistan. Ataur Rahman Khan, a former Chief Minister of East Pakistan (Awami League) on March 19, 1956 said to the Constituent Assembly of Pakistan:

> As a matter of fact, I may tell you it may be a great weakness with me that I feel a peculiar sensation when I come from Dacca to Karachi. I feel physically, apart from mental feeling, that I am living here in a foreign country. I did not feel as much when I went to Zurich, to Geneva, or London as much as I feel here in my own country that I am in a foreign land.

As late as 1963, Robert Campbell could still write of Pakistan:

> ... Her leaders started with a traditional society—illiterate farmers of great ethnic diversity and political parochialism, people who had in common only Islam, and they have managed somehow to produce a national consciousness. They started with two territories a thousand miles apart, separated by an unfriendly India, and they have managed to hold these together as one nation (Campbell, 1963:3).

Obviously, we can say today that Pakistan did not "hold together." As a matter of fact, as we have shown, Pakistan faced an explosive situation right from the very creation of the nation up to its final complete breakdown in 1971. The conflict between East and West Pakistan continued simmering through the *entire* history of the country, and the effect of this conflict touched even the most remote villages.

Before turning to the main subject of this book, conflict and cohesion at the village levels as displayed in Badarpur, I shall first attempt to place Badarpur in the national setting and give an account of the various reports on land-holding composition, population density, language, census and ecology.

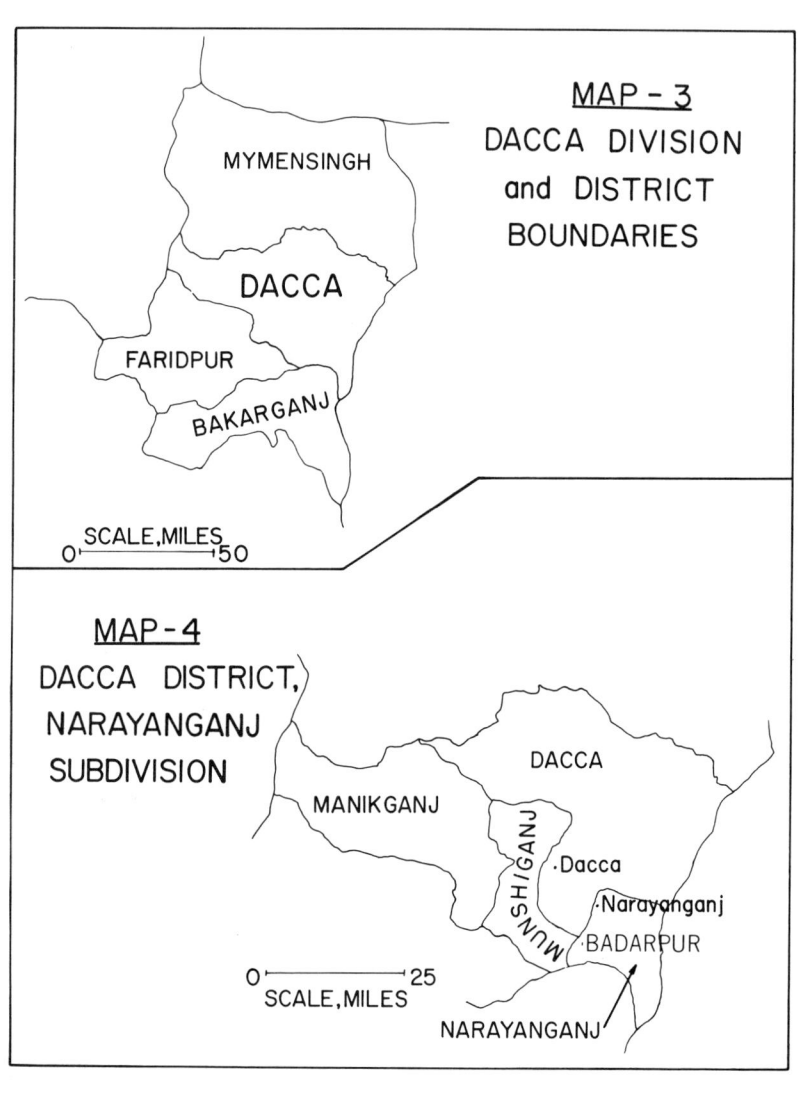

CHAPTER THREE

Badarpur in the National Setting

Badarpur has obviously been affected by the developments in Pakistan; but in its political life the influence of East Bengali culture and political set-up clearly shows through. This chapter spells out the culture common to Badarpur and to thousands of other Bengali villages, and shows the extent to which findings based on Badarpur can be generalized more widely to nearby villages and even to those throughout the country.

Badarpur is one of the 1,490 villages of Narayanganj sub-division of East Bengal. In many ways it is a typical village. It depends largely on its agriculture, and its inhabitants are rustic. They fit the common saying about Bengalis being candid and cordial but lacking in courtly manner. The rural temper of the village has been subject to gradual change during the last few decades, however, as the urban people began to take more interest in the countryside, and played a larger part in determining the pattern of village life.

Like all other villages, Badarpur forms part of a uniform national administrative structure. In this structure, villages are grouped together to form "unions"; several unions form a "thana"; and several thanas form a "sub-division." A number of sub-divisions form a "district," and several districts again form a "division." Five divisions make up the "province" of East Pakistan, now known as Bangladesh. On the following page, Table 2 illustrates this grouping, and shows how Badarpur village is part of Jampur Union, in the Baidyar Bazar Thana of the Narayanganj sub-division of the Dacca District of the Dacca Division. Narayanganj also is the name of the largest city, with important government offices only six miles away from Badarpur. It is the center of activity for the entire sub-division.[27]

Although Badarpur is only six miles from Narayanganj, communications between the village and the city are difficult since there is no all-weather road by which even a bullockcart can get to the village. There are no reasonably good roads within three miles of Badarpur and the village population is thus quite isolated; free movement be-

TABLE 2
Village Badarpur in the National Administrative Structure

BANGLADESH
- Chittagong
- Khulna
- Dacca
  - Mymensingh
  - Faridpur
  - Dacca
    - Narayanganj
      - Baidya-Bazar
        - Araihajar
        - Manahardi
        - Sibpur
        - Baidyar-Bazar
          - Alampur
          - Parabo
          - Kazipara
          - Jampur
            - BADARPUR
            - Kanchpur
            - Sadipur
            - Noagon
          - Burundi, etc. a total of thirty-three Villages
        - Jampur
        - Sanmandi
        - Mograpara
      - Rupganj
      - Fatullah
      - Narshingdhi
    - Munshiganj
    - Manikganj
  - Bakerganj
- Rajshahi
- Chittagong Hills

Narayanganj
- Pirizpur
- Shambhupur
- Raipur
- Aminpur

Baradi

Country ← Divisions ← Districts ← Sub-Divisions ← Thanas ← Unions ← Villages

Photo no. 2.   All items must be carried by head loads.

tween city and village is difficult. Over many years only a narrow path has been created by human and animal footsteps; articles of any size must be carried manually across land that is a knee-deep marsh. (Photo no. 2.)

The village extends for about a mile from south to north, and is cut in half by the path. In fact, the path goes through the center of many dwelling compounds in a zig-zag fashion. In the south the village fans out like a fork (see map no. 5), the densest population being in the most easterly branch of the fork. From east to west the longest distance is approximately 200–300 yards. This estimation, however, does not include the paddy fields which are mainly on the west side, with a narrow strip in the east, again extending from south to north along the stream which the villagers call the Brahmaputra river. According to villagers' testimony the main channel of the powerful destructive river, which now flows approximately thirteen miles northeast of the village, once ran right by the village. They still call the stream by the same name Brahmaputra (son of the God Brahma) and I shall follow their usage.

The houses in the village are clustered together in three major sections called *Uttar Para* (northern enclave), *Dakshin Para* (southern enclave) and *Nama Para* (low enclave)[28] with paddy fields distributed in the adjacent area surrounding the village. Sometimes villagers do include in their conversation a fourth section as *Maiz Para* (center enclave), taking part of the northern and southern enclaves together; but I could not find any consistency in their dividing line and in their usage. (See map no. 6 on p. 95.)

Demographic Features

Badarpur, like many other villages, is quite crowded and has a total population, according to my own census of July, 1966, of 2,101. This may be compared with the 1961 *Census of Pakistan* figures given in Table 3.

There are 383 households in the village, and Table 4 lists the occupations of the heads of these households, and the size of the domestic groups. It will be seen that most families follow traditional callings.

Agriculture is predominant, but there are also the traditional village occupational groups of barbers, weavers, fishermen, boatmen, and shopkeepers and a few landlords and priests. The table includes the two remaining Hindu families, one of which is that of a former Zamindar (landlord) and the other that of a tailor (in the table given above, the tailor's household is included in the households of the six shopkeepers). Before partition, however, there were about twenty Hindu families

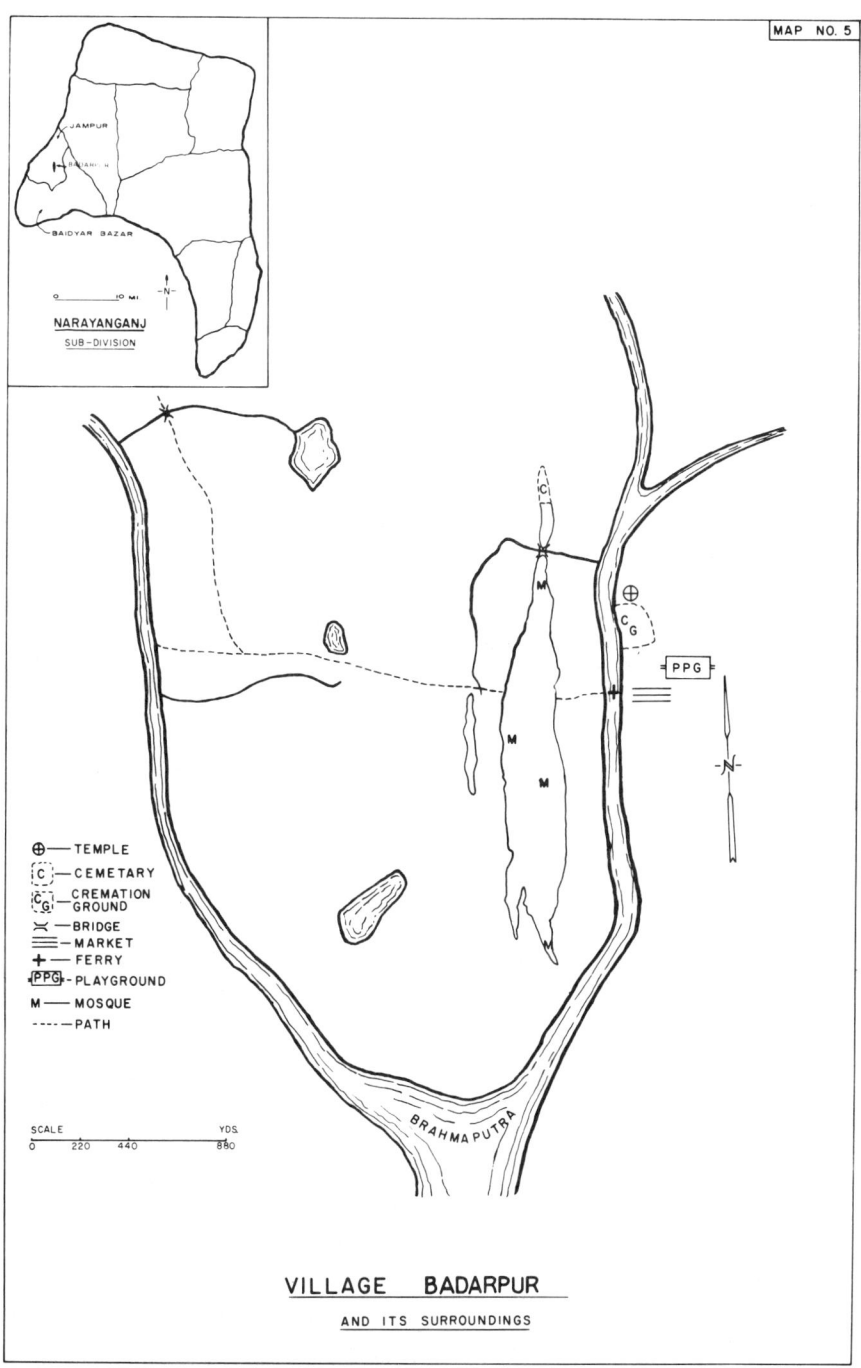

VILLAGE BADARPUR
AND ITS SURROUNDINGS

TABLE 3
Badarpur in Relation to a Few Other Villages of Jampur Union

Name of the Village	Area in Acres	Population in 1961	Male	Female	Literate	No. of Households
Burundi	391	1,914	1,006	908	200	368
Badarpur	520	1,786	991	759	175	346
Kazi Para	266	1,000	541	459	182	206
Alampur	28	89	47	42	4	16
Union Total	5,438	17,880	9,474	8,406	2,732	3,369

Source: *Pakistan Census,* 1961, Vol. 11:IV–67 (the village, however, is given under a different name).

mostly barbers, fishermen and of other occupational groupings. Only nine of the 383 families (households) pursue the "modern" occupations of teachers, officials or doctors.

Today it is difficult to reconstruct the position of Hindus in Badarpur before 1947. They had been very powerful, and all the Muslim villagers were subordinate to them. The two families still remaining never participate in any of the village functions and are mainly concerned with protecting their property—the reason they stayed on—and looking for an opportunity to dispose of it for a reasonable price. In

TABLE 4
Occupational Groups Living in Badarpur

Occupation	No. of Household-heads	Males	Females	Total	% of the Total
Landlord	2	14	12	26	1.237
Weaver	3	5	6	11	0.523
Barber	1	1	1	2	0.095
Boatman	14	17	14	32	1.523
Teacher	6	6	2	8	0.380
Laborer	20	36	37	73	3.474
Official	1	1	0	1	0.047
Doctor	2	3	3	5	0.237
Fisherman	1	2	2	4	0.186
Farmer	320	1,013	872	1,885	89.719
Munshi (priest)	3	9	7	16	0.761
Shopkeeper	6	14	13	27	1.285
Visitors	4	6	5	11	0.523
Total	383	1,127	974	2,101	99.990 (100)

spite of their position today, and the fact that they now live on the fringe of society, they still feel that they have high standing in the village. A number of villagers, when asked, told me about these Hindu families of Badarpur and how they used to treat the poor Muslim peasants:

> Muslims in this village always had to go to the market around the Uttar Para (Northern settlement of the village), although the market is in the central position (opposite side of the river), only because Biswanath (the Hindu Zamindar) did not like to see Muslims walk in front of his house.

Although they expressed themselves in this way, none of the villagers appeared, as far as I could observe, to have any suppressed feelings of hostility against this small minority. When riots and communal disturbances would start in the city or in the neighboring villages, the Muslims of Badarpur were even concerned about the safety of these people and would do everything possible to save them from the wrath of their hostile neighbors.[29]

The Badarpur population is one that has long ties with the local area: 381 of the 383 household-heads were born in the village, the remaining two immigrating with their dependents when they inherited some landed property through an affinal relative. Nine of the 383 household-heads actually live in the city for occupational reasons, but maintain a house in the village and every year, more than once, spend some time at their village home with their own kith and kin. All maintain ties with a household that they regard as home; all, that is, excepting the eighteen or so Hindu families which have left Badarpur permanently since 1947.

Of the dependent members of households, the majority have always lived in Badarpur, although about fifty per cent of the wives in the village were born in nearby villages.

Language and Literacy

In its school system and in its level of literacy, Badarpur was much like other villages of East Pakistan, where school education had never been the prime objective of the villagers' life in the past. During the British rule, and particularly at the beginning of it (during the end of the eighteenth and the beginning of the nineteenth century) all the Muslim leaders of the Indian subcontinent declared any sort of western education anti-religion and anti-Islam.[30] Thus the Muslims of East Bengal, and particularly the villagers, were very reluctant to send their children to school, and as a result the vast majority of the adults

38   A Bangladesh Village

Photo no. 3.   Village School.

in Badarpur are illiterate. On the other hand, due to local differences in the availability of schools or family ambitions, the degree of education actually found can vary quite widely.

There are two primary schools in Badarpur (photo no. 3), one for boys and the other for girls. In these two schools village children can study up to Grade five (previously they could study only up to Grade four, one more year of education having been added to the curriculum since 1964). The occasional exceptional village boy or girl who wishes to go further usually goes to a higher school three or four miles away. There he lives in a lodging house, and pays his board by working for the owners of the lodging house, or by teaching his younger children. For higher education the few who can afford it go to Narayanganj or even to Dacca. At the time of investigation for this study, there were four boys from Badarpur studying at Dacca and six at Narayanganj.

Since the partition of 1947, there has been a growing concern about education, even among the village farmers. Although many villagers need their children's help in farming (photo nos. 4 & 5) and in looking after the cattle, almost all now send their children to school, even

TABLE 5

Level of Schooling in Badarpur and the Number of Literates per Household

Type of Literacy	Number	No. of Households	Percentage of Total Population
Postgraduate	0	0	0
Graduates—continuing	0	0	0
not continuing	1+1	2	0.09
Intermediate—continuing	4	3	0.19
not continuing	2	1	0.09
Matriculation—continuing	14	10	0.6
not continuing	8	4	0.38
Middle (Grade VI)—continuing	50	35	2.37
not continuing	30	20	1.38
Primary—continuing	100	40	4.75
not continuing	51	25	2.42
Enrolled in primary, discontinued primary before completion or never attended, i.e. illiterate	1,840	375	87.577
Total:	2,101	*	99.95 (100)

* Because people of different literacy levels come from the same households the sum of the households does not equal the total households in the village.

Photo no. 4. A village girl husking paddy by having the cattle walk on the grain until it is separated from the husks.

Photo no. 5. During the harvest time even little boys help their elders.

if it means some inconvenience. However, most of the village children continue to go to the school only for a year or two and after that discontinuation is the rule.

To find the literacy level of Badarpur I recorded names and standards of education reached by all persons in August 1966. These figures are given in Table 5. The figures are somewhat higher than those given in the *Pakistan Census of 1961* (see Table 3). This would seem to be partly due to a real increase in the amount of education children receive in Badarpur, as well as to the failure of the census to include some of the better educated villagers who were temporarily absent.

Out of 1,840 listed under "Enrolled in primary, discontinued primary before completion and/or never attended primary," that is, illiterate, 165 (7.85%) boys and 75 (3.57%) girls, a total of 240 (11.42%) are presently enrolled in the village boys' and girls' schools as to the date of investigation of summer 1966.

At the graduate level of literacy I have indicated 1 + 1 because there is only one graduate in the village who received his Bachelor of Science degree from the University of Dacca in 1941. This man works at Chittagong (a port city approximately 150 miles east of Dacca) and only occasionally comes to the village to see his peasant relatives. The other is a licensed doctor who passed the final examination of the National Medical School,[31] having studied for four years after the matriculation. (Normally it takes four years to obtain B.A. or B.Sc. degree from the university after matriculation; this justifies putting the village doctor at the graduate level of literacy.)

It is interesting to compare the three villages, Badarpur, Kazi Para, and Alampur within Jampur Union, since they show how local factors can make striking differences in literacy figures, even among adjacent villages. Thus Kazi Para has a higher literacy rate than Badarpur or any of the neighbouring villages. If we compare Kazi Para with Badarpur we find that, according to the 1961 census (see Table 3), the former has 18.20 per cent literacy against 9.79 per cent. A group of traditional aristocrat families has lived in Kazi Para for centuries and teaching and learning has become a family tradition. The name of the village Kazi Para means "enclave of judges," and appears to reflect this tendency toward education. It is said that somewhere along the line in the past, during the Muslim rule, a Muslim judge (Kazi) migrated to this village and settled there permanently. The story may be mythological, but it indicates the long stand of the educational tradition.

The third village, Alampur, is a small village of eighty-nine people living in sixteen different households. The percentage of literate people in this village is only 4.29% (four out of eighty-nine), but this is an atypical situation. People of this village are all one- or two-generation immigrants from the neighboring villages (although none from Badarpur) and mostly consist of relatively poor people. The main reason for such a low percentage of literacy is that this village does not have any school whatsoever, and the village children either have to go to school in Badarpur or Kazi Para or they are introduced to the Bengali alphabet in addition to the Quran by the Moulvi of the village mosque. Since most of the villagers need their children's help for farming and other domestic work, only a few of them can afford to send their children to the mosque.

The figures for Badarpur can also be compared with those for the district of Dacca, according to various censuses, and for the whole of East Bengal or undivided Bengal. These figures all show a steady rise. Thus for the district of Dacca the figures since 1921 are as follows:

The figures for the whole of East Bengal show that increase in literacy among Muslims has been even more marked. A table from 1951

TABLE 6
Percentage of Literacy in the District of Dacca, According to Various Censuses

1921—	8.43	Source: *Government of India Census* of 1921
1931—	9.01	Source: *Government of India Census* of 1931
1941—	14.59	Source: As quoted in *Pakistan Census* of 1951—Vol. III:10
1951—	22.33	Source: As quoted in *Pakistan Census* of 1951—Vol. III:2
*1961—	20.15	Source: *Pakistan Census* of 1961, Vol. II:IV–67

* Definition of literacy in 1961 census is "Able to read with understanding." In the 1951 census it was "Able to read clear print," and therefore included persons who could read the Holy Quran without understanding.

gives us comparative percentage of literate people in undivided Bengal and in East Bengal which will be of some interest.

TABLE 7
Percentage of Literacy Among Communities. Total Population of Each Community 100%

Types of People	Undivided Bengal			East Bengal	
	1921	1931	1941	1951	1961
All Religions	9.11	9.36	16.30	21.11	18.85
Muslims	5.09	5.71	11.77	19.93	Not available
Hindus	14.17	13.97	22.97	25.28	Not available
Others	8.19	10.26	8.38	20.00	Not available

Source: *Pakistan Census Report*, 1951 Vol. III:111 and 1961, Vol. II:216.

Before the partition of 1947, Muslim literacy was even lower than the average figures given, while Hindus had a higher level. After partition a large number of educated Hindus left East Bengal, and many relatively well-educated Muslims immigrated to East Bengal. Now although literacy is still higher among Hindus, the increase in Muslim

TABLE 8
Languages That Were Commonly Spoken in Pakistan (Percentage of the Total Population)*

Region	Bengali	Punjabi	Urdu	Pushtu	Sindhi	English
East Pakistan	98.0	...	1.1	...	...	1.3
West Pakistan	...	64.0	15.0	16.0	13.0	2.5
Pakistan as a Whole	56.0	28.0	7.2	7.1	5.8	1.8

* Because some people speak more than one language the sum of the percentages is not equal to 100.

Source: *Census of Pakistan* 1951:11.

education has lessened the difference from eleven per cent to six per cent in 1951, and it is still decreasing.

Like the rest of Bangladesh, Badarpur is a unilingual village. Table 8 shows the national pattern of language used. (The two per cent of non-Bengali speakers in East Bengal are mainly city-dwellers, so that Badarpur being 100% Bengali-speaking is not atypical of villages.)

At the same time many Badarpur villagers can read Arabic without understanding it. This is a characteristic of most Bengali villages.

Land in Badarpur

Most of 529 acres of land around Badarpur are used for agriculture. According to my estimate only about ten acres are being used as residential areas, while two acres are covered by natural ponds, mosques and schools, etc., and the rest is used for cultivation. There is no *usar* (barren) land in this area. Because of acute shortage of land and grazing field, the village lads cross the river daily with their cattle. In the field adjacent to the market they play while watching the grazing cattle.

The land is alluvial, and most of it remains under water for three or four months every year. The flooding of the Brahmaputra during the monsoon has brought down clay and built up fertile soil, crosscutting it with canals and ditches in an intricate pattern. The soil yields rich harvests of rice, jute and other crops with a minimum of effort.

Land is the foundation of the economic structure. All the land is in the name of the head of the family, father or grandfather, if he is still alive. No son, even if he is married and has children, can claim any portion of land until the death of this head of the family. According to Muslim Law (Quranic Law, according to Sunna or Muslim Shariat Law) ancestral property must be divided amongst the members of the family in a ratio of two to one in favour of the male members of the family. That is, every son will get double the amount of property of each girl, and each wife (if one has more than one wife) will get the same amount of property as each of the daughters.[32]

Most of the households in the village consist of extended families whereby agnatically related males of several successive generations dwell together with their wives and children. Most frequently siblings, those who are not yet married, as well as some who are, will live together—at least until the death of their parents. After this event, as long as the siblings live together they will cultivate the land together and enjoy the produce in common. This joint ownership of their property allows them security in case of sickness or any kind of incapacity.

This common utilization of the landed property is an institution which ensures rights of equal share to all brothers, and enables the youngsters to receive education as a right during the period that the elder brothers are looking after the family.

Table 9 shows the distribution of Badarpur land among the households of different occupational groups. It can be seen that the occupational groups such as landlords, teachers, doctors, and visitors own relatively larger proportions of landed property in the village than the farmers and others. Out of fourteen boatmen only three households each have a plot of land where they have their own dwelling houses. They could be easily grouped together with the laborers who do not have any land for cultivation other than the land on which they have their own dwelling houses. Out of 320 farmer-households, only a few have more than an acre of cultivated land.

The only official of the village is a bachelor who lives in a room provided for him (against rent by one of the relatively wealthy persons of the village), and does not possess any land of his own. In fact, he is an outsider who lives in the village except when he goes to his own village forty miles away to see his relatives.

The few ponds of the village have been included in this table of landholding. In these ponds people bathe themselves and their animals

TABLE 9

Population of Badarpur and Its Landholding Composition and Occupations

Occupation	Number of Households	Landholding Acres	Total Number of Members
Landlord	2	23.00	26
Teacher	6	10.50	8
Weaver	3	2.00	11
Barber	1	0.50	2
Boatman	14	5.00	32
Labourer	20	3.00	73
Official	1	0.00	1
Doctor	2	4.50	5
Fisherman	1	0.25	4
Priest	3	2.25	16
Shopkeeper	6	7.00	27
Visitor	4	8.00	11
Farmer	320	462.00	1,885
Mosques & Schools (Public Property)	...	1.00	...
TOTAL:	383 (100%)	529.00 (100%)	2,101 (100%)

(often together), wash their clothes, catch fish, and until quite recently (1941–42) got their drinking water. Now nearby tube-wells supply drinking water, all other activities remaining unchanged.

There are several places in the village such as the places where the mosques village schools, and the burial grounds, are situated, which are considered as free property and no villager pays any tax for them. All these public places are from public donations. The Hindus of the village had a cremation ground (see photo no. 6), situated on the other side of the river, which is not included in these 529 acres of Badarpur. The same is true of the Muslim burial ground, which is situated outside the northern border of the village. In fact the geographical situations of both the burial ground (for the Muslims) and the cremation ground (for the Hindus), although very close to the village, fall in the realm of different villages. In the official records the village market, located on the eastern side of the river Brahmaputra, is also in a different union (see map no. 5 on p. 35).

Agriculture in the Village

Land in Badarpur can be classified into two categories: *Tan Zami* (raised land) where varieties of pulses are grown, and *Nama Zami* (low land) where *Aman* (a type of paddy) is the main crop. All lands, whether relatively high or low can produce rice. Jute is also widely cultivated, though less in the low lands. A small amount of sugarcane is grown by the banks of the canals, but the quantity is negligible.

Paddy is the principal crop. The three main varieties are (1) *Aman,* (2) *Aus,* (3) *Boro.*

Aman is by far the most important of the three and may be classified into two types according to the manner of its cultivation. One variety is broadcast and the other is transplanted. *Aman* paddy varies as to size, colour, and taste of the grain. It is a winter crop.

Immediately after the harvesting of an *Aman* paddy, the land is prepared for *Aus,* which is grown in raised land, since the plant cannot grow fast enough to remain above water when the water level rises rapidly, because of heavy and continuous rainfall or floods. *Boro* grows on comparatively lower lands on the rims of the bowl-shaped "beels" (natural ponds or lakes) and on the slopes of the river banks.

The cultivation cycle starts in the season of *Sit* or winter, during the months of November-January. After the rainfall following the harvest the soil is ploughed and left unplanted. At this time temperatures are low, though they seldom go down as far as 40°. Everything is dry and the village lads go out in the field to collect food grains left over in the village fields after harvesting. One of the most pleasurable pastimes

Photo no. 6. Hindus have a cremation ground which is on the other side of the river.

for the village lads is to collect food grains in the evening and to roast them around a central fire where they eat, warm themselves, chat and occasionally sing songs.

At the beginning of the first monsoon in March and after the harvest in winter, manure, mainly of cow dung and ashes, is scattered in the field, and the crops are planted by broadcasting the seeds. This is not the hardest job for the farmer; the most arduous work for him is to clear away the weeds. If he fails to keep them down, within a very short time his valuable crops will be choked by them.

Rice is the main crop, and every farmer will first cultivate rice in his best available land plot. Economically, rice is relatively a less profitable crop than jute. But rice is a food crop, most of which may be used for private consumption and stored for the future, while the surplus amount can be sold in the local *hat* (village market) for cash money or traded for daily necessities. Its cultivation fits into the rhythm of production and requires considerably less labor than does jute.

Cultivation of jute is one of the most tedious jobs for the farmers. Jute needs continuous rain and sun, and the tending of the plants under the heat of the scorching sun, coupled with 100% humidity, makes the work practically unbearable. Yet, the farmers of the village must cultivate jute, since this is their main source of cash money (see photo no. 7), and necessary for such purposes as mending their houses, buying clothes, and buying cattle.

Although rice and jute are the two main crops, some mustard, gram, tobacco and other vegetables and spices such as onion, chili, tumeric, ginger, garlic, etc. are also grown. These spices are grown mostly for domestic consumption and are harvested within two months of the planting just before winter. Usually if a farmer wants to give his field a rest he will also grow crops other than rice and jute on that field. However, every farmer will also have a very small plot of land varying from 20' x 20' to 40' x 100' close to his dwelling house (which he calls *birca*) for growing such crops, particularly the vegetables for daily consumption.

More well-to-do farmers, who have enough land left over after cultivating the necessary amount of rice and jute, will grow any other crop which brings a maximum yield, and thus cash money. In Badarpur, tobacco and gram are two such main supplementary crops. Sugarcane, although highly profitable, is difficult to protect against the village lads, but those who can manage it prefer to grow sugarcane to any other crop for cash money.

This pattern of village agriculture is typical of Bangladesh generally, as shown by Table 10.

Badarpur in the National Setting 49

Photo no. 7. Farmers work from sunrise to sunset.

TABLE 10

Acreage and Production of the Principal Crops in East Bengal
(Average from 1957–58 to 1961–62)

Crop	Acreage in 1000 Acres	Percentage of Total Area	Production in 1000 Tons	Average Yield per Acre
Rice	20,776	87.42	8,397	.27
Rape & Mustard	1,609	6.77	1,042	.41
Jute	563	2.24	91	.11
Sugarcane	269	1.13	3,91	9.90
Gram	140	.59	35	.27
Tobacco	108	.45	32	.20
Tea	77	.32	23	.20
Other crops	255	1.08	51	.19
TOTAL:	23,797	100.00	13,588	

Source: *Economic Survey of Pakistan 1962–63*, Statistical Section, Tables 12 and 13.

Seasons

As spring turns to summer in late February the sky is bare of clouds, and a tropical sun shines with cruel intensity; but the air gets cool after a brisk tropical down-pour and the lush green fields sparkle in the crisp morning sunlight. The trees wake up with birds chattering furiously. The afternoons are hot and at times sultry, with wild winds stirring up dust and dead leaves.

This is a time when every farmer's wife is busy drying and storing the crop. All day, from morning to evening, she is drying chilis and other spices and foods, tending to them with alert eyes so that birds cannot steal any. At any time the sky may become cloudy and rain may destroy their whole fortune. The farmer clears his field, removing the dry straws from the field either manually (photo no. 8) or if it is unmanageable, by setting fire to the field adopting the slash and burn method. The ashes produced by burned straws serve as good fertilizer. Gradually the temperature rises and when it rises above one hundred degrees everyone tries to take shelter in the coolest possible place.

The rains of the main monsoon or *Varsha* come as a welcome relief in early June. The parched earth is soaked with rain and as time passes communication becomes difficult. Yet poets of Bengal somehow have managed to describe it as the most beautiful season. The continuous rain occasionally never ceases for weeks; during this season the whole country is flooded and villages look like small islands in a vast body of water. If the monsoon comes early the villagers are in trouble (photo no. 9). A sudden flood destroys all the paddy fields and a shortage of food results. If the flood intensifies after harvesting in late *Ashar* (late June or early August) the villagers do not face any problem.

The end of the monsoon brings *Sarat Kal,* the season of clear sky, when everything appears clean and spotless with patches of clouds floating in the sky. There is a little rain but it never continues for long. At this time processing jute is the main time-consuming work for the villagers. During the middle of the monsoon (rainy season) the farmer cuts his jute plants and ties them in bundles out of the water and collects the fibers. Washing the jute fibers and drying them is a tedious job. He has to collect the fibers from the jute standing in stagnant water which is full of leeches and snakes. A farmer will start collecting the jute fibers early in the morning and will continue until sunset with a little break for lunch. Every day he will have to pluck out an average of four to five leeches from that portion of the body which remains under water.

The season of *Hemanta Kal,* or Fall, extends roughly from the

Photo no. 8. A village lad carrying a head load of rice (crops).

Photo no. 9. Flood is a constant threat.

middle of September to the middle of November, and is a relatively cool season. At this time the main agricultural activities are growing crops such as gram, lentils, mustard, chili and various types of vegetables for domestic consumption. More than half of this season is spent cleaning the fields, as the flood water brings a good number of shells and dead branches into the field which must be cleared away before anything else is cultivated. A chart below will summarize this seasonal round.

CHART 1. Seasonal Cycle of Agricultural Activities in Badarpur

Seasons in Bengali	English Equivalents	Bengali Months	Approximate Time in English	Agricultural Activities
Grishma	Summer	Baisak & Jaishtya	March-May	Cultivation of Rice & Jute
Varsha	Rainy season (monsoon)	Ashar & Sraban	May-July	Harvesting
Sarat	Autumn	Bhadra & Ashwin	July-September	Collection of Jute Fiber
Hemanta	Fall	Kartik & Agrahain	September-November	Cleaning field and cultivation of winter crops
Sit	Winter	Paush & Magh	November-January	Cultivation of spices and lentils, etc.
Basanta	Spring	Falgun & Chaitra	January-March	Harvesting of winter crops

Fishing

With an abundance of water, and fish as plentiful as the green grass in the monsoon months, the people of the village are fish-eaters. In fact, the people of Bengal as a whole are jokingly referred to by the people of the rest of the subcontinent as the *Machlikhor Bangalees* (fish-eating Bengalis). Yet in Badarpur catching fish as a profession is very much looked down on (photos no. 10, 11) and no villager will take this occupation if he can avoid it. Catching fish for domestic use, however, is socially accepted.

One of the central village sections is still called *Jalua Para* (fishermen's quarters), although today no fisherman lives in it. It is at present occupied by Muslims who purchased the houses from the Hindus. There used to be seven Hindu families of the fisherman caste, but today Badarpur's only fisherman is a Muslim who frequently supplements his income with casual work (photo no. 12). (Muslims have not maintained this industry because of the traditional low standing the

Photo no. 10. Fishing for a living is not an honourable profession, but fishing for domestic consumption is quite acceptable.

Photo no. 11.   A village man fishing for domestic consumption.

Photo no. 12.   Fisherman's net drying in the sun.

Badarpur in the National Setting   55

occupation has had in their eyes.) Previously the Hindus would supply fish not only to the neighboring market, but even to the towns and cities although they did not sell much fish in the village itself.

The abundance of fish means that although there is no great wealth in the village, no one starves. In addition, since all households possess some land, even if only a house plot, they can grow plentiful supplies of green vegetables to supplement their fish diet. Further, all households, whether wealthy or poor, inevitably raise hens, and when possible goats, and cows.

Property Ownership

To give some idea of the level of wealth in a village such as Badarpur, and to establish what the standards are by which "richness" or "poverty" is judged, I shall describe one particular house which is, although not entirely representative, only slightly above the average (photo no. 13).

Kabir and Samir are two brothers, Kabir the elder of the two. Samir, a school teacher, lives in the city and only once in a while comes to the village to see his wife and five children who live with Kabir. Their house is on a flat, plain square field forty feet wide and forty feet in length. There is a large room on the north side of this plot 20' x 14' facing the south, another room on the east side almost of the same size facing west. Between these two rooms is the family kitchen made up of bamboo and straws. On the south side of the plot is another room a little smaller (16' x 12') used as a guest room (*Baithak Khana,* literally: meeting room). Behind the room on the eastern side they have a cow shed where there are two rather sickly bullocks, two cows, and two calves either munching hay given to them by Kabir's nine year old son Wadud, or standing with a sorrowful expression as they wait for Kabir to come and take them to the field to graze. (Photo no. 14)

None of the rooms has any windows, but the bamboo fences have enough open holes to let winter air get in and make the inhabitants shiver. The floors are of plain mud, which is occasionally coated with clay mixed with cow-dung. Corrugated iron sheets form a roof over these rooms, meeting at the top from four sides, and looking more like an umbrella than anything else.

Inside the *bara ghar* (room of the northern side) there is a bamboo partition which divides the room into two unequal parts. This is called *bara ghar* (literally "big room") not because of its size, but because the head of the family (household) lives there with his wife and children. On the right hand side (eastern side) of the partition Kabir's wife

Photo no. 13. A typical village home consisting of a kitchen (center), living room (left), and a bedroom (right).

Photo no. 14. Cattle at Kabir's house are either busy munching hay or remain standing with a sorrowful expression as they wait for Kabir's nine year old son Wadud to come and take them to the field to graze.

keeps all the pots, plates and dishes, and there is a door which enables her to go to the kitchen easily. The partition in the room does not divide the room completely as it does not extend from one side to the other. The rooms are really self-contained huts.

Although these huts in Kabir's house are evenly spaced and there is little room to move around between them, in many of the houses the huts are huddled altogether in a disorderly fashion. Inside the *bara ghar* are the cooking and farming utensils, and household furniture which consists mostly of stitched quilts and two or three pillows, which have never been cleaned since new, and have formed a coating of dirt from the user's hair. A few angling rods and line always remain hanging outside the doorway of the hut just above the head. The angling rods are made from the local bamboos and used only rarely when the household requires fish for its domestic consumption.

In front of the *bara ghar* the neatly kept space is used for the drying of chilis and other crops. The evening will bring people of the neighboring houses or the children of the same house around, and they will spread a bamboo mattress where they will sit and chat. On a moonlit night the children will play there until late.

Kabir is a farmer, and like all other villagers he has a small *dingi* (country boat) which becomes his only means of transportation when the flood waters cover all his fields. Like his neighbors he has been trying to obtain a second *dingi* but he cannot as yet afford it.

The basic diet in Kabir's house, as in most of the villages, consists of rice, fish, lentils, beans and several varieties of spices such as chili, mustard, ginger, garlic, onion, etc. Rice is the common staple food, and the consumption varies sharply from household to household; in rich households rice consumption is reduced by substitution of meat, milk, and other foods which, however, most of the other households in the village cannot afford.

Meat consumption increases during festivals such as *Idd-ul-Azha*[33] when it is obligatory for well-to-do families to sacrifice an animal such as a cow, goat or sheep. One-third (at least) of the meat must be distributed to non-relatives according to religious injunction (photo no. 15). Although this injunction is not followed strictly by every wealthy

Photo no. 15. During Idd-ul-Azha Muslim villagers will sacrifice a cow or goat and distribute meat among the poor.

household in the village, during the festival time all the villagers get some meat.

During other periods, occasionally several villagers get together and kill a cow, dividing the meat according to each one's share or contribution. If a guest suddenly arrives (which happens most frequently), Kabir's wife will kill a hen from her stock which she carefully raised throughout the year.

Differences in status in the village can be observed if one looks at the morning market to see who buys what (photo nos. 16 & 17). A big catch (fish) in the morning market must be sold to the Muslim landlord as no one else can afford to buy it. If the landlord does not come to the market that morning, several people may buy it collectively and then divide it; otherwise the fish will be sent to the landlord's house and the owner will have to accept the landlord's offer whatever it is. Generally it is accepted by the villagers as being the correct price. On other occasions, however, the doctors or the visitors may buy a big catch (if there are visitors in the village at that time), if there are no other buyers.

Clothing is also considered as a status symbol. Almost all the villagers will have nothing covering their bodies above the waistline when they are working, particularly in the field. A *lungi* (loin cloth) tied around the waist and draped down like a skirt, is the normal clothing of the working villagers. But after work they will put on a cotton vest or shirt, according to what they can afford. Only the well-to-do families wear shoes all the time (I did not see the members of more than two families in Badarpur doing so) although a few more could afford it. After work, the villager washes himself and puts on a *Kharam* (wooden made slipper) with his relatively clean clothes and may visit his neighbor's house.

Looking at the economic activities as a whole, it is important to note that except for the one official living in the village the entire population has to depend, directly or indirectly, on agricultural labour and produce. Those who can be considered as the middle class in the village may possess landed property and at the same time may be self-employed in other activities such as working as a family priest and performing annual worship for which they receive remuneration. Most of the time people of this middle class can afford to employ outside workers to work for them at fixed wages for a period, if not for the entire year.

Tools and techniques available to the people of Badarpur are a clear reflection of the acculturation pattern and the changing attitudes of the village. In the entire village there is not a single brick-built

Photo no. 16. Every morning villagers cross the river to go to the market place.

Photo no. 17. Traders gossip in a *hat* (market) before shoppers come.

house, and only in two mosques out of the total four have bricks been used. Even then bricks were used only to pave the floor in one, while the complete brick structure of the other is without any plastering or coating of any kind. Hence, although the mosque is relatively new (newer than the two others in the village) and the bricks reveal its modernity, it has the general run-down appearance of mosques built during the Muslim rule in the country a few centuries ago.

There is a single radio in the village in the house of Karim, the richest man in the village and its leader. There are also five bicycles: one belongs to Karim, another to a village school teacher (who teaches in a neighboring village school and uses it as a means of transport during the dry season), two belong to two students who do not live in the village, but who come home occasionally when their school is closed, while the last belongs to a village doctor, Abdul Gafur.

As will be appreciated, there are many differences between rich and poor within Badarpur, so that it is entirely appropriate to consider it as having a class hierarchy. Yet this class hierarchy has little of the rigidity of the Hindu caste system. On religious and ceremonial occasions the village people all come together inside the mosque, and class differences are ignored.

Religion and Festivals

The festivals of Badarpur are, like the festivals of the rest of the country, based on themes which are followed throughout the Muslim World. Yet, according to local culture and environment there is different local emphasis on different ceremonies, and different local shades of meaning attached to them.

For four months of the year villagers cannot move about freely, as a large part of the village is inundated with water. Since they have little to do at this period it is not surprising that even the average villager turns to thought about life, death and destiny. The dependence on nature for the success of the harvest gives further strength to such musings. From the earliest times, the villagers of Bengal have practised their festivals and religious rites which express a sense of submission to destiny, or the will of God.

Before partition, many Hindu festivals were celebrated, both religious and secular. Since the departure of the Hindus, most of these religious festivals have become defunct, although many secular Hindu ceremonies still occur, or give a local shade and colour to the national festivals. For example, during the night of Sab-e-barat,[34] a Muslim festival, when the Muslims of Bangladesh arrange special prayers and distribute sweets to friends, relatives and to the poor, their practice of illumination at night is a definite indication of the local Hindu festival *Diwali*,[35] when the Hindus of the country perform *Lakshmi Puza* and illuminate houses, shops, and every other possible place.

The most important two festivals are *Idd-ul-Azha* and *Idd-ul-Fitr*,[36] which are religious festivals celebrated by all Muslims the world over. Before *Idd-ul-Fitr,* Muslims fast for a month from dawn to sunset. After the period of one month is over, there is a congregational prayer which all the villagers attend, and then distribute food and good wishes. During *Idd-ul-Azha,* which is considered the most important of these two festivals, well-to-do families sacrifice an animal and distribute meat (see supra; p. 58), and after a similar congregational prayer they wish everyone happy "Idd." These two festivals resemble the Christmas festival of the Christians and *"Durga Puza"* of the Hindus.[37]

There are several other smaller festivals which are associated with religion, *viz.* the naming of a newborn child, circumcision, puberty and marriage, and these are observed by the villagers with great care

Photo no. 18.   Villagers are poor, but happy.

and attention. Friends and relatives are invited according to the economic wherewithal of the individual family.

Life has continually become harder since the last great war, and subsequent political upheavals have considerably reduced the joy of life among the village people of Badarpur. On the other hand it has gradually led them to a consciousness of independence which has made them over-concerned with earthly things. Yet a casual visitor to this village will be struck by the music which seems to make up such a vital part of everyday life (photo no. 18).

The village farmers, as they go out in the morning or return in the evening, sing. Songs are invariably an accompaniment to the work of the fishermen. In the autumn the winds are steady, and boats move across the water with hoisted sails (photo nos. 19 & 20). Relieved of the task of rowing, the boatmen sing of joy and sorrow, of life and death, of faith and destiny. To a visitor it is an unforgettable experience to see the sun waft across the still water of Badarpur.

In the past when the Hindus were in the village, there was community singing during the harvest season. The tradition has not yet died, but is not encouraged by the Muslim elders. Nonetheless, on a moonlit night one can hear the *bauls*[38] (wandering minstrels) singing their religious and mystic songs from the neighbouring villages. It is notable that many of these songs describe some of the highest experiences of man (Mansur Uddin, 1959:13ff).

The songs are inspired by utter abandonment and surrender. Emotions rise to an unbearable intensity, but even in moments of the greatest passion, the sense of community with the soil itself is not lost. In the midst of total surrender and identification with the absolute, little incidents common to rural life are brought in to establish kinship between ordinary and mystic experiences.[39]

Poets and writers of Bengal are very eloquent about their ceremonies and festivals, particularly those related to the seasonal cycle which have already been described.

Summary

Badarpur is a village typical in most ways of rural Bangladesh. Only about ten per cent of the villagers are literate: the language of all of them is Bengali. About ninety per cent are farmers, yet fish, caught mainly for household use, forms a major part of their diet. Above everything else in importance are the seasons, particularly the monsoon, the river whose floods cover the land for some four months, and the land, which gets its great fertility from the river. Rice is the main crop of the village, yet jute provides it with much of its cash income.

64 A Bangladesh Village

Photo no. 19. After having delivered goods,
the boat returns with a hoisted sail.

Photo no. 20. Rivers serve as the main highways.
A loaded boat on to its destination.

In terms of material goods the village is poor, yet food is readily available as everyone has at least a house-plot of land and can always fish. No one need starve. There are marked class differences within the village, yet there are strong bonds holding the village together. Some of these are religious and appear in the common participation in ceremonies at the mosque; some are on a closer human level as higher class families maintain paternal relations with lower class families. The analysis of these relationships, and the extent to which they are breaking down is the subject matter of a later chapter.

CHAPTER FOUR

Social Organization

Knowledge of the physical background of the village is not sufficient. In order to discuss the political activities in the village, we have to know the different types of groupings, the principles for forming and maintaining these groupings, and the relationships between them. The analysis in this chapter will be of static nature. It will be left for later chapters to consider the roles these groupings play in the dynamic process of local politics.

People in Badarpur are members of various groupings which can be hierarchically arranged: *ghar, bari, paribar* and *gushthi*. The meaning of these terms will clarify the social structure of the village as a whole.

Ghar. This word literally means "room," but refers to a husband and wife living with their children. The term "nuclear family" will be used to translate the word, for it fulfills most of the criteria of the popular definition of family:

> A social group characterized by common residence, economic cooperation and reproduction. (Murdock, 1965:1)

The ghar is not always an independent economic unit, however, for it often lives in the same bari (house) with the husband's married or unmarried brothers, his unmarried sisters, and his parents; the family works with them in economic enterprises. A husband and wife and their children always have a ghar (in this case: room) of their own.

Bari. This word literally means "a home," but commonly refers to an extended family group. Its head is usually the eldest member of the bari, and its members are his wife and children, the wives of married sons, grandchildren, unmarried daughters, at times widowed sisters, and as an exception, married daughters whose husbands come to live with them. Although each married son has his own separate ghar within the bari, he does not usually have a separate kitchen of his own. The bari is definitely an economic unit, working under the leadership and guidance of its head from whom it obtains its status in the community. This word shall be translated as "family" since it does not exactly coincide with what previously has been called a household, that is, any unit, be it a ghar or a bari, that has its own kitchen.

Paribar. The literal meaning of this term is a group of houses (baris), where all members are agnatically related (an alternate term for this group is *Khandan* which literally means "lineage," but in this study the term paribar will be used).[40] It refers to all the male patrilineal descendants of a great-grandfather, unmarried sisters, cousins of different baris and ghars, who have a sense of belonging that binds them together. They can trace their common origin to a single male ancestor who may still be alive, or who may have died a generation or two ago.

Gushthi. This term will generally be translated as "kinsmen." It is a more inclusive term than paribar, for while in a paribar all members have a common ancestor, traceable by a genealogical tree, in a gushthi a common ancestor may or may not be necessary. Different paribars in a single gushthi may live in different villages. But the term is also used with a wider meaning. In Badarpur some people who are only affinally related claim to belong to the same gushthi. While genealogical proximity serves to admit people of only casual acquaintance to one's gushthi, close residence or even proximate age and potential friendship can lead people to say they are of the same gushthi as others. In this wider sense it is a term that means that the relationship is somehow more intimate, more demanding of fellowship and special privilege than other relationships.

Gram. In Bengali, the word for village is *gram,* which is pronounced *geram* by the villagers. Outside the gushthi line people in the gram make another distinction as to their own villager or outsider. A man from a certain gram might confide in a fellow villager in preference to a man of his own gushthi who is not living in the same gram. However, a reversal of the situation may also take place.

Although land is owned by household heads, the interaction of all household heads who are members of the same gushthi indicates a corporateness of the gushthi. Since members of the gushthi get together in festivals and ceremonies, any member of the gushthi who is not invited on any particular occasion can easily take offense. Moreover, as there is no strict centralization of village authority, social control is usually regulated on a kind of ad hoc basis by gushthi members, particularly by the paribar or bari heads, when the need arises to square accounts.

The corporateness of the gushthi can also be observed in the attitude the household heads display towards their landed property, especially cultivated land. Since cultivated land is difficult to obtain, easy to misplay, and is the source of much conflict, the household heads of the gushthi agree that land should not go out of the gushthi. This tendency to keep property in the gushthi, even in the absence of collective property ownership by the group, reflects the corporateness of the gushthi.

The delineation of descent may be illustrated by the position of women in the household. An unmarried woman is considered to be a member of her natal patrilineage. When she marries, her children belong to their father's gushthi by virtue of the patrilineal descent rule. Virilocal post-marital residence is favoured, although sporadic cases of uxorilocal unions are found, as will be seen later in the history of the origin of gushthi C.

The fact that women inherit property has crucial implications for affinal and matrilateral ties of their natal and marital households. Even though girls who marry out of their gushthi are theoretically entitled to inherit a share in their parent's property, in many cases, the daughter either does not claim her inheritance or is deprived of it. A reason often given for this is that the girl wants to maintain good relations with members of her natal paribar, especially brothers. Florence McCarthy, who has studied village women in Commilla thana of East Pakistan, quotes one informant:

> Girls don't take their share, but give it to their brothers. Twice a year the brothers have to bring their sisters to their house. They also have to give them saris, and clothes to any children that might have come along (McCarthy, 1967:31).

Village women maintain ties with their fathers' families, even though they spent the majority of their lives in the baris of their husbands (see infra p. 75). This acts as a built-in assurance for them in case of divorce or widowhood. If a woman is married into a family that is well-to-do, and that can provide for her if her husband dies, her future is somewhat assured. However, with the death of her husband the wife loses rank and authority, and in many cases the woman who remains in her husband's bari is allotted the more menial tasks (Bertocci, 1970).

Another option for a widow is to return to her natal paribar. If her ties are strong and the relationship good, her brothers might welcome her home to live with them. If, however, her relationship with them is not good, because she has taken part of her father's legacy, the brothers might not welcome her or take good care of her. In this context it is understandable that women do not generally take the inheritance due them, but invest it in their future security by giving it to their brothers. These security considerations are the same for the ever-present, though relatively small, possibility of divorce, which until recently could be most easily initiated by man than a woman.⁴¹ The result of all these informal rules of inheritance is to keep property in the gushthi, guarding it from loss through females who have married outside the gushthi.

Earlier in the chapter it has been pointed out that the daughters who are married out continue to have a claim against the gushthi, although they do not always demand it. By not demanding, they in fact do a service not only to their brothers, who enjoy their sisters' share, but at the same time to their own gushthi by helping to keep the gushthi land together.

Most villagers do not know their gushthi names, they know only the members of their bari and paribar. Only three groups can be recognized in this village who can trace their gushthi members who are scattered over a number of grams.⁴² These three gushthis consisting of fifty-seven ghars constitute approximately fifteen per cent of the total population of the village.

The Muslim *zamindar* (landlord) gushthi is one of the eldest if not the largest gushthi of Badarpur. In addition there are two other gushthis which have no names to indicate an occupation. In fact the village doctors belong to two different gushthis most of whose members are involved either in agriculture or in other occupations such as shopkeeping, *munshi* (religious teaching), etc.

These three gushthis in Badarpur function as semi-political units and are loci of power and decision-making; also, they contribute to the segmented and compartmentalized nature of village social organization. They help us to understand the channels of communication in the village through which the villagers express their ideas and thinking. At times they become the key for decision-making in social, religious, economic conflicts between factions.

This study gives an account of the collected histories of these three gushthis, which for convenience shall here be named *A, B,* and *C*. In all cases the informant himself was a member of the gushthi whose history was being investigated. *A* was the only gushthi in Badarpur where it was possible to trace a genealogy of six generations.

Gushthis of Badarpur

It is said that the zamindar of Badarpur, who was a Hindu, used to torture the Muslims with or without reason. He was so intolerant of them that the poor Muslim peasants could not perform their religious duties even in the seclusion of their own residences. Though sacrificing an animal during the Idd day was a very important religious function for Muslims, it was prohibited and the Muslims, being desperate, sent a messenger to various places to tell of their difficulties and to request the help of anyone who could help them out of the situation.

A man called Rahim is said to have been the first man to respond to the Muslim villagers' call and he came to Badarpur with ten of his followers, equipped to fight the Hindu zamindar if necessary. Rahim entered the village from the southeast corner, walked through the village once with his party, sacrificed a cow right on the compound of the Hindu zaminar and washed the blood-stained knives in the zamindar's pool. The infuriated zamindar immediately ordered his *Paiks* (guards) to capture Rahim. When the paiks approached Rahim, he single-handedly felled them all.

Many of the villagers who gathered out of curiosity witnessed the strength of Rahim, and one by one they began to gather around him. For sixteen days the zamindar and his followers were virtually confined to their house; then on the seventeenth day the zamindar approached Rahim for negotiation. They finally came to an agreement that the zamindar would never again interfere with the Muslims' religious activities.

Then Rahim advised his ten followers to leave the village and return to their homes, since they were no longer needed. He decided to settle in the village permanently, choosing the southeast corner of the village through which he had first entered.

Rahim's son, Tora Gazi, was of the same age as the zamindar's son, and the two became very friendly. After the death of the zamindar, when his son became zamindar, Tora Gazi was appointed the zamindar's chief *lathial* (leader of the guards). As long as Tora Gazi lived, the Hindus and Muslims of the village lived in peace.

Tora Gazi's son, Kadam Ali, also worked for the zamindar, but during his last days he accumulated enough money to buy plots of land and preferred an independent occupation to service. Kadam Ali's son, Korban Ali, managed to buy more land and declared himself a *talukdar* (petty landlord). Korban Ali was a first-generation Muslim talukdar in Badarpur, and his son, the present Muslim zamindar, is only a second-generation talukdar in this village.

Rahim and Tora Gazi each had only one wife and one son. Kadam Ali also married only once but had three sons, Korban Ali, Ghani, and Rahmet. Korban Ali, however, married twice and had children from both wives. The eldest son of the first wife is the present Muslim zamindar, Karim, who has a half brother Halim, living in the village. This half brother of the present zamindar's and the zamindar's uncles (i.e. Korban Ali's younger brothers and their sons) together constitute the present zamindar gushthi of three paribars, four baris and twelve ghars, most of them living in the southern end of the village while others are scattered over the neighbouring villages, towns, and cities. To show schematically the members of the zamindar family which constitute our Gushthi *A*, I have added the following kinship chart (see Chart 2 on p. 72).

Clan *B* does not have a legend as to its origin, and its kinship could only be traced for five generations. Khuda Bux was the first man of this gushthi (nobody knows from where he came; he probably was a local convert) and he had four sons. Each of his sons had a number of children and one, Azizuddin, who died in 1963, became very prominent in the village because of his religious devotion, honesty, sincerity and learning.

Azizuddin's father, Hakim, son of Khuda Bux, was also a reputed man of his time; however, it is the general consensus among the villagers that Azizuddin was the most pious man of the village; he was loved by all. Two brothers who died before him left a number of children who grew up with Azizuddin's own children. His children and those nephews and nieces now constitute the most educated section of the village.

Azizuddin's brother's son was the headmaster of the village girls' school, and one of his own sons became a teacher working in the city. The formally schooled village doctor (Dr. Gafur) is the son of Azizuddin's younger brother, who left four sons and a daughter when he died. Of these five children, the daughter is the eldest and is married to a school teacher who lives in a village fourteen miles from Badarpur. Three elder sons went to school for a few years and then began to work on their father's land. The youngest son continued studying and finally became a village doctor.

Azizuddin himself had three daughters and three sons. Eldest among them is a daughter, who worked as a village girls' school teacher and then married a school teacher from the city and moved to the city. The two other daughters of Azizuddin also married school teachers and live far away from their own village. All the children of Azizuddin's daughters live in the city and came to Badarpur only once in a while when their maternal grandparents (i.e. Azizuddin and his wife) were alive. Now they rarely, if ever, come.

Of Azizuddin's three sons, the youngest died before he was married and the remaining two, Kabir and Samir, are still alive; their house has been described in the previous chapter (see supra p. 55).

The descendants of Khuda Bux (i.e. the children of Azizuddin's father, Hakim, and his brothers) are also living in the village. Hakim had three brothers, Afzal, Farhad, and Mubarek. Afzal had only one son and a daughter; this daughter of Afzal was married to Farhad, her

72 A Bangladesh Village

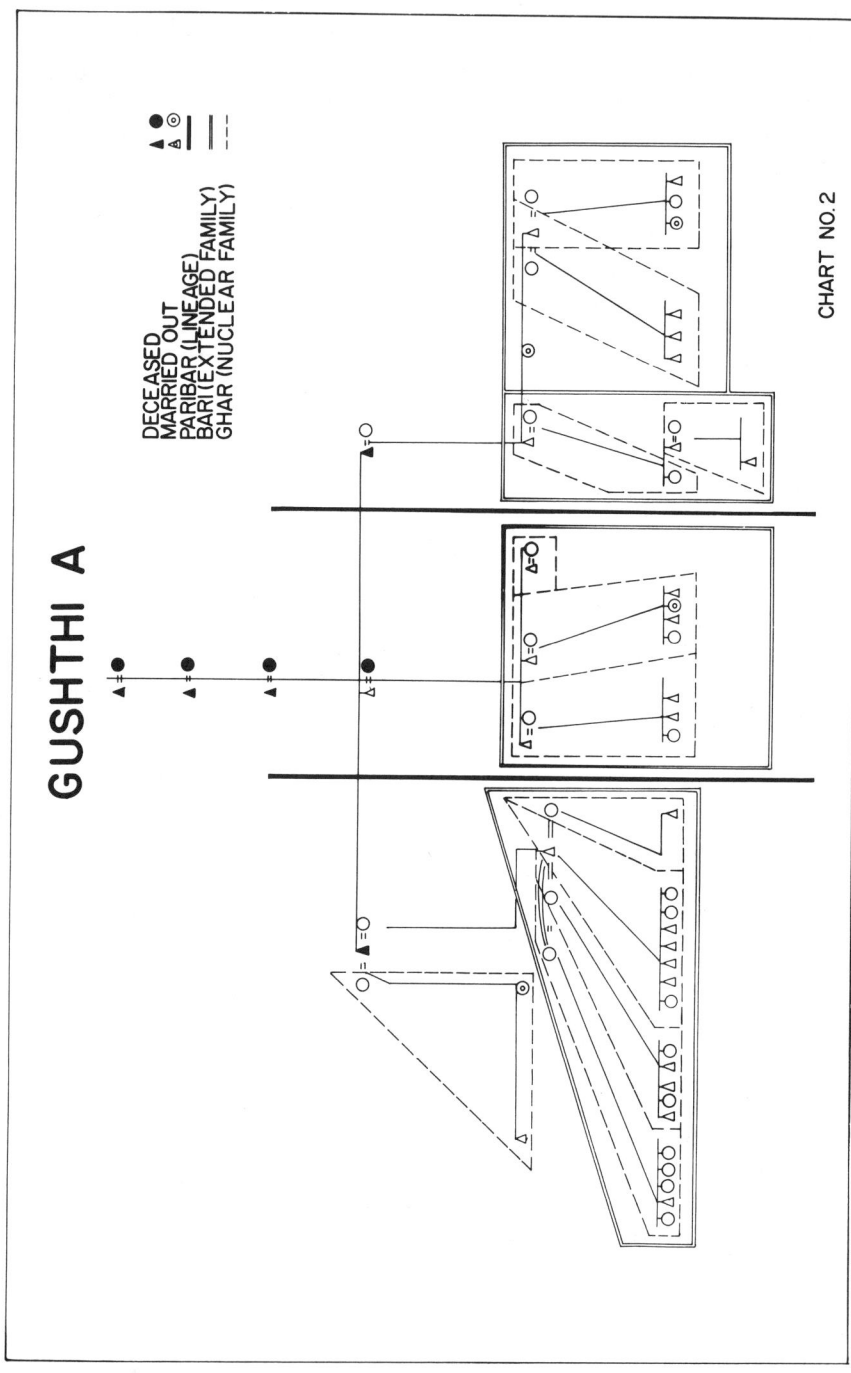

uncle's son whom Afzal adopted after the death of his only son. Here I include another kinship chart (see Chart 3 on p. 74) showing the gushthi of Khuda Bux or Gushthi *B* consisting of 3 paribars, 17 baris, and 31 ghars scattered over all the different parts of Badarpur with heavy concentration in the Maiz Para (central enclave).

The third gushthi in the village, Gushthi *C*, is relatively smaller. However, due to affinal relationships established with Gushthi *B*, this gushthi nevertheless has a definite say in decision-making. Zaman, the present leading member of this gushthi, could not tell me much about his kinsmen, but I reconstructed the history from scraps of conversation.

Zaman's great-grandfather, Kalu, is said to have arrived at the village as a young man; he then fell in love with a village girl, married her and settled permanently. Since she had no brothers, all of her father's property was inherited by her husband. I was unable to discover anything about Kalu's father-in-law or how he came to settle in the village, but I did learn that the family continued to thrive after his initial settlement. Zaman's father, Samu, was a businessman who left much money for his three sons. Zaman, being an entrepreneur, multiplied his wealth a hundred times and is now the richest farmer in the village.

In Badarpur people attach a stigma to men who live in their father-in-law's house or become rich by inheriting the father-in-law's property. Zaman, for instance, has earned most of his fortune through his own entrepreneurship, but because his great-grandfather had inherited his father-in-law's house, a stigma remains in the minds of the villagers. Despite the fact that Zaman, who owns twenty acres of land, is the richest man in the village and his wealthy gushthi relatives are still living in neighbouring villages, in the eyes of the villagers, the people of his gushthi can never again gain the same respect that the people of the other two gushthis have. In fact, when Zaman's father, Samu, came to arrange for the marriage of Azizuddin's eldest daughter and his own eldest son, brother of Zaman, most members of Gushthi *B* were against the idea. But Azizuddin, so it is said, was too affectionate and could not refuse this marriage when he came to know that his daughter liked Samu's son. Moreover, Azizuddin also remembered that in his own gushthi his uncle, Afzal, once adopted a son for his own daughter and then left the couple his property. The marriage took place, but it did not last long, since Azizuddin's son-in-law died within a year leaving his widow and a daughter only a few days old.

Zaman's father, Samu, had four brothers and two sisters. Both sisters are married and live with their children in a neighbouring village. Zaman's three uncles live in Badarpur and their children are all farm-

74 A Bangladesh Village

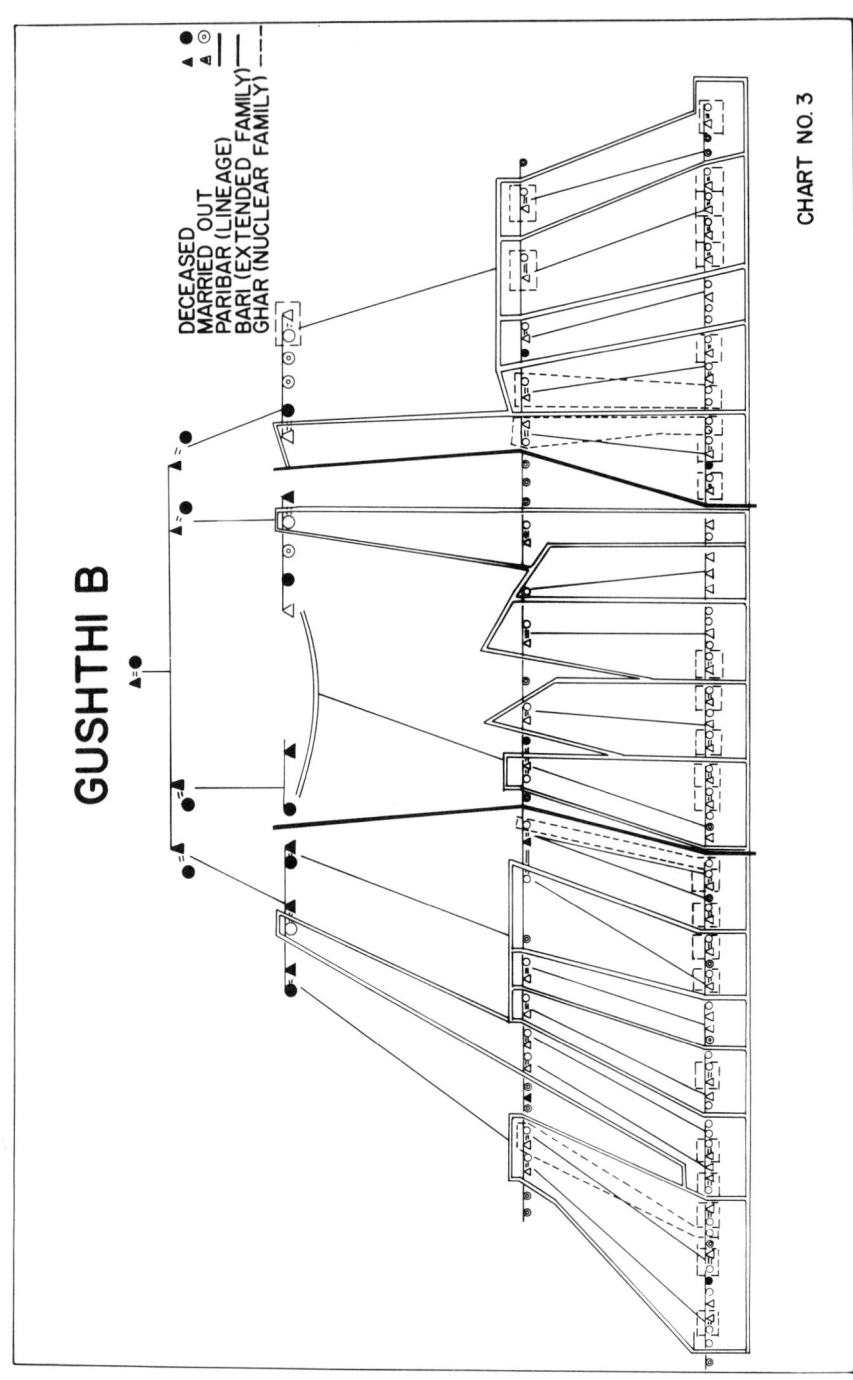

ers. Here I include a kinship chart showing the gushthi of Zaman, Gushthi C, consisting of four paribars, nine baris and fourteen ghars (see Chart 4 on p. 76) scattered over all the different parts of Badarpur, like Gushthi B, with concentration in the *Maiz Para.*

These three gushthis form an old, ingrained pattern in the village life, but are not necessarily political groupings, or temporary alliances of individuals to fight court cases, although they may take on political functions and become involved in power politics. Rather, they are kinship groupings which carry on important social, economic, and ceremonial functions while they are concerned with internal and external struggles or rivalries. Other villagers know their bari or paribar members but cannot trace any further. Here I would like to include another kinship chart showing a Badarpur farmer paribar. And although it does not have any strong power and influence in the village politics, it is the paribar of the largest occupational group in the village (see Chart 5 on p. 77).

Bari or *Family*—Bari, which has been previously translated as "family" is the prime social group in the village and is an institutional basis for most organizations. All the members of a bari who are blood-related through the patrilineal line have a strong sense of consanguinity and feel that their relationship together is much stronger than their relationship to spouses who have married into the bari. For this reason, when a village girl is married outside the village she keeps close ties with her brothers and sisters left at home. Brothers retain strong ties to the girls and stress their links to natal paribars whenever possible. All the girls of the village, after marriage go to their husband's father's homes and live there throughout their life. Yet each will feel that her own home is her father's home, even though she may be a mother of a dozen children. However, in my figures of households, I have included the wives with their husbands instead of with their brothers, as they are normally grouped for economic and political purposes.

In the bari (family) children are supposed to be raised by the grandparents. Grandparents have a joking relationship with grandchildren. A grandfather can tease his granddaughters and grandsons; he might refer to granddaughter-in-law as his youngest wife. Similarly a grandmother may tease her granddaughter that the granddaughter's husband is her own new husband.

Family ties are very close. A man's duties are, in order, to his own family, then towards his paribar, then to his gushthi and then to his village. However, when the line of a gushthi cuts across villages, and the villages are not on friendly terms with each other, what is known as gushthi politics begins.

76   A Bangladesh Village

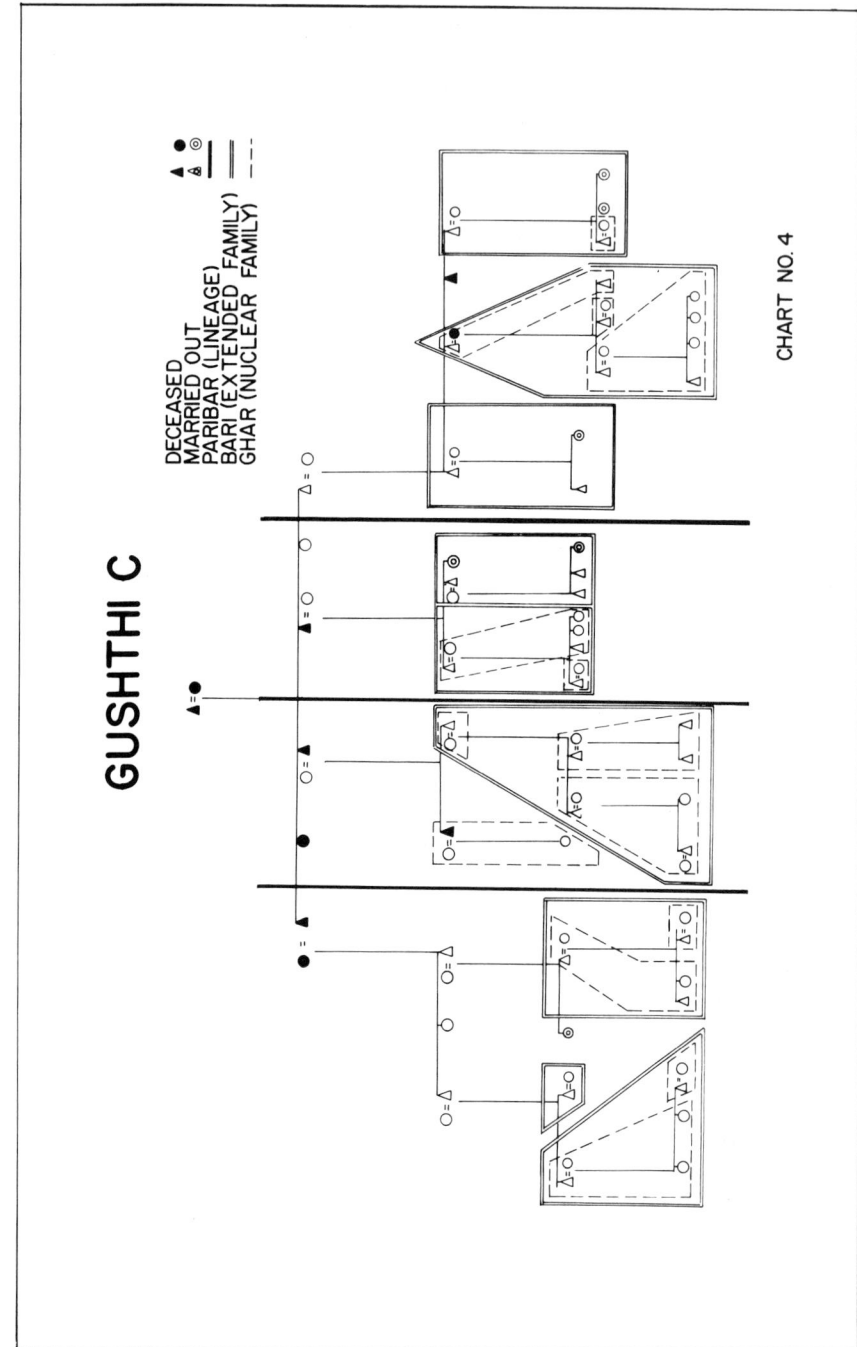

CHART NO. 4

Social Organization 77

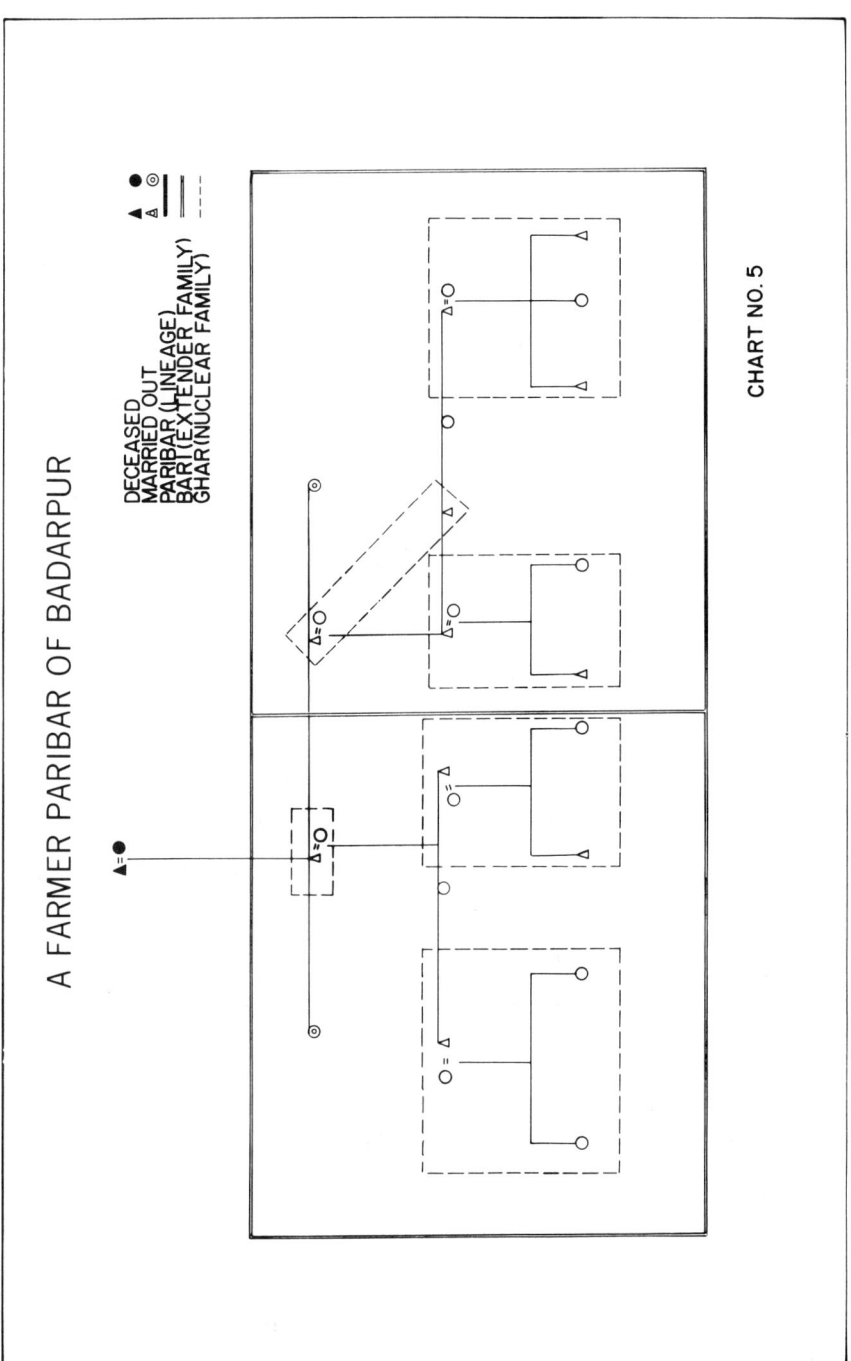

CHART NO. 5

The value orientation of a traditional bari in Badarpur follows an almost classically familistic pattern. The familistic pattern and the attributes of familism could be determined with reference to the maintenance, continuity and functions of the bari (family) groups. On the other hand, a bari in Badarpur can be considered the most important economic unit, wherein its members work together, raise crops, attend livestock and, in fact, produce most of the things they consume.

In Badarpur, a bari is subject to a variety of external controls, some from larger social organizations, such as paribar and gushthi. The responsibilities of the baris are highly inclusive and constricting, consuming much of the people's everyday life. The influence of paribar and of gushthi on the control of the bari in such matters as mate selection, bride-price, pregnancy, birth, legitimation of children, marriage, disposition of children, etc., suggests the very restrictive nature of this social unit.

Paribar or Lineage—The paribar is a strong determining factor of one's prestige and power in the village. A young man who marries a girl from a wealthy, reputed paribar is likely to prosper sooner in his field than one who marries a girl from a less wealthy, less reputed and, hence, less influential paribar. This does not mean, however, that the power and influence of a paribar depends only on wealth and occupation or that a son of a cultivator cannot marry the daughter of a zamindar. Although there is a stigma attached to certain occupational statuses, in Badarpur, there is no strict rule that a cultivator has to obtain a bride from another cultivator's paribar, despite the fact that such a marriage would fit the statistical trend. The marriage of two individuals depends solely on the consent of the paribars of the boy and the girl concerned.

To become a prestigious man in the village it is necessary for one to have a network of affinal relatives. Careers may be built, in agriculture or in any other field, by managing and dealing with relations, either affinal or blood. Hence, the desire and effort to elevate kin relationship are continuous on the part of the villagers. The best way of expanding this relationship is through marriage of daughters and sons to wealthy, and powerful, already-established paribars.

Marriage and Selection of Mate

Men in Badarpur take wives from surrounding villages. I collected data of 882 marriages covering 3 to 4 generations, regardless of whether the participants were dead or alive. Data are presented in Table 11 showing the location of marital ties as derived from the place of birth of spouses.

TABLE 11
Locations of Marital Ties of Badarpur

Place	Nos. of Marriages	%
Same village	58	6.58
Badarpur, Kazi Para, Parabo, Mahajampur	300	37.41
Jampur Union	106	12.02
Baidyar Bazar Thana	346	39.23
Outside of Thana	42	4.76
	882	100.00

Analysis reveals that if one combines intra-village marriages with immediately adjacent villages, 43.99 per cent of all reported marriages fall into an area of about 5 square miles. This same area is the largest, micro-regional, multi-village complex of which Badarpur forms a part. Thus it can be seen that mate selection leads to a network of kinship ties over the immediately surrounding area, where other kinds of social relations are also important, such as the *majhab*,[43] gushthi and paribar relations around Kazi Para, Parabo and Mahajampur.

The next most significant regional clustering of marriage ties, 39.23 per cent, is the area of Baidyar Bazar Thana, 125 square miles. Badarpur, Kazi Para, Parabo and Mahajampur villagers contract marriages anywhere within the Thana, but the tendency to venture beyond the immediate border of the Thana is rare.

Two types of marriage take place in Badarpur: the wealthier group always attracts brides and grooms from non-related villagers or, if possible, from wealthier paribars or baris living outside the village, while another group tries to select mates from their already established affinal relatives. In the latter group cross-cousin marriage is very frequent. In fact, according to the village custom, it is possible to marry anyone of the same generation if the individual is not the child of the same parents. The only restriction the Badarpuris observe in mate selection is the restriction prescribed by Islam. Islam permits beyond the limit of twelve prohibitive relatives of the opposite sex and they are that a girl cannot marry her: brother; father's brother; mother's brother; mother's father; father's father; brother's sister. A boy cannot marry his: sister; mother's sister; father's sister; mother's mother; father's mother; brother's sister. Chart 6 on page 80 shows one type of marriage which takes place frequently, almost inevitably, when the situation permits.

Suppose A is married to B and they have a daughter E. After the death of A, B is married again to C who already had a wife D. C and D

CHART 6. One Type of Marriage in Badarpur

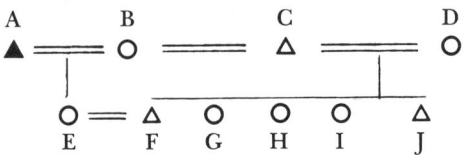

had several children. C and D's son F will now marry A and B's daughter E, although B and D are co-wives of C and living in the same bari.

Although plural marriage has been prohibited by the government of Pakistan since 1961,[44] there are still some people in the village who have more than one spouse alive and living in the same bari. Below I shall list the names of people, the number of times they married, and the number of wives they are cohabiting with, as found and recorded during the summer of 1966.

TABLE 12

Plural Marriages in Badarpur

Name	No. of Total Marriages	Present Wives
1. A. Karim Talukdar	4	3
2. Latif	20	1
3. Amu	2	2
4. Chan Miah	5	1
5. Samu (Pahlowan)	3	1
6. Zaman	3	3
7. Benga	3	x
8. Johar Ali	10	3
9. Lal Miah	4	1
10. Kabir	2	1
11. Kafiluddin	2	2
12. Kalai	6	3
13. Kitab	2	2
14. Osman	2	2

Before the new "Marriage and Family Law" (Government of Pakistan, 1961) anyone could marry up to four wives, as permitted by Islamic Shariat Law or Sunna. There are quite a few men other than the ones I have listed above who married more than once, but they did so only after the death of or their divorce from previous wives. In the list above I have included the names of persons who married more than once while their first wives were alive and were not legally divorced, although five of them are now living with a single wife.

In Badarpur the oldest male of the bari or paribar is the negotiator or arbitrator in selecting future mates for kith and kin. A marriage is still regarded not so much as a union between two individuals as the establishment of a relationship between two baris and thus two paribars and gushthis. However, in Badarpur, people construct their marriages to last, and they are not bound to any fixed system that dictates marriage in which young people are the wrong age.

During the year 1965–66, seventeen marriages took place in Badarpur, but ten of these involved remarriage of widowed or divorced spouses. Of the seven first marriages in Badarpur all were negotiated by the parents or grandparents of the principals. In all seven cases the bridegroom had to pledge *Rasooli Mehr*[45] for the bride. The amount of mehr promised is directly related to the political motivation of the contracting parties, and indirectly to the prestige and status the parties hold in the villagers' eyes. In Table 13, all seven marriages are shown together with the amount of mehr promised by the bridegrooms' families, the amount of land owned by both parties' parents, and the respective ages of the brides and grooms.

TABLE 13

Seven Marriages of Badarpur During the Years 1965–66

No.	Relationship	Mehr	Land Owned by Bride's Father	Land Owned by Groom's Father	Ages of the Bride & Groom	
1.	Cousins	Rs. 100	1 acre	1 acre	14	20
2.	nil	1000	4 acres	3 acres	14	20
3.	nil	1500	3½ acres	5 acres	15	19
4.	nil	2000	6 acres	4 acres	14	25
5.	nil	3000	4 acres	1 acre	16	22
6.	Cousins	3000	4 acres	2 acres	14	20
7.	nil	5000	5 acres	1 acre	16	22

Out of these seven marriages only two (nos. 1 & 6) involved were cousins. Number 1 took place between very poor households of the village who could not possibly acquire a spouse from anywhere else. Numbers 2, 4, and 6, acquired mates from the neighbouring villages. In each case guardians of the principals knew exactly for what reasons they had arranged the marriages; the receiver was aware of how much the giver was worth; the donor knew how much the receiver was worth to him. In the case of Number 2 and Number 6 the bridegrooms' fathers wanted to have the support of brides' fathers in the village council elections, and as a result they had to promise a relatively high amount of mehr.

Numbers 5 and 7 involved bridegrooms who did not have any prestige but had steady income from their mill jobs. Here the objective was to get recognition in the village by marrying daughters of relatively well-respected villagers, thus gaining prestige and influence. Possession of agricultural fields is a precious heritage; the major means to prestige and upperclass status rests heavily on the amount of land and property owned, and marriage is a useful means of augmenting the status of the next generation because it combined the land resources of two families.

Marriage Number 3 took place between two households of equal status in the village. This marriage, however, was arranged by the grandfathers of the two principals, who had been friends since childhood. In fact this is the only case where the groom's father had more land acreage than the bride's father. There is a general tendency in the village for all the brides who come from relatively low prestige groups to go to higher prestige groups and the brides of higher prestige groups to move to still higher places.

This can be linked to claims that a girl has against her brother, hence her natal paribar, and which, by extension, her husband has over her brothers and her gushthi. Since the husband is supporting his wife, she does not have to claim her brothers' assistance. By supporting his wife, a husband is doing a service to his wife's brothers who otherwise would be obliged to assist their sister. This naturally obliges the wife's brothers to be on good terms with their brother-in-law who could otherwise demand that his wife claim the portion of her father's property which she would have inherited legally. Hence a man who has a number of wives can call for assistance and support from his wives' brothers, whereas a man with a number of sisters is in a disadvantageous position, since he has ever increasing obligations to his brothers-in-law (sisters' husbands).

In Badarpur, although inter-gushthi competition is rather conspicuous, there is no restriction whatsoever regarding intermarriage between gushthis. Three wives of Gushthi A came from Gushthi B; four brides from Gushthi A came to Gushthi B; and one and three brides from Gushthi C went to Gushthi A and B respectively; also two brides from Gushthi A came to Gushthi C. Also, there are a few marriages between members of these gushthis and individuals from other families.

Kinship relationships are so strong in Badarpur that a minor insult to a member of the paribar will soon mobilize all other members for retaliation. Accordingly, situations arise when it becomes impossible for the villagers to settle problems; yet most of the time the village disputes are settled in the village through affinally related kin and by the members of the paribar.

Frequently members of the gushthi exchange gifts and invitations. During Idd-ul-Azha meat will be exchanged amongst them. If someone is forgotten he will take offense. During the festivals and occasions such as marriage, circumcision, and naming ceremonies, all the gushthi members expect a formal invitation which will be reciprocated on similar occasions. It is the duty of all the gushthi members to attend the funeral of a fellow member. Since the hearth of the deceased will not be lighted in the ghar or bari for three days following the death, it will be the duty of the paribar members to cook and supply food.

In other words, bari and paribar ties are the strongest of all the ties that the villagers enjoy. In another sense, however, the villagers consider themselves members of one solid group whenever they need to show a joint effort against a neighbouring village.

Religious Groupings

O'Malley (1934:45) writes "Religion is still the Alpha and Omega of Indian life." In a way statements such as this one are very accurate for describing Bengali life; but perhaps such statements are not at all applicable to the Bengal situation.

Religion may not today be the Alpha and Omega in the life of the people of Badarpur, but not long ago it was. For instance, the village is not only structured in terms of ghar, bari, paribar and gushthi; it is also divided in terms of religious faith and practices. Although most of the villagers are Muslim, and Islam does not approve of social discrimination in terms of wealth and birth, social differentiation can be observed in Badarpur in terms of their affiliation to different *majhabs* (sects), even though the line of demarcation may be somewhat blurred.

As to the origin of majhabs in Badarpur, no coherent history can be traced; the most that could be gathered was that many years ago there was only one mosque in the village, that being the mosque in the center of the village, where all the Muslims used to gather during any of their festivals and ceremonies. People belonging to this mosque are all Muhammadi (name of the majhab) and do not follow any of the Muslim Saints who came after Muhammad.[46]

After the death of prophet Muhammad, the Muslim community was divided into two major subdivisions, Shiah and Sunni.[47] The Sunni group was divided again into four sects, the first three of which

(Safi, Hanafi, and Hambali) were the followers of the three great Saints of Islam: Imam Safi, Imam Abu Hanifa, and Imam Ahmed-Bin-Hambal. The fourth sect Muhammadi did not recognize any of these three Imams and continued following only Muhammad the prophet.

When Rahim, who was a Hanafi, came to this village and founded Gushthi *A,* many villagers grouped themselves with him and changed their faith from the Muhammadi to the Hanafi sect. The Hanafis for some fifty years prayed in the same mosque with the Muhammadis; but during the lifetime of Korban Ali, around the turn of the century, the task of appointing a new Imam (priest, the man who leads prayer) arose. When Korban Ali chose to support a Hanafi for the job, a dispute broke out between the Hanafis and Muhammadis.

The Muhammadis who had established the mosque did not approve of Korban Ali's choice. However, the dispute was settled rapidly without coming to a head, when Korban Ali together with his group decided to establish a new mosque at the extreme southeast corner of the village, where his ancestor first arrived and entered the village. Thus the second mosque was established in the village.

During the early 1920s after the end of World War I and with the downfall of the Khaliph of Turkey, a revivalistic movement amongst the Muslims spread over all the world (see supra Chapter two). Many missionaries set out to revitalize the faith of the Muslims. One of them, a follower of the Safi sect, came to Badarpur and converted a small group to his own faith. Thus the third sect of Muslims started in the village, establishing their own Safi mosque near the Muhammadi one.

The Muhammadis were the first in this village and are the largest in number. Recently (1954) they found it difficult to accommodate all the members of their faith in their small mosque and decided to build a second Muhammadi mosque in the village. Hence they established the fourth mosque close to the extreme northern border of the village. There are no people in this village belonging to the Hambali sect of Islam, and, hence, no mosque of this sect.

From this history of the origin of these mosques it is apparent that there cannot be any one-to-one relation between a gushthi or a paribar division and that of a majhab division. It will thus be seen that although Gushthi *A* can be loosely identified with the Hanafi Majhab, and the rest of the village with Muhammadi, this is not a one-to-one relationship between gushthi and paribar divisions and majhab divisions. Although the Hanafi majhab in the village owes its origin to Rahim, most of his followers were the local inhabitants either Hindu converts or followers of the Muhammadi sect. Thus members of approximately 10 per cent of Gushthi *A*, the descendants of Rahim, are in fact the Muhammadi majhab and 4 or 5 per cent are of the Safi sect. All individuals of the same paribars were not necessarily converted; consequently most paribars in the village have both Muhammadi and Hanafi members.

Members of a single ghar in the village always belong to the same sect. This is usually because sects tend to be endogamous and Hanfi or Safi men marry Hanafi or Safi girls. If a member of a Hanafi majhab decides to marry into a Muhammadi majhab, there may be politicking between the two groups against such a match. In no case will the individual be ostracized from the village activities, although he may be teased by the members of his own majhab. In such a case the bride takes up the majhab of her husband. Majhabs are in many ways loose organizations, and any individual member can move from one sect to another for convenience and personal gain. The gushthi kinship is not necessarily a determining factor in this shifting affiliation.

Within a bari, members of different ghars may choose different majhabs, and most frequently they do so. In fact, over the slightest misunderstanding between two bari members, one may for some time attend a different mosque. However, as soon as the misunderstanding is over, he may come back to his original faith. It is also common for affiliation with different mosques to create factions within the bari, or within the paribar, as will be shown later. In other words, bari, paribar, and gushthi often cut across majhab lines, giving rise to conflicting loyalties and possibilities of friction and/or solidarity.

Mullahs and Maulanas, who lead prayers, always try to differentiate between the villagers in terms of their affiliation with different sects; these leaders often accuse sects other than their own of being sacrilegious and un-Islamic.

During festivals and ceremonies mosques become busy. Especially in the month of Ramadan,[48] people become particularly religious and spend considerable time in the mosque. Most of the villagers fast during Ramadan, and the scorching sun makes them tired and unable to do much manual labour. They go to the mosques, all of which are situated in relatively cool, shady places in the village, and lie on the floor until the time for *Iftar* (at sunset, the time for breaking the fast).

Gathering in the mosque gives the villagers a chance to gossip and to maintain a form of social control in the village. After Iftar, however, they do not find time to gossip, firstly because they have to perform their prayers, and secondly, because they are too tired to socialize after fasting for the whole day.

Non-Muslim Religious Leadership

There are some people in the village who neither go to the mosque for prayer nor believe in any supernatural power, but most of the villagers are devoted Muslims. There have been a series of personal and community-wide crises that lead some to fear the unknown. Many of these believe that sickness, death, crop yields, and individual fortune depend on some powers which can be appeased through specific ritual behaviour. Although ritual performance and similar activities other than direct prayers to God are not sanctioned by Islam, a number of people in this village practice such rituals, not only for their own gain but also for the good fortune of others.

There are five or six healers, *fakirs,* and *sadhus* in Badarpur of whom Idris Kabiraj is perhaps the best known. The way he controls his following will serve to illustrate workings of a group which focuses on healers. Idris Kabiradj preaches that there is a direct relationship between the crises of life and a world of supernatural beings and unseen forces. He insists that a systematic ritual can link men and supernatural beings in order to modify or if necessary control events causing uncertainty, pain, or fear. God created human beings, but He also created Zins,[49] Idris Kabiraj would say. Zins are responsible for all pain, fear or uncertainty, and are controllable through rituals. The differences between zins and man are due to the circumstances of the creation of each group.

Members who believe in such supernatural beings also claim to be Muslims by religion and go to the mosque more frequently in this village than people who do not have any faith in the rituals of Idris Kabiraj.

I interviewed one of the followers of Idris:

Q. Why did you first go to Idris and what was your trouble?
Ans. I don't know! Someone used to call me at night, mostly at dusk, and I used to go out of my house and most of the time used to end up in some ditches or bushes, senseless.

Q. What has Idris done for you and how?
Ans. He recited *doa* (chants) for me and has given me these *tabis* (omens, talismen) which saved me from that horrible trouble.

Q. Did you ever consult a doctor?
Ans. Yes! but, to no effect.

I interviewed five persons in the village (all males) and all of them gave me similar stories. All are between twenty and thirty years of age and are either bachelors or divorcees. It has been reported to me that most of Kabiraj's patients are females, whom I could not interview. All their relatives were reluctant to discuss these things with me.[50]

I asked Idris to explain his technique and to tell me names of the shrubs and plants he uses as medicine (or talismen). First he refused to disclose his professional secret; however, finally he agreed to give me his secret for twenty rupees (roughly four dollars). He gave me the names of the following medicinal ingredients:

1. Dhutra leaves (a poisonous tree leaf)
2. Liver of Bhetki (a kind of river fish)
3. Roshun (garlic)
4. Purana Ghee (very old purified butter)
5. Supari (Betal nut)

Idris declares that only the pungent odor of his medicine can control the supernatural powers that visit the village occasionally (see photo no. 21). In this village Idris is so famous for his skill in controlling

Photo no. 21. Idris Kabiraj (the traditional healer) believes that only the pungent odor of his medicine can control the supernatural powers that visit the village occasionally.

supernatural zins that even the most religious Muslims as well as the most agnostic villagers talk about him with a sense of respect and fear. I could not find a single person complaining that Idris had tried to harm anyone in the village with his power. Belief in Kabiraj is a most effective means of social control in Badarpur's life, particularly in the context of poisoning, soul stealing and the effect of zins. Kabiraj works with confidence and his followers in Badarpur form a special class in the village.

Those who are the poorest in the village, who hardly have any say in the village disputes, form a large part of this class. Second, other people of this group are those who go to the mosques for prayer, but at the same time take advice from *Sadhus, Fakirs* and from anyone else they think is more capable than themselves. And third, the group consists mostly of the fishermen and agriculturists who are the least educated of the village.

All these groupings may be considered independent social units comprised of a number of individuals who, at a given time, stand in definite independent statuses and role relationships with one another, and who possess a set of values regulating the behaviour of individual members, at least in matters important to the group. Hence, specific attitudes, sentiments, aspirations, and goals are implicit in the common values and norms of these various groupings. Such a grouping in Badarpur, as in every part of East and West Bengal, is known as a *dal*, literally meaning a group or faction.

The word *dal* would be translated as faction when applied to village groupings, and as political grouping when applied at the provincial or national level. Dals are not necessarily created just for opposition and hostility; nor are discord and dissension the distinguishing qualities of dals in inter-faction relations. Frequently dals are cooperative economic, social, and religious-ceremonial groups.

> While hostility towards other groups is a common attribute of factions and new factions are often formed as a result of quarrels and disputes, this is seldom the only or even the major force which holds factions together (Dhillon, 1955:30).

The factions in Badarpur are generally referred to by the names of their leaders or in some instances by the nickname of a gushthi, sect or occupational group. This may be the case when faction and gushthi, sect or occupational group are synonymous; for example, Bhuyiar dal (faction of Bhuyian); Hanafi dal (faction consisting of the Hanafis); Majhir dal (factions consisting of the boatmen) etc. Hence it is possible to look at these different factions of Badarpur from an entirely different angle, taking the economic and occupational factors into consideration.

Occupational Groupings

In the previous chapter we looked at the population of Badarpur and its land-holding composition and occupations. Table 4 lists the thirteen different occupations of household heads in Badarpur. These occupations are ones that the individual can choose for himself, and not occupational caste groupings which individuals are committed to at birth and which are connected by *jajmani* relationship.[51] There is, nevertheless, a statistical trend for a farmer's son to become a farmer, a barber's son to become a barber, and a boatman's son to become a boatman. Individuals and occupational groups are not committed to other occupational groups: a weaver in the village does not have to supply certain of his products to be assured of getting some products that he needs. A teacher in Badarpur is not committed to teach the village boys in exchange for certain facilities extended to him by the villagers; rather he is supposedly regularly paid by a bureaucratic educational system which encompasses the whole country.

There is in Badarpur a sense in which the occupations form groupings for particular social activities in informal interaction and in economic affairs. These groupings can be labeled "the outside oriented occupations," "the internal service occupations," and "agricultural occupations."

Outside Oriented Occupations

The outside oriented group of the village consists mostly of shopkeepers, labourers, "visitors," and teachers. Although they have land in the village, the main economic enterprise for these four occupational groups lies in the shops, in manual labour outside the village (normally in jute mills), in occupations in other villages, in town (in case of the "visitors" group all of whom may be considered white-collar employees), and in pay cheques from the office of the District Education Officer.

For various reasons members of this group are frequent visitors to the cities, and most have an interest in what is going on in the outside world. Having the most contact with city life, through their own occupational channels they try to keep themselves informed. They socialize in their spare time, particularly in the evening, either in the village market drinking tea or at the house of one of the "visitors" or teachers.

Frequently in such gatherings people discuss matters of interest inside the village realm although occasionally they do discuss internal village affairs. The frequency of their discussions of internal or external subjects fluctuates according to the overall current trend. For example, during a flood most of their discussions may revolve around the flood situation, while the topic of a quarrel between two of the villagers may not be discussed at all. This may be reversed, however, if an influential member of their group becomes involved in the internal conflict.

The Internal Service Occupations

The internal service group consists mostly of the zamindar, priests, doctors, boatmen, the fisherman, weavers and the barber. All these people are directly or indirectly under the control of the zamindar. The boatmen, the weavers, the fisherman, and the barber in the village cannot live on the income from their occupations alone; they are also dependent on their own or others' land and land produce. The zamindar, being the Chairman of the Union Council, controls the taxation of their land, and thus easily controls these people.

The two doctors of the village, though not dependent on their land products, find it economically to their advantage to group with the zamindar. Occasionally all these people go to visit the zamindar to discuss village matters and to participate in the settling of disputes. The priests of the village, who also find it advantageous to group with the zamindar, are the most vocal in such gatherings, their discussions mostly focusing on village affairs, religion, the negligence of religion, private conflicts, and inter-village conflicts.

The zamindar is not only the discussion leader, he is also the main patron of these people. The zamindar's patronage is not necessarily financial help, but it does involve economic assistance in terms of supplies. Doctors will get relief medicine through the zamindar; the priests will get donations for the mosque; and the weavers will get weaving thread at government controlled rate. The boatmen will win contracts to bring merchandise from the city; the fisherman will find his best customer in the zamindar; and the barber will live under the protection of the zamindar.

Agricultural Occupations

The agricultural group consists of the farmers of the village, who are busy from early morning to sunset in ploughing, tilling and caring for their land (see photo no. 22). In the evening, when they have some

Photo no. 22. Farmer clears his field, removing the dry straw by hand.

time they tend to congregate in their neighbouring mosque or join in *hookka* (locally made smoking implement) smoking with their neighbours.

Most of their discussion centers around their land, their crop, rainfall and drought. Matters such as country politics or economic supply and demand, being too complicated, are carefully avoided by them in their discussions. Occasionally they may talk about inter-village conflict, but mostly their conversation remains confined to their own personal problems and plans regarding their land and crop.

Farmers also participate actively in the mosque affairs, considering themselves an important part of their own mosque. They are interested in knowing what is happening outside the village, but with their limited time they find it hard to discuss such matters. Members of the outside oriented group are a puzzle to them, and members of the internal services group a terror. Being sandwiched between these puzzling, and often terrorizing groups, they try to avoid social intercourse with both these groups as much as they can. They regard the other groups as something mysterious, as something beyond their capacity to understand.

92 A Bangladesh Village

Hence, theoretically, it is possible for us to divide the villagers into three different groups as described above. To show this schematically, a table is added below:

TABLE 14
Occupation and Social Organization in Badarpur

Outside-oriented Group	Number of Households	Internal Services Group	Number of Households	Agricultural Group	Number of Households
Labourer	20	Zamindar	2	Farmer	320
Teacher	6	Doctor	2		Total: 320
Shopkeeper	6	Priest	3		
Visitor	4	Fisherman	1		
		Weaver	3		
		Barber	1		
		Boatman	14		
Total:	36	Total:	26	Total:	320

This is a hypothetical construction. Not all the 36 households of the outside oriented group will group together; nor will all the 26 households of the internal services group stay together; nor will the 320 of the agricultural group always remain together. In fact, they overlap both in groupings and in occupations. The functions, activities, and personnel of these groups overlap and interweave in a bewildering intricacy.

There are approximately 10 per cent of the farmers in the village who feel more at home with the members of the outside oriented group than with the internal services group, or with the agricultural group. One or two teachers, on the other hand, feel more at ease with the people of the internal services group or even with the agricultural group. The same is true for a few shopkeepers (particularly the two who act as government dealers for rice, wheat, and sugar). About 40 per cent of the outside oriented group, 50 per cent of the internal services group and a good majority of the agricultural group are members of Gushthi *B* and Muhammadi majhab, while about 40 per cent of the outside oriented group, 10 per cent of the internal services group and approximately 20 per cent of the agricultural group are part of Gushthi *A* and Hanafi majhab. The rest of the villagers are unevenly distributed and are affiliated with Gushthi *C*, Safi majhab, the followers of Kabiraj and other Sadhus.

These three groups can also be seen to have three different types of social backgrounds. The outside oriented group consists of the village entrepreneurs, professionals, teachers and others who are less concerned about religious ceremonies and functions. They never try to avoid people of any other group, despite the fact that rivalries, although usually inconspicuous, do exist between occupational groups. People of the outside oriented group are very reluctant to accept the supremacy of the internal services group (for example, in genealogical or religious fields) and will try their best to protest anything in which the initiative has come from the members of the internal services group.

The internal services group consists of the village aristocrats, priests and remnants of the dead jajmani occupations, all of whom claim to have hereditary aristocracy or position in the village, and most of whom have some landed property to depend upon. The very few who have sold their property still try to maintain their affiliation with their own group. In social gatherings they will expect to have the best seats in the village. Although many of them do not perform regular prayers, they easily become critical of others who do not observe prayers regularly.

The third group is not particularly concerned about earthly matters; their demands are less and they try to console themselves in every difficulty by shifting the responsibilities to an unknown power, the God. According to them everything is done by God. People have no hand in matters; it is beyond their power to regulate the will of God.

In this chapter we have looked at the social organization of Badarpur and have seen that groups formed by different households cross-cut their bari, paribar, gushthi, religious or sectarian faiths, and occupational groups. None of these groups, whether affinal (paribar or gushthi), religious (sectism) or occupational, are closed, and thus no two groups' memberships are actually exclusive.

Although the functions, activities, and personnel of these groups overlap and interweave in a bewildering intricacy, nevertheless, a crude formal classification has been attempted in Diagram I on p. 94, in an effort to differentiate these groupings.

We have seen so far that geram or village of Badarpur is not an unsegmented unit but is a combination of a number of smaller units. Yet, the whole village constitutes a very distinct unit in which the villagers have both a feeling of strong solidarity against other villages and a great affection for their village folks. Members of Badarpur fight side by side to support each other in feuds against a neighbouring village, thus strengthening the solidarity of the village. This will be taken up in Chapter six.

The intricate behavioural and interaction pattern of these groups and subgroups both creates integration and binds them in solidarity.

DIAGRAM I
Cross-Cutting Groupings

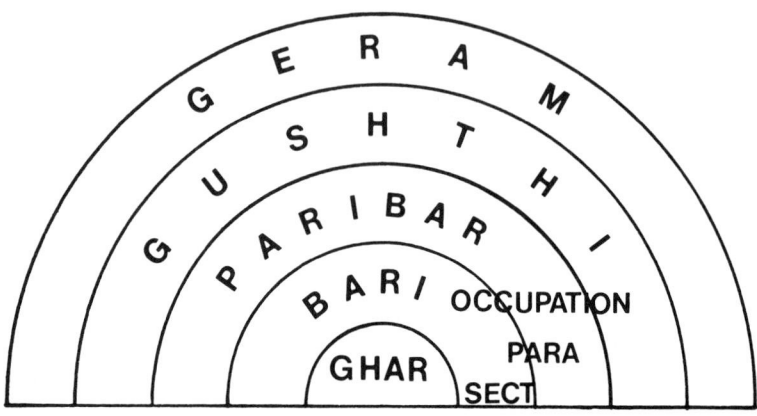

To understand this pattern it will be necessary to turn first to the growth and development of the traditional village political organization, the subject of Chapter five. This will lead us to look at the political organization of the village in its historical perspective, and to examine the manner in which that organization changed its structure. Because of the non-bounded quality of the groups and because there are alway some individuals who are members of some group other than the expected one, the sixth chapter will be concerned with changing village political structure and the maneuvering by individuals who wish to get decisions made in their favour. Finally, the subject of chapter seven will be the shifting loyalties of the individual and the relationship between village politics and the changing national political ideology.

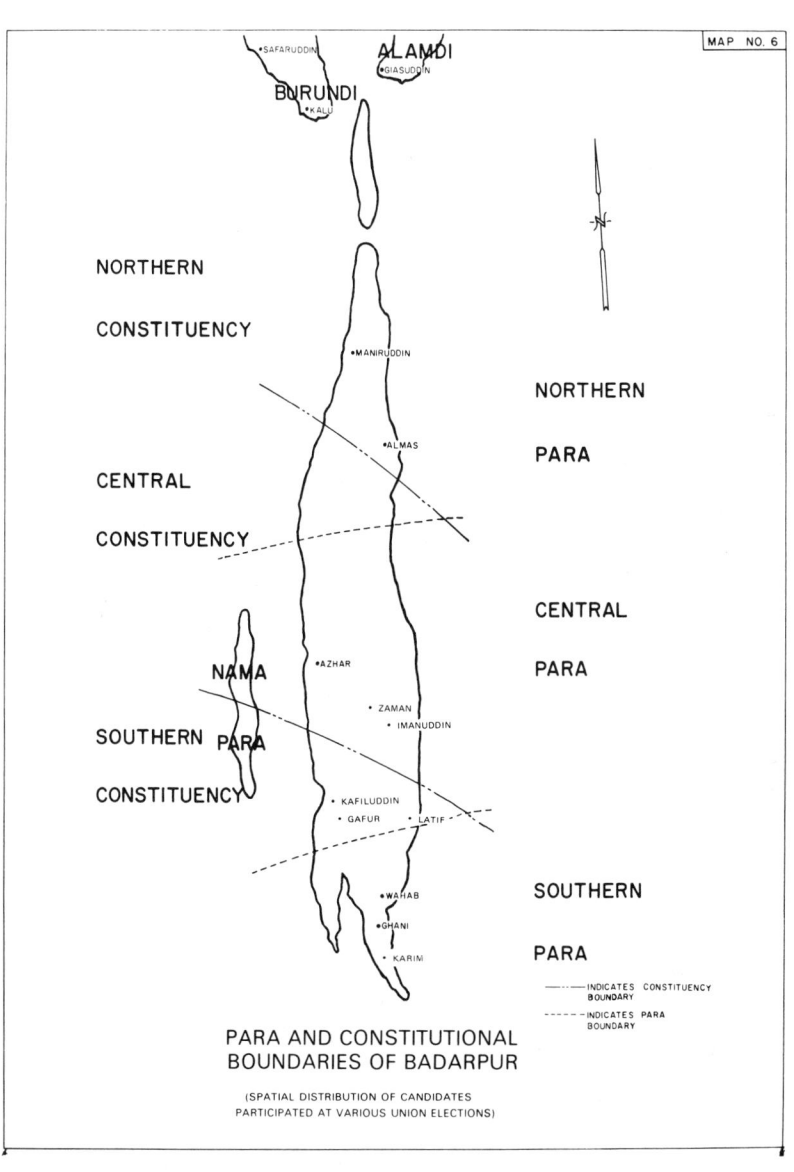

CHAPTER FIVE

Political History of Badarpur

In the previous chapter we have looked at Badarpur as a series of groups which are cross-cutting. This chapter will describe how, over the course of history, these groupings and the roles which have composed them have changed their relationships. Coming down to the recent past it will introduce the recent political history of the village, the various village and national elections that have occurred since 1947 and the individuals who have been the chief actors in the politicking. For this purpose the present chapter is divided into sections and sub-sections beginning with the functions of zamindar-talukdars of the late eighteenth century (1793 A.D.) showing their power and influence in the village politics, together with the development of the Panchayat system in 1871 and the way in which nominees of the zamindar used to dominate over the panchayat. The development of Union Boards in 1885 and the way the villagers used to elect the members of the Board is then described, after which we take up the changes that took place in 1919 with the establishment of the village Self Government Act which changed the judicial power of the panchayat. Finally we study some points in the development of politics from 1947 to 1961.

1. Pre-Partition Village Politics in Badarpur

(a) *Zamindar, Talukdar, Mollahs and Moulvis*

The Zamindar system was established in Bengal in 1793[52] with the Permanent Settlement Act of Lord Cornwallis. At that time the villagers of Bengal were usually ruled by the most powerful man and the most powerful man in the village was necessarily the zamindar if he lived in the village or his representatives responsible for collecting taxes for the zamindar.

The government was not particularly interested in the protection and welfare of the cultivators as opposed to the zamindar as the government did not consider that to be its business. Thus when Lord Hardinge questioned Bayley his collector (District Magistrate) about the welfare of the peasant class (Woodruff, 1964:2:51) ". . . he laughed and said it was no business of ours; the zamindar has a right to do what he liked with his *ryots* (subjects)."

In the village Badarpur, the Hindu zamindar was the most powerful man, and he dominated village affairs without challenge. Only when there were conflicts of religious interests, would the Muslim majority village rebel against the zamindar and threaten the peace. As we have noted earlier (see supra p. 70), it was in such circumstances that the villagers invited Rahim from outside to defend them against the zamindar.

Thus the descendants of Rahim, particularly after the time of Kadam Ali, became a talukdar family, the leaders of the Muslim community. They defended the Muslims against the power of the Hindu zamindar, but also acted as the zamindar's assistant where Muslims were concerned. Likewise, though, they had a political and economic role, particularly when Kadam Ali bought land rather than continuing being "leader of guards" as his ancestor Rahim did. This change probably took place around the middle of the 19th century, definitely after 1850.

In religious matters the Muslim community was led by Moulvis and Mollahs (priests and religious scholars). These were not appointed by the government, but were appointed from the local or neighbouring villages on the basis of their knowledge of religion. Mollahs and Moulvis may be self-educated persons, or may go through formal schooling in the cities, or adopt a hereditary profession.

Mollahs and Moulvis in Badarpur were not formally educated in any religious institutions. They were self-educated persons from the village, specializing in religious matters. In fact, they were the only literate Muslims in the villages—the only people to whom the farmers could go to get their letters and tax notices read. Although with the spread of education in the village this particular function of the Moulvis was greatly reduced (and, in fact, is hardly perceptible today) until recently they used to think of themselves as the leaders of the villagers. Education is the magic which dispels the mystery of the world of print and sets people free from dependence on Moulvis willing to interpret at the expense of the clients' freedom of thinking. Nevertheless, to the illiterate villagers of Badarpur the prestige of the Moulvis and Mollahs was very high.

(b) *Village Panchayat*

All disputes and matters where a decision was to be taken by the entire village were brought before a panchayat. Although the power of the zamindar used to make itself felt in all village activities (for example, the panchayat always met in front of the zamindar's house and either the zamindar or, in his absence, a member of the zamindar family used to preside over it), most of the decisions regarding religious questions involving only Muslims were normally made by the Mollahs and Maulanas. When the disputes involved both Hindus and Muslims, the Muslims of the village used to gather at the talukdar's house and the Hindus at the house of the zamindar.

The traditional panchayat did not have any fixed membership; the zamindar or in his absence a nominee of the zamindar, the talukdar, Moulvis of the village mosques, and a few village elders used to participate in the panchayat meetings. Any villager could attend to hear the panchayat's decision, but only certain ones could participate in the decision-making, since as has been mentioned earlier, the decisions of the panchayat depend exclusively on its members, the zamindar or his representatives, the talukdar and the Mollahs and Moulvis of the village. In 1871 the Chowkidari-Panchayat Act was passed by the government and this traditional system was formally included in the government structure.

(c) *Local Government 1871–1947*

The Chowkidari-Panchayat Act of 1871 nominally created a five-man Panchayat Committee embracing several villages (or a Union) and superior to several village panchayats. This five-man committee was responsible for maintaining village peace and was entitled to collect taxes. In practice, Badarpur was in no way affected by the Act. The zamindar or his nominees still settled internal disputes at the village level without bringing them to either the village panchayat or the Union Panchayat Committee. The Panchayat Committee itself was entirely composed of people pre-selected by the zamindar himself from among men whom he trusted. In other words, although the Panchayat Committee was formed as far back as 1871, the power of the zamindar did not recede to a fraction of a degree.

The local Self-Government Act of 1885, instituting elections and higher level bodies at the District and Local Board levels, also, as in most rural areas, meant little change for Badarpur. Although any taxpayer was eligible for election to the District, local or Union Boards, hardly anyone would dare to contest in the elections from the villages because of the risk of incurring the displeasure of their local zamindar; after all, the zamindars always did want to have their own candidates elected for these committees. Only in the cities, where people were relatively more educated and where the power of the zamindars was not so strongly felt, could one feel free to seek election. But in a country where more than 90 per cent of the population were villagers under the direct control of the zamindar, a few city elected members in different organizations could hardly exert any pressure to change the structure. Moreover, one-third of the members of the District, Local and Union Board were nominated by the District Magistrate, Sub-Divisional Officer and the Circle Officers, and all of these had usually been selected from recommendations of the local zamindars and were from the educated class.

Even the advent of education brought little change in Badarpur. Before Azizuddin, Amir Ali and several other Muslim villagers first organized a school in Amir Ali's house at the beginning of the century, only the zamindar's children were able to go away to school; and up to 1947 only children of six Muslim paribars of Badarpur had gone to school.

In other words, the power and authority of the zamindar had never been challenged effectively by anyone in the village. For violations of the law, an ordinary farmer (villager) would be beaten with a cane or shoes whereas relatively powerful ones were fined. This type of discrimination (against the less powerful farmers) as well as the ignominious punishment of being beaten with a cane or shoes infuriated the Muslim villagers and they began to express their discontent with the Hindu zamindar in every way they could. The political movements of the country after 1914 added fuel to the villagers' discontent. Muslim national leaders at that time were trying to popularize the Khelafat movement in the country—a movement against the British rule and in favour of the Turkish Empire. The non-cooperation movements of Gandhi, although they first sought for Muslim support, gradually took a different turn and the Hindu-Muslim clash burst out throughout the subcontinent. As rumors from other provinces began to pour in, the Muslim majority in the Bengali villages gradually became more and more jaundiced of the Hindu zamindars. The talukdar Kadam Ali and other Muslim leaders of the village gave active support to the villagers at this time and asked them to boycott any kind of dealings with the Hindu zamindar. The Hindu zamindar, as a result had to hire labourers for his fields from outside Badarpur. The time was ripe to look at the village situation and the British government made a major change in the village administration.

Village Self-Government Act of 1919

The first major change in the village administration came after the Village Self-Government Act of 1919—which marked the first British attempt to intervene in village political affairs in order to remedy the ineffectiveness of village Panchayats in the struggle between Hindu zamindars and Muslim peasants. This Act decreed that the village disputes should be settled by the Union Board whenever possible. When they could not be settled there they should go to higher courts. In no case however, was the zamindar to settle a dispute arbitrarily or exercise physical punishment to any accused offender. The victim has the right to be redressed, but the offender has also an equal right to be heard by a legitimate authority such as the Union Board. This increase in the powers of the elected Union Board and the decrease in the powers (particularly in that of summary punishment) of the zamindar dominated village panchayat did indeed serve to diminish the prestige of the village zamindar.

Yet, the zamindar still retained much of his power and could manipulate villagers to get decisions made in his own favour. In particular he could exercise power by nominating candidates, by instructing villagers to vote for them, and by keeping villagers ignorant of the implications and importance of their votes. (This was possible because few in the village could read or write either Bengali or English, and those who could did not have access to elected members of higher authorities). Thus, the elected members, being the nominees of the zamindars, whose interests they represented, had few links with their constituents,[53] and the zamindars had every interest in preventing them from appealing directly to villagers. Further, as long as zamindar support was required, elected representatives had no reason to risk losing it by appealing to the peasants themselves or seeking their welfare.

Local Government 1918-1947

Even the talukdar's family, though opposed to the zamindars as the leaders of the Muslims against the Hindus, was a landlord family and had many of the same objectives as the zamindars to spreading popular representation. However, the talukdar family had never reached the height that the Hindu zamindar family enjoyed in the power structure of this village.

Another person who wielded influence and power in the village was the Chowkidar. A Chowkidar is the lowest representative of the police at the union and village level. It was his duty, as it is even today, to report all the happenings in or about the village to the police station at Baidyar Bazar, four and a half miles southeast of the village. Unless there was something very serious such as murder, robbery, etc. which necessitated immediate reporting, he made his report when he went there for his weekly attendance.

The village Chowkidar was paid a monthly salary by the Union Board, of which the zamindar or his nominee used to be chairman. Being an appointee of the Union head, the Chowkidar entangled many persons in the village in fictitious cases, and brought government policemen to the village to fleece people. The Chowkidar was an engine of oppression, and prided himself in the reflected glory of the police whom he represented. People were terribly afraid of police and before independence in 1947 the sight of the red turban (police used to wear red turbans during the British rule) made people flee into the paddy fields and bushes nearby. There were many cases in which the police threatened to arrest people, and it was only the payment of heavy bribes that could save them. Certain individual families were financially ruined because of machinations by the police, and a threat through the Chowkidar to call the police made it possible for the Union Board head to get anything done.

Through this Chowkidar, it was told, any party could bribe the Union Board chairman before the formal meeting of the Union Board, and this is what is commonly done. The party who furnished the largest bribe was sure to win the case and gain his point. The other members of the Union Board, less vocal, influential, and domineering than the zamindar, could never have much to say against his decision. Until 1947, the Union Board was only a guise through which the Union head dominated the village and its affairs.

With this fear of the disastrous consequences resulting from the outside police being called in in criminal cases, it is not surprising that the village also feared calling in government officials from the Sub-divisional Office in Narayanganj to settle civil disputes which the village panchayat failed to mediate. Furthermore, any appeal to outside help in settling disputes was felt as making the entire village lose face. Both factors thus tended to make villagers accept the decisions of the Union Panchayat. In a village dominated by "village elders" this could have resulted in considerable democratization, but in Badarpur where the zamindar nominated most panchayat members, it resulted in a panchayat which acted to retard change.

2. Post Partition Village Politics (1947–1961)

After the partition of 1947 the power of the Hindu zamindar, already on the decline, was severely curtailed and he could no longer dictate the voting of the villagers. This shook people's ways of life and thought. Those who were masters were approaching the poorest villager for his vote. There was scope now for talent to show itself. Persons with ability in organization, persuasive power, oratorical skill, some education and knowledge of men and affairs could become leaders. Time was ripe for the emergence of new leadership.

The three-tier power structure of the village, zamindar, talukdar, and Mollahs and Moulvis held more influence in the village decision-making than the legitimate source of power the Union Board. After the partition of 1947 the Talukdar Karim took over the leadership from the zamindar as an automatic and natural transformation. In other words, after partition, at least initially, Karim was the only person in the village who could claim the leadership of the entire village in the secular areas of village affairs. As Mollahs and Maulanas are only involved in religious affairs, they hardly came into conflict with Karim, who in fact used to be urged to represent the Muslim cause to the Hindu zamindar. The only real conflict Karim used to have was the conflict of interests with the Hindu zamindar.

Thus, after the partition, since there were no more any members to fight for the zamindar's cause, the Union Board came under Karim's control. Before 1947 Karim used to be a nominee of the zamindar; after 1947 he became the "nominating authority" replacing the zamindar. In this way both the informal and formal power structures of the village (the village panchayat and the Union Board) at least for some time came under Karim's stronghold.

The nexus of politicians of Badarpur so far had not included the working class, peasants and labourers who constitute the major portion of the village population; it was quite unthinkable for a man of lower strata to contest for the membership of the Union Board. This is one of the main reasons why the Muslim landlord Karim could retain his chairmanship for a quarter of a century, in spite of the earnest desire of most of the villagers to have him ousted. Whenever an election comes he can easily manipulate a group of people to seek election on his ticket.

Thus after the partition village politics became more and more complicated as new people began to get involved in the struggle for power by contesting in the Union Board elections and participating in decision-making at various levels. Here I will try to narrate these events and introduce the chief actors. A later chapter will analyse the processes by which they gained power.

The first person to emerge independently was Maniruddin. Manu (Maniruddin) managed to acquire some Hindu property and soon became financially well-off. In the election of 1953, he managed to defeat an influential member of Gushthi C, Wahab, an uncle of Zaman and Imanuddin, and thus became a member of the Union Board. This was the year in which Karim did not contest in the Union Board election, but was nominated as a member of the Union Board by the government.

1953 Chairman Election

In the chairmanship election of 1953 Maniruddin tried to challenge the incumbent Karim and remove him from the chairmanship of the Union Board. Although the attempt failed, nevertheless, he remained a constant threat to Karim's power.

Maniruddin was the son of a rice merchant. His great grandfather had made a moderate fortune through his rice business, but earlier in the century had become involved in a case with the Hindu landlord of the village. This long drawn-out case sapped the financial strength of the family, which was reduced to great hardships. Although the family had fallen upon evil days, Manu's education was not neglected. He was sent to a middle school six miles from the village, but could not complete his education due to the death of his father. From the rank of a practically known agriculturist of the village, Maniruddin suddenly came to power and influence and challenged Karim's leadership in the Union. This was in fact the first time an ordinary villager had dared to contest in an election.

1956 Membership Election

After a span of four years in 1956 another election in the Union Board took place. During this election Karim was challenged by Dr. Gafur of Gushthi B while Kafiluddin, cousin of Gafur was nominated by the government as a member of the Union Board on the recommendation of Karim.

The growing popularity of Gafur made him an irritant to several other villagers and particularly to the members of Gushthi A and their political head Karim, whose power, influence and prestige had declined due to Gafur's activities. The members of Gushthi B, all of whom lived in the Dakshin Para of the village, started to create trouble for Gafur in every way possible and began to campaign to discredit him. The realization that Gafur was so popular and would have been elected so easily if Karim had accepted government nomination gave Karim grave concern about the situation. Karim and Mafiz (the Chowkidar) were the two who were most affected by Gafur's popularity: they could no longer frighten the villagers by calling the police on the slightest pretext.

To avert this eventuality Karim himself decided to run in the election against Gafur, instead of seeking the government nomination which he had secured previously. Karim, a shrewd politician, nominated Kafil (Kafiluuddin) and recommended him for the government nomination, and thus was assured of Kafil's allegiance to him. Kafil, himself an influential member of Gushthi *B*, created a faction and thus split Gushthi *B* members into two groups, one favouring Karim as their candidate and the other supporting Gafur. Mafiz, although he was a member of Gushthi *B*, joined with Kafil against Gafur because Gafur's exhortation to the people to shed their fear of the police and resist temptation to offer any illegal gratification was a threat to Mafiz's income.

Thus with the help of Kafil and Mafiz Chowkidar, Karim was able to divide the votes from Gushthi *B* while his own Gushthi *A* supported him in a block. As a result Gafur lost the election and Karim became an elected member of the Union Board together with Kafiluddin as an ally in the contest for the chairmanship. Although Gafur lost in the election, this election established the fact that in Badarpur, Karim no longer was an unchallenged leader, and it will be seen that whenever occasion permitted, people came forward to challenge Karim in his leadership fight, the climax of which took place in 1965.

Karim's unsuccessful opponent for membership in the Union Board, Abdul Gafur, was a doctor and the agent for the Muslim League party. He had read medicine in the National Medical School (see supra, Chapter Three, p. 42) and could make fiery speeches. But he had hardly any roots in the village. Although his ancestors had all lived in the village and he was a nephew of Azizuddin, he himself since his childhood had been out of the village studying at the neighbouring schools, and later studying medicine in the city. He had gained some prominence in the village when he came back to practice there in 1955. Moreover, his contact with the city, the members of the legislature or prominent men (such as ministers and officials) and participation in the Pakistan movement helped him. If a member of the legislature visited the village, normally Gafur would arrange for his accommodation and public meetings. These contacts gradually but considerably increased his importance in the village. Yet, when the election came the villagers chose their old member, that is the Muslim landlord, Karim, instead of choosing the doctor.

Early in 1958 Zaman, a member of Gushthi *C*, came into contact with some officials at the Sub-Divisional Officer's (S.D.O.) office at Narayanganj which further buttressed his position. The Sub-Divisional Officer had to come to a neighbouring village for a government enquiry, and ordered the Waterway Supervisory Official to have all the water hyachinth cleared from the river to allow his boat to pass. The chairman of the Union Board, Karim, took the clearing contract from the official but the progress of the work was so slow that when the official came to inspect the work a week before the Sub-Divisional Officer's arrival he became unnerved at the prospect of the Sub-Divisional Officer's wrath. He at once went to Badarpur to contact Karim (the Chairman of the Union Board) but met Zaman instead, since Karim was absent at Narayanganj at the time. Zaman assured the official that the work would be completed in five days if assigned to him. The official asked Zaman to begin at once and save his prestige. The work was completed in record time and the Sub-Divisional Officer was able to go on his visit. The achievement established Zaman's reputation with regard to influence and organization, and thereafter all the officials from the Sub-Divisional Officer's office began to get their work done through him. This recognition by government officials strengthened his position at home as he could now offer jobs when a government contract came up.

Whenever authorities introduced new measures, Zaman was the first person to accept them. For instance, he was the first man to use chemical fertilizers. After some time others followed suit. He was the first to adopt the Japanese method of paddy cultivation. Later on others took it up. In earlier times, when government officials came to the village, they were viewed with suspicion and indifference, and people were reluctant to accept any scheme, even if it were suited to their needs and resources. But this use of chemical fertilizer, and the introduction of the Japanese paddy method not only rewarded the villagers financially, it made the innovator popular, and also made him a favourite of the development officers at the headquarters. Yet, neither Zaman nor Gafur nor anyone else could really compete with Karim in the race for village political power. From time to time, there was discontent in the village; Karim's incumbent was challenged (first in 1953 by Manu in the chairmanship election and second in 1956, by Zaman who as a member of Gushthi *B*, and nephew of Azizuddin, could claim almost similar traditional background). Yet, the administrative machinery at the village level was unchanged until 1959.

Administrative Change of 1959: Basic Democracies System

Until 1959 only those who paid a tax of six annas (approximately 7.8 cents) or more per year on their landed property could vote. Hence the number of voters was very limited and the Jampur Union Board had a total of only six elected members, while the remaining three were nominated by the Circle Officer on the recommendation of the local zamindar or talukdar. In fact, in most of the cases, the elected members were also the nominees of the zamindar or talukdar. Karim himself was first nominated by the zamindar.

The Circle Officer could, if he wished, choose the three "nominated members" according to his own choice on the basis of education and respect in the community. But since the Circle Officer had always been an outsider (a government officer) and was frequently transferred from one Thana to another Thana, he could hardly know the popularity of any individual in a union. Naturally, Circle Officers used to consult the most prominent local man (the zamindar or talukdar) as to whom should be offered a government nomination.

Earlier in 1958 in a coup-d'etat, Field Marshal Muhammad Ayub Khan overthrew the then parliamentary government of the country, and took power in August 1958. The next year, in October 1959, he formulated the Basic Democracies System.

The Basic Democracies Act of 1959 changed the name of the equivalent of Union Board to Union Council and the Union Board Chairman to Union Council Chairman. According to this system every resident adult may vote whether paying taxes or not and every 1,000 adults constitutes an electoral constituency which can elect a person as a member no matter whether that person is a taxpayer or not. Badarpur, with a population of more than 2,000 could now elect at least two members to the Union Council. Not only has the franchise been made universal, but there were also more openings for talented villagers to gain positions of political importance.

The constituencies in terms of which the village was divided roughly coincide with the Para divisions which have been mentioned earlier (see supra Chapter Three, p. 34). Not all Para boundaries coincide with a constituency, nor are the Para boundaries well demarcated. After 1959 South Para, the core of traditional Badarpur, elected a member for a constituency that included part of Central Para and part of Nama Para. The bulk of Nama and Central Paras, together with part of Northern Para formed a new constituency. Some Northern Para residents vote in a third constituency the majority of which is made up of two other neighbouring villages. Occasionally candidates from Badarpur contest this third constituency.

Thus, in 1959 there were three different constituencies where Badarpur is contested for the membership of Jampur Union Council. For the sake of convenience I will henceforth refer to these constituencies as South, Central and Northern constituencies.

In the Southern constituency Karim was opposed in the election by his uncle Ghani and Imanuddin of Gushthi C. In the Central constituency a school teacher Latif of Gushthi B ran as a nominee of Karim against Doctor Gafur of the same Gushthi, and in the Northern constituency one Kalu of the neighbouring village of Burundi stood as a nominee of Karim against Safaruddin Master and Giasuddin. None of these three candidates was from Badarpur.

In the Southern constituency Imanuddin could have given Karim a good fight had there not been Ghani to split his supporters. It was the consensus of the villagers that Ghani, the uncle of Karim and the brother of Korban Ali, had decided to contest in the election only in order to divide the voters of the northern part of the Southern constituency, who otherwise would have voted for Imanuddin. As the oldest member of Gushthi A and as a younger brother to Korban Ali, Ghani had relatively greater influence amongst the villagers than Imanuddin. It was Karim who requested Ghani to seek election so that the voters of Gushthi B in the Southern constituency would be divided, and with the solid votes of Gushthi A in the south he could be elected without much trouble.

In the Central constituency, however, Doctor Gafur was too popular for Latif, a village teacher; even Karim's support and backing did not help him against Gafur. In the Northern constituency all the candidates were from outside Badarpur. Kalu, as Karim's nominee, hoped to get a solid group of voters from the northern enclave (Uttar Para) of Badarpur, while the other candidates split the remaining votes so as to make way for him as Karim's nominee. But when the results were in, to his dismay, he found himself a loser to Giasuddin of Alamdi.

Before the 1961 election Ghani died, and in the elections in the Southern constituency, Imanuddin again ran against Karim, but lost the election this time as well, although he did much better than he did in 1959. In the Central constituency Imanuddin's brother Zaman fought the election against Latif, who again was a candidate on Karim's ticket. As Gafur did not contest the election this time, Latif thought that he would have a better chance to be elected against Zaman, a member of Gushthi C. Being a member of Gushthi B, Latif was confident of a majority since Gushthi B had the largest number of voters in the constituency. Moreover, Latif had the support of Karim. Yet, Latif lost, and Zaman was elected. The influential members of Gushthi B, particularly Doctor Garfur, were the main spokesmen for Zaman against their own gushthi member Latif.

In the Northern constituency three people contested the election. Among these was Almas from Badarpur. Originally an agriculturist, he had managed to become a businessman by starting as a small trader.

CHART 7
Change of Structure of Village Administration in Jampur Union

(Pre-1871)	(1871–1959)	(1959–)
1. *Village Panchayat*	2. (a) *Traditional*	3. (a) *Traditional*
Zamindar—head	Talukdar—head	Talukdar
Talukdar	Moulvis	Teachers
Zamindar's nominee	Teachers	Any number of villagers
Moulvis	1 or 2 village elders	
1 or 2 village elders		
	(b) *Union Board*	(b) *Union Council*
	6 elected members	Elected members
	3 nominated members headed by an elected president	(one member per 1000 votes) headed by an elected chairman
TOTAL:		
No limit in number	No limit in number	No limit in number
	9 members per Union	Number fluctuates according to population of the Union

His opponents were Kalu and Giasuddin from the two neighbouring villages, Burundi and Alamdi. As the majority of the voters in this constituency live in Burundi, the Burundi candidate was almost certain of winning the election without even counting on the support of his own gushthi (Gushthi *A*), or the support of Karim, and he did.

With this extension of franchise and the villagers' relative awareness of their political rights, the traditional Panchayat system did not die out totally but its power in decision-making became less and less effective. Most of the time, many of the same people served on both institutions—the traditional village Panchayat and the Union Council.

Chart number 7 shows the changes in the structure of the village administration at different periods.

Chart number 7 not only indicates the village administrative structure for the period prior to 1947, but also the structure of the Union Board and Union Council responsible for the maintenance of peace and order for Jampur Union. While the Union Board and Union Council members' authority was extended over the entire Union, the authority of the traditional Panchayat members was restricted to their own village. The two Union Council members of the village Badarpur were frequently included in settling disputes in the village Panchayat, but in that case they generally acted as villagers instead of following the dictates of their membership roles in the Union Council.

Since an individual may have to take different roles at different times his stand on issues may not always follow the same pattern; occasionally individuals group together to form a dal to get decisions made in their favour. This tendency becomes particularly apparent in the village elections. Chart no. 8 on p. 110 indicates candidates who contested the different constituencies in the various elections as well as the results of these elections.

Earlier, three different roots of leadership were pointed out. First, the traditional aristocracy, dominated by the zamindar and talukdar; second, the Mollahs and Moulvis, whose power and influence is more or less restricted to the religious group; and third, the emerging leaders who are gradually challenging the occupants of the Union Council positions; the old power structures persist but become restricted in scope.

The three different leadership structures are based respectively on authority, loyalty and persuasion of the group, and competition, and can be considered as active political groups of Badarpur, organized and maintained by lineage, religion and personalities (gushthi, sect and individuals) who are successful in manipulating and mobilizing the villagers. Retention of the loyalty of the group depends on factors such

CHART 8
Election: Participants and Elected Members

Election	Candidates	Constituency	Elected Member
1953	Wahab (B) vs. Manu (Maniruddin)	(N)	Maniruddin
	Nominated member	(S)	Karim (A)
1956	Karim (A) vs. Gafur (B)	(S)	Karim (A)
	Nominated member	(M)	Kafiluddin (B)
1959	Karim (A) vs. Imanuddin (C) vs. Ghani (A)	(S)	Karim (A)
	Latif (B) vs. Gafur (B)	(M)	Gafur (B)
	Safaruddin vs. Kalu (A) vs. Giasuddin	(N)	Giasuddin
1961	Karim (A) vs. Imanuddin (C)	(S)	Karim (A)
	Zaman (C) vs. Latif (B)	(M)	Zaman (C)
	Almas (B) vs. Kalu (A) vs. Giasuddin	(N)	Kalu (A)
1965	Karim (A) vs. Halim (A) vs. Latif (B)	(S)	Karim (A)
	Gafur (B) vs. Imanuddin (C) vs. Almas (B) vs. Azhar	(M)	Imanuddin (C)
	Zaman (C) vs. Kalu (A) vs. Safaruddin	(N)	Kalu (A)

A—Member of Gushthi *A*
B—Member of Gushthi *B*
C—Member of Gushthi *C*

S—South Para (Constituency)
N—North Para (Constituency)
M—Central Para (Constituency)

as financial support, compulsion and threat, and the heritage, and effectiveness of which today is in the same order.

Even in 1953 Karim's wealth and particularly his heritage as a member of Gushthi *A* were the main factors which enabled him to retain his position. His contestant, Manu, though later a rich man, was far behind Karim in the race for wealth; moreover, Manu's family tradition was not that attractive to the villagers. He could not claim any hereditary aristocracy and it became hard for him to contest the chairmanship in spite of the fact that he managed to become a member of the Union Board.

In the contest for chairmanship, Karim was helped by the elders while Manu was openly bullied as a *chasha* (son of a cultivator) trying to upset the village tradition by contesting the chairmanship. On the other hand, open gossip prevailed in the village that Karim had "purchased" all the votes from the elected membership for the chairmanship, and managed to eliminate other prospective candidates. After this defeated attempt (until 1965), Karim never again was opposed by any other candidate for the chairmanship of the Union.

Karim's success in the chairmanship contest of 1953 however, indicated a picture of the political life of the village immediately after partition. The political prestige was monopolized by aristocracy and tradition, creating a hierarchy of power structure in the village politics. There was no rotation of the elite in this village; tradition and aristocracy had the greatest say. Although the numerical strength in the village was with the cultivators, they were politically inarticulate. To the elderly people representing the traditional village gentry, Karim was important on account of his wealth and noble birth.

Although Karim was no longer an unchallenged "dictator" in the village and was being opposed by others, he somehow managed to keep the village power structure in his control. His technique of gaining power and maintaining it seemed to many villagers something more than "natural" and many villagers, particularly the most uneducated agricultural group, thought he had a divine sanction.

A typical response was that of a village farmer, Afiruddin by name, when asked:

> "Afiruddin, what do you think of Karim and his dealings with the villagers?"

he replied:

> "What can we think of big people? God has given them power and influence and we are only to obey them. By disobeying them we will

be incurring God's displeasure and we Muslims are not supposed to do that."

An average village farmer who is totally preoccupied with cultivation and who considers the village leadership to have a divine sanction naturally tends to follow the traditional ways of supporting the leader without question. Only on occasion, when they are confronted with two leaders at the same time, do they get unsettled and it becomes difficult for them to conform to their usual ways—a fact which is particularly noticeable when the new leader is of charismatic type.

When two leaders of two Gushthis *A* and *B* compete against each other, it is easier for the gushthi members to take sides, but for the rest of the villagers it is a real conflict situation. They are reluctant to change the village leadership which has "divine sanction"; on the other hand, they may find the new contestant a charismatic, benevolent individual who seems to have been fighting for the villagers' cause.

Leadership based on the power of gushthi is the traditional leadership of the village, the strength of which today may fluctuate with the loyalty of the gushthi members and so decrease the power of the leader without much prior notice. Two individuals from the same gushthi may come into conflict, and the marshaling of people behind two conflicting leaders can be considered as an indication of support and loyalty. However, as we shall see in the following chapter, in many cases inter-lineage, inter-village, and inter-sectarian antagonisms are countered by other groups whose interest it is to seek resolution of disputes between opposing groups.

CHAPTER SIX

Political Processes

In the preceding two chapters, we have discussed the structure of the village, and have placed some of the politically active individuals of the village in the context of the groupings. In the present chapter the focus will be on the political processes in which the structural groupings and the individuals act. We will show how these individuals utilize the groups and how they mobilize support for action in particular cases.

In the ordinary run of events, individuals do not have to do anything special in order to mobilize support; they exercise legitimate authority and are backed as leaders of particular groups, or of particular aggregates of people. On the other hand, in situations of conflict they have to work to mobilize support and to promote particular courses of action. The cases in which the struggle for support occurs involve, in the normal run of events, not merely overt conflict but also special situations such as the one I observed in 1965, the situation of election. What I shall try to do in this chapter, then, is to survey disputes, conflicts and elections in a series of case studies and analyse the processes by which individuals seek to gain support from numbers of uncommitted individuals, how people use their patronage and how people without any support behind them either from gushthi or from patrons tend to yield to one side and shift their loyalties. Success comes to the person who has support from the largest number of uncommitted individuals.

Gaining support means getting people involved on one's own side. Individuals do not merely have to get the uncommitted to *involve* themselves in the issue, they must also work to get the committed to come out on their side rather than on the side of their opponents. These two aspects of gaining support appear differently in different situations.

A. *Situation of Straightforward Confrontation*

The situation in which there is a straightforward confrontation of one group against another group is the one that has usually been described with segmentary societies (Fallers, 1956; Frankenberg, 1957; Salisbury,

1962). It is the situation in which an individual precipitates conflict and gets his group to support him.

Case 1: Awal and the Trader

During the summer of 1966 Awal went to the neighbouring village market at Mahajampur, one and a half miles north of Badarpur in the same Jampur Union. It was a sunny day, very hot and humid. Awal went to the market and began bargaining with a trader over the price of jute. During the bargaining the following conversation took place:

Trader: I'll buy your jute at the rate of thirty rupees per maund (approximately 82 lbs.)

Awal: I wouldn't give it unless you pay thirty-five rupees.

Trader: I went to Badarpur yesterday and several people sold their jute at the rate of thirty rupees per maund.

Awal: No. They told me that you paid them thirty-five rupees.

Trader: Badarpuris are liars. I didn't pay them thirty-five rupees.

Awal: How dare you say Badarpuris are liars, you scoundrel?

Trader: Of course they are liars. All Badarpuris are liars; their fathers and forefathers were all liars.

At that point Awal could not take any more and slapped the trader. The trader was a Mahajampuri man, and once in the past he had been harassed (as he reported later) at Badarpur. He immediately started shouting and his Mahajampur kinsmen, who were nearby came to his aid. At that early hour there were few Badarpuris present at the *hat* to help Awal, and he was badly injured.

Humiliated, Awal returned to Badarpur, limping and crying and then burst into tears. This was enough to arouse youths idling about in the village. Immediately a number of them, led by some from Awal's gushthi, armed themselves with bamboos and other weapons and without enquiring further about the matter, started for the market place at Mahajampur. They arrived, beat up the villagers, and destroyed much property. When the older people of both villages heard of the young men's fight, they brought the entire populations of each village onto the scene. The older people of Badarpur realized that they could not afford to quarrel with the Mahajampuris since Mahajampur was the only market close to their own village where they could trade their village products. It would have been too inconvenient for them to use any other market. At the same time they realised that it was difficult to cool down the younger people who were furious and wanted to retaliate even further for the humiliation of Awal (the younger people behaved as if they had all been humiliated). The older group of Mahajampur at the same time realized that they could not afford a quarrel with the Badarpuris since the Union Board Chairman is from Badarpur and it is through his office that they get their government aid. Both Mahajampuris and Badarpuris needed each other.

Older people of both the villages talked to each other for some time while a group of them tried to calm down the younger members of their group. Finally the older people of Badarpur managed to calm down their youths by promising them that justice would be had and Awal would be compensated properly; the older people of Mahajampur sought to calm down their younger group (who, in fact, were no less excited than the Badarpuris) by saying that their village was certainly on the wrong side since a Badarpuri had been humiliated on Mahamajampur grounds while he was a stranger and deserved to be treated as a guest. Even if Awal was in the wrong he should not have been beaten, as it does not speak well for villagers to mishandle their village guests.

For about four months following the disturbance there was a peculiar sense of internal solidarity in each of the two opposed villages. They avoided entering each other's territory until finally elders of these two villages actually met, negotiated and made Awal as well as the trader apologize in front of all the inhabitants of the two villages. Although a few of the Badarpuris present insisted that the trader pay a compensation to Awal, it was the general consensus of the elders of both villages that Awal bore the main responsibility since the trader had actually never paid thirty-five rupees for jute as Awal had accused in the first place.

Case 2: Grazing Rights in the School Yard

When Latif became contender for the leadership of the area in 1965 and decided to contest the village election in the southern constituency, he did not have the support of his own gushthi members, nor were his gushthi members numerically strong in that constituency. Yet, Gushthi *B* of Latif wielded prestige and power in the village. He liked neither Karim of Gushthi *A* nor Gafur of his own Gushthi *B,* both of whom at least had some support behind them. Latif's objection to Karim's leadership was that he had dominated over the village for too long a period, creating difficulties in building a democratic trend in the village. His complaint against Gafur was more personal; Gafur did not allow Latif's cattle to graze in the village school compound which was situated on Latif's ancestral property. The school headmaster had objected several times when Latif, his assistant, let his cattle into the school compound, but the headmaster could not do anything as Latif was a violent man.

The affair came to Gafur's notice. He called all the villagers together and eloquently convinced them that a place for the education of the village children should be looked after by the entire village. He argued that the school compound, as the future hope of their children, is a sacred place for the entire village, and that everybody in the village should see to it that nobody's cattle graze there. Both Latif and Karim were present at the meeting and realized that gradually they were being left far behind in the race for leadership.

During the time of this disagreement between Gafur and Latif, Karim did not become involved openly. Probably he was thinking that if this misunderstanding were increased, the two would try to destroy each other and make his own field clearer. Karim was said to have promised Latif the chairman's support against Gafur whenever needed; but when he found that Gafur had convinced all the villagers by his eloquence, he decided not to get involved, even at the expense of infuriating the school teacher. As a result, Latif became determined to contest in the election against Karim.

Case 3: Case of the Flood Victims

An inter-sect conflict between two dals became apparent in 1966. During the flood in the summer of 1966, a village conflict developed over the resettlement of flood victims. One portion of the village is relatively low lying (Nama Para) and gets flooded earlier than the other parts. Approximately thirty per cent of the people of this area are of the Hanafi Majhab, and the rest are the Muhammadis. Housing for flood victims was provided in the village school, which is situated on the property of a Muhammadi man, Amir Ali of Gushthi *B*. Amir Ali's sons, together with other Muhammadis, were very reluctant to accommodate the flood-affected Hanafis. One specific reason for Muhammadi antagonism to the Hanafis was that the Muhammadi school teacher, Latif (on whose ancestral property the school was situated) had planned to contest the 1965 election against the Hanafi chairman, Karim, but could not do so because of interference by the COP and particularly of other Hanafis who wanted Karim's step-brother instead.

When the situation grew worse and people were suffering seriously, a group of the Hanafi flood victims became impatient; with the help of Karim they tried to mobilize support against the Muhammadis who were opposing their presence in the relief camp. Now it happened that some of the flood-affected Hanafis were related to Muhammadis of the non-flood-affected areas and told them of the disturbance which was about to break out. All was set for a major confrontation. But before anything could get started, a police officer from Baidyar Bazar Police Station arrived and said that all government help for the village would be stopped unless the villagers stopped fighting against each other. The whole affair subsided without violence.

This little threat from an outside authority acted as a tonic, and all the villagers under the leadership of the elders of various Majhabs agreed that for the sake of the village they should agree to accept the disadvantage of living with people of the other Majhab. The villagers realized that they had to remain united in order to get benefits from outside.

Case 4: Hafez[54] Abul Basir vs. Karim

Hafez Abul Basir of Gushthi *B* wanted to get the Moulvi's position in the Muhammadi village mosque. He was the only Hafez living in the village, and he maintained his family by working on his one and a half acres of land. He had long been a political opponent of Karim and although his appointment was really only an issue for the Muhammadis, since Karim was a Hanafi, politics became involved. When the question of the new moulvi appointment came up for decision, a village woman who had lived at Abul Basir's house and worked for his family, suddenly left. A rumour started in the village that the servant had gotten pregnant by Abul Basir and to save face for herself and for Abul Basir she had left the city to get an abortion. This was a very serious allegation in the village, particularly when made against a man who wanted to be the villagers' Moulvi. Basir was furious but he was helpless as he could not produce the woman to prove his innocence. As a result someone other than Basir was appointed village Moulvi.

After some time the woman returned to the village. When she was interrogated by the villagers she said that she had gone to see her relatives in neighbouring villages and that all the allegations made against Abul Basir were totally unfounded. No one could trace the initial responsibility for this scandal, but the general consensus amongst the members of Abul Basir's gushthi was that Karim had paid the woman to leave the village for a while and had then spread the rumor in order to prevent Basir's appointment as Moulvi. Karim had said that he did not approve the appointment although strictly speaking it was not his concern. But to have as a Muhammadi Moulvi an individual who was a potential rival would certainly have harmed Karim politically. Basir and his gushthi members have been waiting to retaliate ever since, waiting to get back to the Moulvi's position after the expiration of the contract of the new appointee. Basir is now working as a Moulvi in a village of a neighbouring union on the other side of the river.

The cases cited above involve individuals in face to face disputes, mobilizing behind them the groupings of which they are members and turning the disputes into confrontations of groupings. Closer analysis of each case reveals specific principles at work. We notice in the case of the trader in Mahajampur, that Awal managed first to get his gushthi behind him, and that then he and the gushthi got the whole village's support. Such disturbances reveal one thing: a villager's kinsmen do not include only blood related or affinal relatives; rather all the villagers are like members of the same, single family whenever a quarrel develops with some outsider. Had there been such a quarrel within the village, however, all the affinal or blood relatives would have grouped together to fight for their own paribar or gushthi people. Since Awal, a Badapuri, was humiliated in another village, the Badarpuris felt as though they as a village had been humiliated. It was not a problem of Gushthi B alone; rather, it was a problem for the whole village. The younger group did not even take time to think before taking action to retaliate for the humiliation they felt. Yet, eventually the case was settled by the elders of the two villages, who through negotiation realized and convinced those persons involved in the conflict that both villages could benefit only from peace.

The second case, the dispute of Latif and Gafur over grazing rights, started as an intra-gushthi dispute between two families of Gushthi B. It could have escalated into a confrontation between two gushthi groups A and B, if Karim had overtly come in against Gafur. However, as soon as Gafur appeared in public to have more support on his side, Karim withdrew entirely from the dispute and thus made it clear that Gafur had won over Latif. The dispute was resolved by Gafur getting enough outside support to render his gushthi opponent ineffective. As this support was clearly visible in public, the issue went no further.

In the third case, that of the flood victims, the issue between Latif and Karim at first seemed to crystallize majhab groups against each other. In Nama Para, where the flood victims were, the majority majhab, the Muhammadis, were able to triumph over the Hanafis until the Hanafis were supported by their more powerful sect-brothers of South Para, under Karim. But when both sides stood to lose all flood relief aid from the Government the conflict stopped escalating.

In the fourth case, involving Basir and Karim, the dispute was a purely personal one in which it would have been impossible for

Karim to have mobilized to any effect either his gushthi or the Hanafi sect, since neither was relevant to the issue of appointing a Muhammadi Moulvi. By using tactics to discredit Basir, Karim in fact appealed to the widest group, the whole village, which could be mobilized on the basis of an affront to Islamic morality.

On the other hand even a straightforward confrontation may not crystallize to form any clearcut factional conflict and may die out if one of the conflict groups does not have any gushthi or other support and the leader is himself a non-entity. The following detailed case study will clearly illustrate the position of a villager who does not have any gushthi support behind him and whose initial patron withdraws in the face of conflict, since he does not feel it worthwhile to back him all the way. In such a situation the man without any support has no other alternative than to shift his loyalties to another patron who appears to be generous at that moment.

Case 5: Man without Gushthi Support

June 12, 1965. It was raining relentlessly. The whole village was drenched by monsoon rain; the temperature was about 100° and the humidity was probably 100%. I came out of my den and started towards the doctor's quarters. I was sure that Doctor Gafur would not go to his dispensary this morning and that patients in need of him would go to his home. Since the doctor's compounder had not come for the last few weeks, I had the opportunity to assist him.

As I approached his house, I could hear a boy crying, soon I could also hear the conversation inside. Dr. Gafur, seeing me as I entered the room said: "Islam Shahib, look how badly this man has been beaten."

"But why doctor, and who has done this?"

Before the doctor could say anything the ten year old boy who was crying aloud said: "Kitab (Bhuiyan) came to our house this morning, called my father out of the room and beat him with a stick."

"But why, why should Kitab beat your father?"

"For nothing," he said.

It was hard to believe, but I did not requestion him at the moment, since it might have increased the loudness of his cries, already too loud for both the doctor and myself.

I assisted the doctor in bandaging the wounded man's head after the application of tincture of iodine. After about half an hour Geda, for that was the name of the wounded man, left for home. Dr. Gafur offered me a cigarette, lighted one for himself, and said:

"Islam Shahib, you must be wondering about all this, but it is a very common scene in village life, it is a part of the ongoing process." He continued:

"You know Kitab, cousin of Bhuiyan, who has a store in the *hat*. Geda also started a store last month, and the people of Maiz Para and Utter Para all go to his store to buy their necessities (mostly salt and oil) instead of going to Kitab's store as they used to do. Two weeks ago Kitab offered to buy Geda's store from him, but the latter refused to sell it. Yesterday morning while the children were playing in the field Kitab's son got hurt and accused Geda's son of being unfair to him, of pushing him too hard, throwing him to the ground. Kitab's son lost a tooth. Geda was not in the village yesterday as he went to shop for his store at Narayanganj. Kitab tried to get him all day yesterday but could not do so. This morning, Kitab went to Geda's home and without even asking anything beat him with a stick."

"But what about Geda's relatives, why didn't they come to assist Geda? What about Bhuiyan? Is he going to see that Geda is redressed?"

"Well, the roots of the matter go back further, I'll tell you this if you would like to hear, in a minute. Geda does not have very many relatives, at least not to quarrel with Kitab and his kinsmen. And as for Bhuiyan, he might like to avoid the whole thing by labelling it as childish and probably would just scold both Kitab and Geda to settle the matter."

"You said that the roots of the matter go further—how is that?"

"Geda could not possibly have any store in the *hat*, had not Azhar and Almas both helped him to get the store. Azhar and Almas gave him money to start that store so that they could use it as a centre for their publicity in the last election. Imanuddin could use Kitab's store, I could use my dispensary there for campaigning, but Almas and Azhar did not have any store."

"But Almas and Azhar do have a store there too, for their rice business."

"Yes, but that is just a godown (warehouse) which they open only on the *hat* day, not in the morning bazaar."

"Almas and Azhar were contesting against you too, right?"

"Right, but they thought their main opponent was Imanuddin and not me, which in fact was true, since I was never serious in that election. Almas requested me to withdraw in his favour, but I could not possibly do that as that would have probably offended Azhar. If only one of them had contested, I would have been glad to withdraw on his behalf. In any case I just wanted to see that Imanuddin was not elected. But unfortunately for Azhar, Almas and I split our own votes to make room for Imanuddin."

"But what has this got to do with Geda and Kitab's quarrel?" I asked.

"Kitab and Imanuddin are related. Kitab approached Azhar to withdraw on Imanuddin's behalf, which he refused to do. Moreover, Kitab was contemplating having Geda's shop space as an extension of his own shop. Geda could never have got that place, if it were not for Almas and Azhar's money."

"But Doctor, all this does not justify Kitab's beating. Who is now going to stand for Geda? Will Almas or Azhar stand for him? Will Geda be redressed?"

"Islam Shahib, this is not a serious quarrel at all. Almas, Azhar or even I might call a meeting of the villagers to settle this quarrel. But I know what's going to happen; as I told you before, both of them will be asked to forget and forgive. Old grudges will be at least temporarily forgotten only to erupt again suddenly. Fortunately, this quarrel is between Geda and Kitab, and not between Kitab and me or Kitab and Azhar or Almas."

"Doctor, what do you mean? What difference would this have made?"

"A lot of difference Islam Shahib; first of all Kitab would not have dared to beat anyone in the village who has strong relatives; secondly, neither Almas, Azhar nor I would have tolerated such a thing. Poor Geda. We can all sympathize with him, we can console him, but none of us would like to stick our neck out for him or for anyone like him. We just cannot afford to risk that!"

After three days, on June 15, 1965, while I was packing up to return to Canada, Geda's son came running to my den and said:

"Master Shahib, my father wants you to be in the *shalish* (village conciliatory body, Panchayat) this evening; *Matbars* (village elders) will gather at the school to 'punish' Kitab."

I noted his use of the word "punish" but told him, "Safi, I should love to be in the Shalish, but unfortunately I'll have to leave before noon to catch my plane from Dacca!"

* * *

In July 1966, after a year in Canada, I came back to Badarpur. As I came out of my den, Safi, son of Geda was standing at my door.

"Safi, how are you? How is your father?"

"Master Shahib, my father died last year, after you left; he was bitten by a snake, and Idris Kabiraj could not save him."

I felt really sorry, and was recollecting the events of last year when Geda, Safi's father, was beaten by Kitab. I could remember the very face of Safi saying, "Master Shahib, my father wants you to be in the shalish this evening. Matbars will get together at the school to punish Kitab."

I was wondering if Kitab was ever "punished" or if Geda had ever been redressed. I was wondering if Geda was the prototype of the majority of the Badarpuri "Chasha" (farmers) who were always being "used" by "Bhadralok" (gentlemen) for their own purposes, but who are hardly given any support if they become involved in a dispute with another "Bhadralok."

"Master Shahib, Uncle sent me to tell you he would like to have you join at lunch."

First I could not understand who this uncle could be, since I could clearly recollect that Geda had no brothers. However, Safi continued, "Uncle will return from his dispensary and on the way back he will come here and take you with him." There was not a bit of doubt in my mind, Dr. Gafur had become Safi's uncle. In Badarpur villagers do address each other in kinship terms of uncle, brother, aunt, grandfather or grandmother, etc., depending on the age and sex of the individual, but this does not necessarily indicate a real kinship relationship.

"Well, Safi, I'll be glad to. Please tell your uncle I'll be waiting for him."

Dr. Gafur arrived at about 12:30 p.m. and we began to walk towards his home. Dr. Gafur said: "Islam Shahib, I was happy to hear from Safi that you have come back. He saw you getting out of your boat and going with Karim. I wanted to see you earlier but could not."

"Yes, I came day before yesterday and spent my first night at Karim's house. I expected to see you there last night; Karim told me you were also invited for supper."

"I am sorry, I had to go to Parabo to see a patient. He is alright now."

Immediately, I thought of Geda again and said: "Safi said his father died from a snake bite?"

"You know Idris. Instead of sucking the poisonous blood out, he tried to feed him some juice of shrubs. I was out of the village at the time. When I returned Geda was already buried."

"Who is looking after the family now?"

"Geda's wife went back to her parents' home. As I hear from Safi, she works there at her brothers' house (since her parents are dead), and lives with her little daughter. Safi lives in my house as an aid."

"Doctor, what happened at the shalish last year, when the matbars were supposed to meet in the village school to settle the dispute between Geda and Kitab?"

"Nothing much. Kitab said he became angry to see his son's tooth knocked out and could not control himself, but now he was sorry. Imanuddin, even Zaman, Azhar and Almas advised Geda to forget and forgive. Karim gave Geda a new lungi, and Geda was happy."

"Just like that?"

"Islam Shahib, no, not only that, within a week after that Geda gave away the occupation of his shop to Kitab which made Almas and Azhar unhappy. They wanted to file a suit against Geda and Kitab, and I was drawn into the picture. Both the parties wanted me to be their witness." He continued:

"Almas and Azhar wanted me to say on their behalf that Geda's shop actually belonged to them, since they paid the price of the shop in the first place. Kitab, on the other hand, had on his side the previous owner of the lot who would swear that he received the price of the shop from Geda and not from Almas or Azhar, and that Geda had every right to dispose of it in any way he wanted."

"But what did Geda say, did he lie?"

"Well, he said to Almas and Azhar, 'Why should I be with you any more? You did not come to my support while I was beaten. If you can't fight someone, fight with him. Kitab beat me, but now he is kind to me. If I give him this shop-space he will give me one acre of his land to till."

"How did you manage this dispute then, did it actually go to court?"

"No, finally, we met in another shalish and decided that Kitab would give Geda one acre of his land to till at least for two years and after that Kitab could renew it. But the actual proceeds of the sale would not go to Geda for he would have to give the money to Azhar and Almas. They all agreed."

The above case indicated that even Dr. Gafur, who appeared to be the most democratic individual in the village, who always in the past tried to help the victim to get redress, did not want to push Geda's case further since Geda's initial patrons Almas and Azhar were not backing him up any more. Under these circumstances, Geda possibly did not have any other alternative than to make the best of the situation by changing his loyalties to Kitab from Almas and Azhar. Almas and Azhar used their patronage to achieve their goals only as long as they did not have to encounter any problem or risk. By being a patron to a man without any gushthi link, Almas and Azhar avoided any risk of too much criticism for not backing up Geda in his trouble. In other words, it can be stated that in Badarpur people like Geda, although they constitute the majority of the village population, and although they are needed by "brokers" like Almas, Azhar, and Kitab, do not have any real say in the village politics and are like pawns in the hands of the brokers. In time of danger or threat they have only one alternative to save themselves from the threatening situation, that is, to change their loyalties to a more powerful or to a new patron after they have been used and rejected, uncared for, by the first one.

B. Situation of Conflict Using Cross-cutting Ties

But in many situations it makes no sense for the principals to a dispute to mobilize their groups for straightforward confrontations, either because those groups are too weak to constitute a majority, or because they are not solidly behind the principal. In such cases the winner is often the individual who in the course of the conflict can involve ties which cross-cut sect or gushthi as a means of gaining support. This support group is heterogeneous and by involving individuals who according to some principles of grouping, would be on the opposite side, he can often weaken his opponent sufficiently.

Case 6: Conflict and Cohesion in the Gushthi

An earlier chapter showed how the Muslims of the village formed a united body under Rahim's direction and fought for their causes against the Hindu zamindar. After the death of Rahim the leadership of the Muslim villagers fell to Rahim's descendants, the members of Gushthi A. But the numerically stronger, as well as the earliest Muslims in the village were the members of Gushthi B. They never liked the idea of being dominated by the members of Gushthi A, although they did lend their support to the Muslim talukdar whenever he needed it in opposing the Hindu zamindar or whenever there was an inter-village conflict. Inter-gushthi competition and rivalry in this village was simmering for a long time, but had been suppressed in favour of unity against the Hindu outsiders.

The change in the political structure of the country after partition meant that the Hindu zamindar in the village no longer presented a common threat to the villagers against which they could unite. And so rivalry between Gushthi A and B became more conspicuous. Muslim villagers, particularly the members of Gushthi B no longer needed the assistance of the members of Gushthi A to establish their claims against the authority of the Hindu zamindar. Hence the leadership of Gushthi A was no longer looked to for assuring the solidarity of the village, and the numerically superior Gushthi B might have been expected to take over control of the village. Members of Gushthi A, however, adopted a new technique to maintain their leadership. They nominated candidates from Gushthi B, and caused a split in the votes of the gushthi which enabled Gushthi A to win. Thus, as we have already seen, in 1956 Karim nominated Kafil of Gushthi B and competed against Gafur of the same gushthi, and in 1959 Karim invited his uncle Ghani of Gushthi A to contest against him in order to split Imanuddin's voters.

This politicking within and between gushthis can be best illustrated by the events of the election of 1965. The details enable me to analyse how such conflict works in the context of free elections.

Several techniques are used by villagers to win an election. The most popular is the spreading of rumours against opponents, in order to alienate their supporters. It comes into play particularly when a candidate finds his supporters decreasing in number while the popularity of his rival is on the increase. It is then important to dig up some family or personal scandal to counteract the rival's popularity at its core in the paribar or gushthi. The skill and effectiveness in spreading the rumours of this scandal may determine the political future of the individual.

In order to counteract the rumour spread by one candidate, the best technique adopted is to spread another. Several rumours were publicized against Karim. These ranged from incidents connected with his personal life to others involving misappropriation of Union Council money and acceptance of bribes. Action with its counteraction by opposing candidates continues in the village until each election is over. Sometimes the bitterness resulting from scandals prevails long after the election, and occasionally the members of the whole gushthi take them as an offense against themselves and try to retaliate whenever time and opportunity permit.

In November, 1965 just before the election, the prestige of the chairman, Karim, was running low for a number of reasons. Karim had greatly expended his assets, houses, and land since partition. With his three wives and several dependents his expenses had risen quickly. In a poor village like Badarpur where people live just above the subsistence level, it was only too natural for people to become suspicious of him, of his honesty, and of his integrity. There were whispered accusations that he was not utilizing the money of the Union Council properly. But the most vital blow to his prestige was in his personal life. In 1965 he was maintaining a number of mistresses in different parts of Jampur union. Thus rumours about Karim spread quickly and were widely believed. His reputation was considerably harmed.

Although Gushthi A is powerful, aristocratic and normally solidly behind its chief member, Karim, intra-gushthi antagonisms against him began to appear. Many of its members were infuriated by the accusations which seemed to be justified, and felt that Karim was damaging the reputation of the gushthi. Together with the other villagers they began to think that this election offered a golden opportunity to get rid of an undesirable member, at the same time chairman of the Union Council who had been dominating the entire union for decades.

The growing unpopularity of Karim encouraged the school teacher, Latif, a member of Gushthi *B*, to offer himself as a candidate. But Latif was in no way a more likely winner because many people in the village disliked him and thought him arrogant; even his own kinsmen were hostile to him because it had been he who on Karim's ticket opposed Gafur in the 1959 election and Zaman in the 1961 election. Further, although the members of Karim's gushthi did not approve of Karim's behaviour and practices they did not relish the idea of the Union Council member (and thus the chairman) from another gushthi. They would have liked to eliminate Karim, but at the same time they wanted to keep the position of chairman within the gushthi. In a straight confrontation between Gushthis *A* and *B* Karim would have won in the South constituency.

In the meantime Karim's step-brother, Halim of Gushthi *A*, expressed his desire to contest the election. To many in the village, especially those of Gushthi *B*, this wish of Halim came as a relief. By supporting this young man, the villagers on the one hand could eliminate Karim, and, on the other, would no longer have to vote for Latif. Also members of Gushthi *A*, who comprised the largest number of votes in the constituency, could keep the office within the gushthi. Halim was a young man backed by the younger generation not only of his own gushthi, but also of the whole village, together with other villagers who would no longer support Karim.

The unpopularity of Karim and the cross-cutting nature of his support group gave Halim positive hope of polling a majority of votes. Upon the insistence of the Combined Opposition Party (COP), the dissidents and opponents of Karim persuaded Latif to withdraw his candidacy so that there could be a straight contest between the two brothers. Latif himself realized the likelihood of losing the election in a straight gushthi contest and withdrew.

During the early stage of the election campaign Halim felt almost over-confident about his success. Out of some thousand voters he hoped to have a solid block of votes from the villagers outside his own gushthi, and he hoped that those from his own gushthi (which was also the gushthi of Karim), would be fairly evenly divided, thus assuring his victory. But although he had the support of the younger members of his gushthi in addition to the support of other villagers, many elderly gushthi members continued to support Karim in the belief that Halim was too young.

This initial conflict between the two brothers was in no way confined to Gushthi A, nor did it simply divide the Southern constituency into two groups of known strength. Rather by involving other cross-cutting groupings and by splitting Gushthi A it meant that the outcome was not clear at all. Either side could have had a majority. The general discontent in the village had a chance to show itself and as a result a larger number of people than ever before came forward to participate in the Union Council elections of 1965. Politicking reached its climax in 1965. Never before had this village shown such political consciousness.

The presence of Halim made it a real possibility that Gushthi A would be split. And if Gushthi A would split then there was every possibility that individuals antagonistic to Karim might rally behind Halim. In such a situation no one could predict the outcome of the election. As he realized the situation and was incited by the threat, Karim was determined more than ever to succeed.

Karim was a shrewd politician who had always shown a brilliant capacity to play with villagers' sentiments and feelings and as he knew the election techniques, he began by spreading a counter rumour of his own. After Halim decided to oppose him, he went to the city and somehow managed to spread the news that he had been killed by bandits. This false alarm was strong enough to bring his relatives together in the village to await mournfully confirmation of the story. And this illustrates another election technique—the attempt to have some sort of conciliation among the candidates, so that all but one will withdraw, thus making for an uncontested election.

Although Halim was contesting against Karim, he immediately forgot all rivalries and went to Baidyar Bazar Police Station where he found Karim playing cards with his friends. The alarm of course had been a false one. This false news, however, brought Halim and his brother together again. Halim was ready to contest against his brother but definitely did not want to see him dead. All the way from Baidyar Bazar to Badarpur they talked and talked. When they reached home all their assembled relatives from different parts of the country were jubilant to see the chairman alive and insisted that Karim should be given another chance to be elected. In the face of united pressure by his fellow gushthi members and just twenty hours before the polling Halim withdrew his name. His brother, the chairman, was elected unopposed.

In this fight between Halim and the Chairman a solid group of people was determined to remain behind the Chairman, not because they like him but because the other rival, Halim, though amiable, and bold, was too young to contest for the chairmanship. On the other hand, the most active support for Halim came from a group composed of students, cultivators, and members of a few families (paribars) of the village that had personal hostility towards the chairman, because some of their fellow members had been harassed and embarrassed by the Chairman and his Chowkidar. Specifically, individuals from these families had experienced either arrest for a short period because of suspicion of being connected with village burglaries, or an unfavourable judgment from the Union Conciliation Court.

In the campaign for election the followers of Halim showed logic in presenting his candidacy. They argued that Halim was veracious, frank, honest, sincere, and ready to meet the wishes of the people. His activities were described in pamphlets which were widely circulated; and the building up of a political image was greatly helped by the students of the local school. There were meetings on the eve of the election where his supporters spoke on his behalf.

There were innumerable meetings in the village held either in front of the school or at the mosque. Everybody apparently talked about the uselessness of elections in such meetings. The candidates, as a rule, did not talk much in such meetings, but their agents and supporters were most articulate. The agents of the chairman presented the argument that he had been an experienced member of the Council and chairman for so many years and as such deserved re-election. In fact, they pointed out, he had been a member as well as the chairman since before the birth of his opponent. His supporters further argued that the chairmanship of the Union would go to some other village if he was not elected. The supporters of Halim presented the plea of electing new blood to the Union Council. The discussion in those pre-election meetings continued for several hours, often ending in a hot exchange of words between groups. The candidates nearly always remained cool and calm in public. In private they would promise a "good lesson" to one another when the election was over, but in public they spoke with humility. For example, Karim always said that he had no desire to contest the election but was doing so only under public pressure. He further said on innumerable occasions that he would withdraw if the villagers so wished.

Most conflicts that involve cross-cutting loyalties are not as complicated as that between Halim and Karim. Most often they involve the mobilization of affinal relatives. The following case will illustrate just such a dispute which started off as a majhab conflict, but which, as affines were called in, eventually got solved because the same individuals were affines to both sides.

Case 7: Majhab Conflict

The undercurrent of hostility between the Hanafis and the Muhammadis of the village has been expressed a number of times by their attitudes or actions, sometimes through a simple disagreement (see supra p. 84) and occasionally through violence and disruptive activities. Yet, there have always been difficulties for any sect leader wishing to achieve lasting sect group loyalty since sect membership tends to cross-cut kinship groupings. In the village social organization an individual's primary loyalties are at his own bari, paribar and gushti.

Although the Muhammadis are the oldest sect-group in this village, the Hanafis claim to be the most respected group, since it was a Hanafi who came to the village to save the Muhammadis from the wrath of the Hindu zamindar (see supra p. 70). However, the numerically stronger Muhammadis never liked the power and influence of the Hanafis. This was the main reason that the Hanafis had to compromise with the Muhammadis in the conflict regarding appointment of a new Imam for the village mosque (see supra p. 84). The roots of this sectarian split go back to the middle of last century, immediately after Rahim's arrival in the village.

The conflict between the sect groups in Badarpur reached its climax in the early thirties when the whole village was divided into two distinct groups, leaving a microscopic and indifferent third group (the Safi). Actual quarreling started in the *milad* arranged by the Hanafis of the village. They brought to the village a visiting Hanafi moulvi who declared all the sect-group activities other than those of the Hanafis to be un-Islamic upon which he then advised the villagers to accept the faith of the Hanafi majhab. A Muhammadi Moulvi who was present (it is a general consensus in the village that anyone from outside is more learned than the local people) could not restrain his temper and openly protested against the speaker. The tension became very high and a quarrel seemed about to break out; but it was avoided by the intervention of Azizuddin Munshi of Gushthi *B*. By stressing that argument with a visitor would damage the villagers' reputation, Azizuddin Munshi quieted the Muhammadi Moulvi who apparently gave in and withdrew. The Muhammadis avoided physical violence but immediately afterwards sent for an eloquent Muhammadi Moulvi to come to the village to speak in a second milad.

The Hanafis planned to retaliate for the disturbance at their milad by creating a disturbance in the second one. But Azizuddin's nephew, himself a Hanafi, disclosed the plan to Azizuddin, who had raised him and his orphan brothers after the death of their father. This gave the Muhammadis enough time to prepare themselves in case there was an inter-sect riot, and no disturbance occurred. For some time the Hanafis and the Muhammadis tried to backbite each other and avoided each other's invitation. But the gushthi line cross-cuts the majhab line in such an intricate way that the inter-sect quarrel could not last long. Yet, even today when there is a religious discussion (milad) in the village, believers of different sect-groups exist in a penumbra of uncertainty about the numbers on each side which can never be fully relied upon. Some individuals may always prefer to support an individual of the same gushthi against someone of the same majhab.

When gushthi, majhab, or para loyalties coincide there is a strong likelihood that a dispute will become a confrontation. But even then, affinal ties may effectively cross-cut the loyalties, and so resolve the issue.

Case 8: Case of the School Renovation

In 1965 a quarrel broke out in Badarpur over the question of renovating the village school. The debate was at the beginning one between north para and south para. The school is situated on the south side of the village, and some northerners were reluctant to contribute for its renovation. In a village gathering, Kitab, a southerner, of Gushthi *A* and cousin of Karim, made a scornful remark to Samu, a powerful man of Gushthi *B* from the north; Kitab was beaten on the spot. The two sides in what had been an inter-para debate, became quarreling gushthi groups each of which is strongest in its particular para.

As all the relatives got involved in the quarrel it became almost unmanageable as it escalated. However, other people began to talk about the two quarreling parties being affinally related (Kitab's youngest brother, Salam, had married Samu's niece), and Kitab and Samu both realized that the quarrel between them was doing harm to their gushthi reputations. They immediately stopped quarreling, and all the misunderstandings faded, and nobody ever brought that event back into notice.

Thus when affinal ties can be traced and uncovered, disputes can be avoided. So too the creation of affinity can help people to forget a conflict, and induce opponents to support one another.

Case 9: Case of Two Bhairas

In the 1961 Union Council elections, Imanuddin of Gushthi *C* contested against Karim of Gushthi *A*. Soon after however, Imanuddin's younger brother, Altaf, married the sister of the husband of Karim's third wife's sister. A man's wife's sister's husband in Bengali is called *Bhaira*, and the bhaira relationship is very intimate. Since Imanuddin's brother married Karim's bhaira's sister, Imanuddin and Karim themselves became bhaira and came to have a joking relationship with each other. Hence, in the 1965 elections when Karim wanted Imanuddin to contest against Gafur (Karim's most formidable opponent in the village political field), Imanuddin assented. Soon Karam Ali, who was from Gafur's gushthi, offered his support. Karam Ali, an official living at Chittagong, was the only graduate of the village other than Gafur himself (see supra p. 42) and was related to Gafur affinally. Karam Ali used to think that he was more qualified (learned) than Gafur since Gafur had only graduated from the National Medical School (see supra p. 42). Students of that school were not regarded as equal to the qualified graduates of the Government Medical School or Medical College. Moreover, Karam Ali, as a government official felt higher than that of the village doctor, Gafur. Gafur, however, did not think in the same light and felt equal if not higher in status position than Karam Ali. Therefore, even though he was not enthusiastic about it, Karam Ali joined in the alliance with Imanuddin and hence with Karim (because Gafur had not cared to humour his in-law without any reason).

When the election was held, the majority of the voters supported Karim's candidate, Imanuddin. The affinal relationship created by the marriage of Imanuddin's and Karim's relatives thus cut across and was stronger than gushthi ties.

Since marriage and marriage relationships determine to a great extent the prestige and power of the individual, many a time a candidate will try to disrupt a possible marriage negotiation which might make his opponent stronger in the future. Karim has always shown a mastery in selecting people and tying them to a kin-network so as to get a maximum support in every village quarrel. He has also worked hard to attempt to stop possible marriages which might strengthen his opponents.

When two individuals negotiate a marriage for the purpose of enhancing their power in the village, the rival group certainly will try to prevent it, as will be seen in the following case when Imanuddin and Zaman negotiated a marriage between their children to gain each other's support.

Case 10: Case of the Political Marriage

Imanuddin's son, Kemal, a young man of twenty-one, attended school up to grade seven and was a worthy groom for many girls in the village.

Zaman's daughter (fourteen) was an eligible bride, and moreover she was Zaman's only child. Zaman, who was Imanuddin's brother, had made a fortune by his trade and was a well-to-do man in the village. Although Imanuddin had received half his father's property, he was not as wealthy as his brother. Zaman and Imanuddin had not been on good terms with each other since the death of their father; but there were good reasons for both of them to want to get their children married to each other.

By marrying his son to Zaman's daughter, Tahera, Imanuddin would get Zaman's wealth as she was the only child and would inherit her father's property. Also this would bring more power for securing votes in the Union Council election.

Zaman, on the other hand, would get for his only daughter one of the most eligible grooms, Imanuddin's son Kemal who was both educated and handsome. Zaman himself was thinking of contesting in the Union Council elections at the time, and the marriage would make his brother an ally, rather than an antagonist who might divide the gushthi vote in his own paribar.

Almost everything was finalized and a date was fixed for the ceremony. Just a few days before the ceremony, however, a rumour spread in the village market that Zaman's daughter and Imanuddin's son were having an affair and that the parents did not have any other choice than to agree to such a marriage. Gossip spread like wildfire and the prestige of both Zaman and Imanuddin was at stake.

Villagers consider a love affair not only anti-religious (in Badarpur the bride and groom are not to see each other before they get married), but they consider it a serious corruption which might endanger all the villagers' lives. Love affairs in the village are talked about with sarcasm, and a verbal harangue calculated to draw an audience may be started by pleading that the morale of the village is being ruined by such actions. As a consequence, the parents of the two principals not only lost face but also the chance of support from individuals and/or paribars who could have been useful through a bond of matrimony between their children. To continue with the marriage would have appeared to confirm the scandal, and the marriage was called off.

In actuality what happened is this:

Zaman's opponent in the Union Council election was Kalu of Gushthi *A*. If Zaman's gushthi, Gushthi *C,* had solidly supported Zaman, it would have ensured his election. To get Kalu, of Gushthi *A,* elected from the Northern constituency, Karim employed people to go to the village market during the *hat* day (on Tuesday, when the market took place) and spread the scandal regarding Zaman's daughter. At this the girl's relatives (i.e., the relatives of Zaman and Imanuddin) became very angry and beat the people allegedly employed by the chairman. Karim then came into the picture and very cleverly rescued his men by asking them to apologize. He skillfully pretended all the time that he did not know anything, and scolded the men for spreading the scandal. But the harm was already done. News of a scandal is like wildfire; you stop it on one side and suddenly it will break out on the other side. Despite Zaman's efforts, the scandal reduced his support in his gushthi, completely alienated the uncommitted voters of Gushthi B, and thus ensured Kalu's election. The marriage did not take place and Zaman and Imanuddin stopped negotiating.

This also had an impact on the Central constituency election, where Imanuddin was contesting the election on Karim's ticket with Gafur as his main opponent. Zaman and Gafur were close friends, and both were antagonistic to Karim. In this situation, Karim wanted his nominee, Imanuddin from the Central constituency, to be elected, but he did not relish the idea of Imanuddin being an affine of Zaman. The breaking of the marriage meant that Karim and Gushthi A could support Imanuddin without reserve.

The mobilizing of affinal relatives is thus extremely important in Badarpur politics. Conflicts can be resolved and problems can be solved by tracing some sort of link on an affinal basis between the parties. A man can get position and prestige in the village by maneuvering within kinship lines. Extension of kinship brings new allies all the time; new relations are created and also the bondage of the older kin can be threatened as seen in the relationship between Imanuddin-Karim and Imanuddin and Zaman. Imanuddin became an ally of Karim against his own gushthi members (his brother Zaman supported Gafur) when the two became affinally related. There are many examples of how different individuals have used affinal ties to gain support, but perhaps the best example of the effective use of affinal ties in all various circumstances can be seen in the history of the rise to power of Karim.

Case 11: Karim and His Several Wives

Karim left home while he was in the tenth grade. That was in 1930, when a good number of Hindus still lived in the village. His father, Korban Ali, searched for him in all possible places, but without any success. After two years, Karim suddenly arrived at the village with his bride, a Hindu woman of twenty-six (Karim was only eighteen at the time). The Hindus of the village became furious, but the Muslims thought that Karim had done a great thing by converting a Hindu girl to Islam. Villagers believed that converting a non-Muslim to Islam is clearing the way for heaven.

The following year there was an election. Despite the violent protests of the Hindus, Karim got solid support in this Muslim village and got himself elected for the first time. When Karim married again in 1935 (on the plea that his Hindu wife could not manage a Muslim household) his first wife committed suicide. This new marriage enabled him to open up another field of influence. Karim was already a rich man since his Hindu wife, as an only child, had inherited all the property of her wealthy father. The father of his second wife was also a wealthy businessman, and helped Karim build his political career. In 1943 Karim married again. The new wife was also the daughter of a businessman, a businessman from the neighbouring village, Parabo, who had wanted Karim's favour for a long time. Now Karim could be sure to get all the votes from the Parabo area, formerly the most difficult area for him. An important man of Parabo who had always opposed Karim in the past, and prior to that had opposed Karim's father, was a distant cousin of Karim's new wife. Karim could now easily control the cousin and soon became very powerful in village politics. Karim's fourth marriage in 1954 brought him power and influence in still another part of the Union, making it nearly impossible for anyone in the Union to successfully contest an election against him.

Marriage not only helps to extend kin relationship, it also helps to resolve conflict and bring two quarreling parties to an understanding. Links established through some affinal ties bring people close to each other, and misunderstandings between two parties or groups who have affinal ties are normally settled without any outside intervention.

Affinal ties are not the only ties which cut across groupings. Friendship is another such tie. Personal friendship between individuals may be so strong in the village that friends may go out of their way to help each other. Personal friendship or loyalty can be a strong determining factor in the village politics, and often helps to predict dal composition.

Case 12: Story of Four Friends

Gafur has always had solid support in his political struggles from three of his childhood friends in Badarpur: Kabir, Abul Basir, and Zaman. Kabir was a traditional leader of the village; his father was a Mollah and used to lead prayers in the village mosque. After the death of his father in 1963, he began to lead the prayers in the central mosque. He had all the weight of traditional authority and prestige which did not diminish even after the charge against him of first-degree murder. Kabir himself never contested any election and was well respected and admired by his neighbours; so he had been a helpful friend to Gafur.

Abul Basir, another childhood friend of Gafur, was a Hafez and had been trained in the traditional system. Yet, he became interested in the new system and the new ways of life, and was the only villager to subscribe to a weekly journal. Whenever he had a chance he used to read this to other villagers in the evening. His idea was that Islam does not wish anyone to remain stagnant by sticking to old traditions; rather, as he puts it, "change is the rule of law and Islam is no contradiction." He and Gafur had always helped each other in times of need. When Basir was going through a difficult period (due to the scandal spread against him), it was his friend Gafur who, putting no faith in the accusations, would console him and reassure him that one day the truth would prevail.

The wealthy Zaman was the third childhood friend of Gafur. Their friendship remained strong even in the days of inter-gushthi quarrel and Gafur was supported by Zaman in 1965, when Imanuddin, his brother, contested against him. In face of anything that might happen in gushthi or any other type of conflict, these four friends considered their friendship above all other alliances and tried to help each other in time of need.

By 1965 the people of the village had come to realize that their future prosperity depended on their ability to market their surplus produce. Due to many improvements in agriculture (such as adopting the Japanese method of paddy cultivation) a surplus had already begun to show. But it would have fetched poor prices if sold in the local markets to which goods could be carried in head loads. If they could take it to neighbouring towns and cities, Narayanganj and Dacca, it would fetch higher prices. Rice could be transported by carts if there were link roads connecting the village with the neighbouring markets as well as with the big market centres.

Under the initiative of chairman Karim, the Union Council tried to build a new road connecting Parabo and Baradi, two centres six miles apart. Since Parabo has a road to Dacca and Baradi to Narayanganj, this connecting road between Parabo and Baradi passing through Badarpur would have completed the road from Dacca to Narayanganj. It would also have connected other smaller centres, and hence would have been most helpful. However, Gafur and Zaman and later Kabir objected to it until finally the project was abandoned. Zaman, Gafur and Kabir usually form what may be called the progressive faction; so that their attitude in this matter was a puzzle to many.

Their argument, however, was that the Union Council wanted to build the road without paying compensation to villagers through whose paddy fields the road would run. Karim's interest in the road was not altruistic, they argued, but based on the fact that he wanted to connect Badarpur, his home, with Parabo, the home of his second father-in-law. Gafur and his dal opposed the project not only because the proposal came from Karim, but also because all the land that would have been commandeered would have come from the northern enclave (Uttar Para) of the village, where most of the supporters of Gafur and Zaman lived.

This politicking within the village, between Karim, Gafur, and Zaman, did not create any clear-cut division between the two dals supporting them; rather there was an entanglement of interest-groups working against and counteracting each other. Although all these three individuals came from different gushthis, attitudes towards the road were not simply split along gushthi lines. There was also a major split in terms of Para affiliation, with people from North Para opposing the road. The young people and the progressives were also split in spite of their usual course of supporting Gafur and Zaman, as many could see the long-term benefits from the road. In this situation Karim could not form an idea as to whether he had a majority support or not, and the project was quietly dropped.

C. Situation of Conflict and Outside Links

Although most disputes are within the village, between people of the village, some individuals with prestige or contacts call in certain influential outsiders to help settle disputes. These outsiders may often act to the advantage of a particular individual or village group, but as has been pointed out in connection with police intervention their presence may harm the entire village. Hence the decision to call in an outsider is always considered carefully, but the ability to call in one gives great power to those villagers who can do so.

Case 13: Hadudu Game

A fight between two villages took place in the summer of 1965. The details are vividly remembered by the people, since many villagers had to leave the village temporarily for fear of the police. The following informant's account is clearly one-sided, but it will indicate the effect of outside intervention in settling disputes:

> Last summer (summer of 1965) our village "Hadudu"[55] team went to play a trophy match against the Murapara (a neighboring village)

team. We were very proud of our village team and were sure we would win the game.

Murapara is about five miles from our village, so we started quite early as we wanted our players to have a little rest before the game started. However, when we were only two miles from the village, suddenly it started to rain with thunder and lightning. After the rain was over we started again, almost running, to reach Murapara in time.

When we reached Murapara, to our dismay we found that the referee had already declared the Murapara team the winner because we were late in arriving. We were completely drenched by the rain, yet ready to play. A protest was lodged with the game committee, but the committee did not favour our request. We then started shouting protests against the committee, the Murapara team, and the Murapara people, and a quarrel broke out. The game was scheduled in the Murapara school field and most of the villagers who came to watch the game had already left the place by that time since we were late and the Murapara team had already been given a walk-over against our team. Since the few people who were there were not strong enough to fight our group, we beat them right and left, and then hurried back home before the rest of Murapara could come and catch us. We almost ran all the way back home.

We reached home safely but the trouble soon started. One of the players of the Murapara team was the son of a *Daroga* (police inspector) who was stationed at Dacca. This inspector learned about the fight from his son who had been badly injured, and he immediately advised the police station of Baidyar Bazar to arrest all of our players. Our players were mostly farmers and laborers and were very much afraid of the police. For about six months many of us, including me, had to remain outside the village in relatives' homes in neighbouring villages, or hidden in different houses whenever the police came in search of us. A compensation was paid by us to the Murapara players with an extra amount for the inspector's son. When we collected the compensation money, all the villagers contributed even though only a few were actually involved.

This incident also indicates that during inter-village disputes the villagers not only forget their internal conflicts and help hide their people amongst themselves to save them from the threat of police, but also at the same time, they do not hesitate to contribute cash, the rarest commodity in the village, to save their fellow men. And during all such conflicts it was Karim who came to the forefront to lead the village, and it was Karim who negotiated the deal on behalf on the entire village.

It is also evident from this case that an outside link or familiarity with influential outsiders is a very important factor if one wishes to have decisions made in his favour. For the people of Murapara it was important and useful to have the contact with the Daroga who supported their side. At the same time, it was Karim's power, his ties with the police and outsiders and his support for the Badarpuris that enabled the case to be resolved the way it eventually was.

The importance of this ability to contact outsiders can also be noticed in the rise of Gafur. It's largely because of the help he once gave a fellow gushthi member to get him out of a police case, that he later ended up as the acknowledged leader or spokesman for his entire group (gushthi).

Case 14: The Emergence of Gafur

In 1959 a quarrel broke out between the supporters of Husen Ali of Gushthi A and of Kabir of Gushthi B over the ownership of a vacant lot. Several persons were injured as a result and one of the injured, Awal, a ninth grade student and the son of Husan Ali, died in the hospital. Kinsmen of both Husen Ali and Kabir took part in the actual fighting, and the case went to court as a murder case with Husen Ali as the plaintiff and Kabir as the defendant.

Kabir was a religious and devoted man (See supra, Chapter three: p. 55) and he had never before argued or fought with his neighbors. On being involved in a first-degree murder case, he became terribly frightened, and fled from the village. A warrant was issued, and ultimately the police arrested him together with his twenty-one supporters, incidentally all members of his gushthi. Gafur (a newly elected Union Council member at the time) went to see him in the police station and was convinced that in reality, the vacant plot did belong to him, and that Husan Ali was the trespasser. Accordingly, if Kabir had hurt anyone it had been only in defense of his own property. Moreover, the boy who died in the hospital had been mortally wounded by a spade; Kabir had been empty-handed.

From the very beginning of the quarrel Kabir's efforts had been aimed at cooling everyone down. But the argument had become too heated; the mob had become too excited; and violence had spontaneously erupted. Because of Kabir's past record for mildness, Gafur believed in his innocence, and decided to help him and his family defend themselves. He went to the city to consult government officials and lawyers.

Husan Ali, on the other hand, paid, according to informants' stories, a huge bribe to the police and to Karim, the chairman, to have the chowkidar Mafiz of Gushthi B on his side, and he literally purchased a number of witnesses from among the villagers outside the gushthis involved.

Gafur's involvement in the case gave Karim a golden opportunity to embarrass his opponent. Karim at one stage advised Husen Ali to add Gafur's name to the charge, as advisor of Kabir's party. The allegation was that Gafur was directly responsible for the mob action. This was a serious charge. The warrant was issued in the name of Gafur, but as he was not physically present at the fight or even in the village, it was a bailable warrant. Gafur bailed himself out, went to Dacca, and saw the Superintendent of Police and the Sub-Divisional Officer. It was because of the intervention of the latter that the police case against him was finally withdrawn, and he was set free.

Finally, after a year and a half, the case was settled at Dacca Sessions Court: Kabir and his party were acquitted, and Husen Ali and the members of Gushthi *A* were branded as trespassers. For some time the Chairman, the Chowkidar, Husen Ali and the others remained aloof and sullen, but Gafur was friendly in his behaviour towards them. Actually, neither Karim nor Gafur wished to pursue the case any further. Gafur had been accused by Karim, and after the acquittal, could easily have filed a damage suit against him and his supporters. But instead he silently bore the whole thing and was satisfied with a simple acquittal. Both Gafur and Karim realized that the whole thing was exacerbated before the trial. If Gafur had pursued the case further and brought Karim to trial for the harassment, it might have induced many to believe that Gafur was helping Kabir only because of kinship. On the other hand Karim did not pursue the case further because he knew that further instigation could lead Gafur to file a defamation case against him.

However, the concrete results of this case were that Gafur came to realize how important friendship ties had been in helping him win the case, and that he became the leader of Gushthi *B;* he unified all members of his gushthi, including the chowkidar. We have already seen how it was Zaman's successful contacts with the Sub-Divisional office at Narayanganj because of clearing the water hyacinth (Chapter five, p. 105) that enabled him to become the leader of Gushthi *C*. The ability to call in outside support is decisive in ensuring support for a leader within the village, as Karim's long career shows.

Discussion

This chapter has shown—especially through the example of Karim— the manner in which disputants or political leaders within the village try to get majority support for their actions through such devices as the appealing to the sense of village patriotism; the exploitation of affinal ties and gushthi ties; the division of opponent's gushthi loyalty; personal appeal to individual supporters; and manipulation of sect loyalties. The analysis of issue after issue has shown how Karim as the leader of Gushthi A, of the South Para, of the conservatives, and of the Hanafi majhab could not hope to get a majority behind him. Even his skill at using affinal, or patronage ties would not have secured him a majority. Yet Karim and his dal won the elections, and their overall success can be attributed to extra-village ties and to inter-village conflict which feeds into the villagers' desire to keep the Union chairmanship in their own village.

The villagers of Badarpur, whether they did or did not like Karim, enjoyed and boasted about the fact that the chairmanship of Jampur Union had always been held by their village. They relished the prospect of Union domination by a Badarpuri. If Karim's nominee could be elected, there would be no doubt about Karim's chairmanship and Badarpur would be able to boast again that since the establishment of the Union Board, the leadership of the Union had not been taken away from her. More practically, his chairmanship would bring patronage benefits to Badarpur, rather than to other villages. This attitude by the villagers was responsible for the thumping victory of Karim's nominees and the defeat of Gafur and two of the other candidates, Almas and Azhar.

Thus village patriotism was one of the main factors which together with the splitting of gushthi loyalty led Imanuddin, Karim's candidate, to victory. The fact that Karim held the leadership of this village for more than thirty years was not due to accident, but rather to factors which led the villagers to place him in the leadership position. Village patriotism may be considered the most important of these factors.

In a quarrel between people of two different villages all the villagers forget their internal rivalries and jealousies to group together against the other village. The villagers will automatically unite and fight tooth and nail not simply for their relatives but for the interest and prestige of their own village. During such inter-village conflicts Karim becomes the main spokesman for the village, and becomes indispensable to the villagers. It is Karim who, in such a situation, can direct the villagers and make a decision. They look to him for leadership, and they give him their enthusiastic support.

However, in elections on a higher level than that of the Union Council (e.g. District Board and/or Provincial or Central Legislature), villagers would not hesitate to bring in from the city or from a neighbouring village a spokesman whose name was already identified with a national political party. People from outside the village occasionally came to address the villagers to get support in favour of their party's candidates. It is only on issues where there is inter-villager rivalry that Karim's ties are important.

As we have seen, the apparent conservatism of the village in continuing its support for Karim over thirty years led to a continuous political process of dispute and struggle for support. The status quo was maintained only by astute use of all the political techniques available and by the importance of certain issues where extra-village ties were important. The following chapter will consider village reaction to issues which are national and not just local.

CHAPTER SEVEN

Village Politics and National Issues

This study has so far focused on the internal processes of village politics. Even so the importance of events outside the village has been apparent. National politics constitute one, and by no means the least important, of these outside events. Village politics certainly are influenced, though not directly, by the national politics which sometimes create conflicts even at the village level and always feed into the existing conflicts present in the village. In this chapter an attempt will be made to use the 1965 election as a case study from which to analyse the interaction between national and local politics. This analysis has been divided into three sub-sections:

1. 1965 election from the East Bengali national standpoint
2. Intermediaries between villagers and the national parties
3. Reinterpretation of national issues by the village

1. 1965 Election from the East Bengali National Standpoint

The national issues of the 1965 election as viewed from Dacca, the capital of what was then East Pakistan, involved a dispute over the Bengali language and the contention that insufficient attention had been given by Pakistan to the economic and social needs of its eastern region. These two issues resulted in an antagonism to Ayub, and as a consequence, the COP (Combined Opposition Party) was organized and presented Miss Fatimah Jinnah, sister of Muhammad Ali Jinnah, as its Presidential candidate.

The younger generation of East Pakistan, and particularly those who lived in the city, were determined to achieve economic and political control over their destiny. Their determination was so strong that "there was no denying that a number of the younger generation under twenty-five had separatist tendencies" (Ahmad, K 1967). The polarization of this separatist spirit of the young Bengalis, however, was counteracted by the older generation who had earlier gone through the

Village Politics and National Issues 143

terrible civil war in the wake of partition, and who thus were still looking toward a kind of federation of the east and west. In this conflict, the younger generation (mostly students; the labourers and farmers had not yet developed any organized body) divided up into groups of separate student wings in favour of various political groups. The Students' League organized under the patronage of the Muslim League tried its best to level the opposition and maintain more or less unchanged the existing governmental system. On the other hand, the Awami League recruited a majority of the East Bengali students and organized its own students' wing, the Student Federation. A third student organization, *Tammadun Majlish* (literary meaning: the Cultural Assembly) was affiliated with the Islamic group.

As the 1965 election approached, the national political groups became more and more involved in politicking; they began to send student representatives to the rural areas of East Bengal to organize support in their favour. As leaders of West Pakistan, members of the Muslim League with the student counterparts in the Students' League, were unanimous in their firm resistance to grant more power to East Pakistan. To counteract the demands of East Pakistani nationalists, they reminded the people that East Pakistan made up only one sixth of the territory, and that even though it had a population majority, a part of that population (the Hindus), was not loyal to the country. In reply, the Awami League leaders and their student counterparts in the Students' Federation maintained that the alternatives to giving East Pakistan more power were at best unrest, instability, with a consequent decline in economic growth, while at worse they threatened the break-up of Pakistan.

The East Pakistanis who opposed the break-up of the country argued that as often pointed out by leftist intellectuals, separation would be a retrograde step since small countries have a tendency to become authoritarian. For them blind nationalism was retrogressive, and not a solution to the problem of an increasingly modern nation.

On the other hand, those who favoured separation cited arguments such as the following:

1. The link between the east and west wings is religion, and the central government and the West Pakistani government will always use Islam for their own political ends.
2. The industrialists and commercial magnates of the west will always use Islam for exploiting the illiterate masses of the east.
3. The peasants and workers of all of Pakistan will never be able to

unite to fight against the united "reactionary" forces or vested interests, whereas the high cost of communications between the two wings is no hindrance to the capitalists and feudal lords.
4. A central government will always be able to find "a dangerous common enemy"—Chinese communists or Indian Hindus—to keep the two peoples together.
5. Freedom of expression, of assembly, of conscience, etc., will always be in danger.
6. Political parties not based on religion, but stressing secularism and social and economic problems will have no chance to succeed.

The East Pakistani intelligentsia realized that neither the "integration theory" of the Muslim League nor the "separation theory" were totally acceptable or even practicable under the circumstances. The majority of the people were illiterate, and East Pakistan with her population density had to look to West Pakistan for food supplies. Thus groups such as the Awami League seemed at least for the time being, to abandon some of their separatist tendencies, and combined with Nizam-E-Islam and a number of other groups to counteract the Muslim League which they considered their most dangerous rival. The Combined Opposition Party (COP), mentioned earlier was the result of this opposition to the Muslim League.

Although the national political parties had always been reluctant to get involved in local elections, such as those of the Union Council, they realized that the 1965 Union Council elections would be of vital importance. Accordingly, the national political parties appointed overseers to observe indirectly the Union Council elections of that year and to report on the possible candidates for future party recruitments. This was the first election of the Basic Democrats (see supra p. 106), who were going to elect the President of the whole nation, and it was important for the national political parties to see that the elected Basic Democrats of the grass-root level in village politics became members of their particular party and finally voted for their presidential candidate. In cases where the national political party organizers realized that the village man expected to get the most votes would probably not support their party ideology after election, they advised the overseers to do everything possible to see that this "unwanted man" should not get elected in the first place.

The East Pakistanis, though somewhat indirectly, thus felt the influence of the national political parties, and local elections were thus affected by national issues.

2. Intermediaries between Villagers and the National Parties

There were in East Pakistan people who served as intermediaries or "brokers" between the villagers and their interests, and the national political parties and national issues. For example, individual candidates often invited students from outside the village and usually from the city to speak in their behalf. The national political parties were always happy to help recruit student supporters for village candidates because the students could serve as brokers between the parties and the villagers. Students are accorded a good image in the minds of the villagers who like to hear them speak, and the Union Council candidates who can get support from outside student groups are likely to get a favourable response from the villagers.

If a village Union Council candidate had relatively direct links with the national political parties, then he could naturally recruit many student workers. Since most of the students of East Pakistan were more or less committed to the COP in 1965, a candidate likely to support the "principles" of the COP could recruit such student workers more easily than other candidates. City students helped many village candidates create a better political image. For instance, local candidates were briefed by the students from the city and told to mention in their public speeches amongst the villagers that the government, the administration, and the so-called "respectable" citizens alike displayed a total lack of concern for basic human values, and cared nothing about whether a neighbour was subjected to sub-human conditions or not. Naturally, by "government" they meant West Pakistani government; by "administration", West Pakistani administration; and by "respectable citizens" those who were "big" officials and were in the good books of the administration; "neighbours" referred, of course, to the suffering East Pakistani masses.

The 1965 election in the Central Constituency involved a specific example of students serving as intermediaries between national politics and village affairs. The main contestants were Imanuddin and Gafur of Gushthi C and B respectively. But Almas and Azhar were also candidates. They came to the forefront in village politics during the period 1959–67. Although their traditional occupation was agriculture, these two entrepreneurs, having started as small traders, managed to become businessmen. They derived good incomes from their jute trade and maintained a fair standard of living in the village.

Although they had neither any strong gushthi affiliation nor any strong group of supporters in that constituency, Almas and Azhar did have their business in the village market directly opposite the Central Constituency across the river. And because they were financially well-off and were on good terms with the inhabitants of the village, they thought that they would be able to procure enough votes to win the election.

Almas and Azhar were the only two businessmen at Badarpur who had direct business links with Dacca, where they knew the Awami League office. On several occasions Awami League workers went to gather contributions from Almas and Azhar's Dacca centre, and gradually Almas personally came to know a few of the Awami League officeholders. As the election approached, a number of provincial leaders of the Combined Opposition Party came to the village and stayed with Almas. One of the provincial Awami League leaders persuaded him to accept the local secretaryship of the Awami League party; thus he became the regional spokesman for the COP. Students from the village, particularly those who studied outside the village, were contacted by the Awami League party and sent to help Almas create a political image for himself. The students organized frequent meetings and focused the villagers' attention on Almas, making him the main attraction in all such meetings.

If only Almas, and not also Azhar, had contested in the election, the result might have been different, but unfortunately, with both running, victory was practically impossible. Ultimately both of them shared the vote, and neither was elected in 1965. However, the outside "brokers," linking town with country, helped obtain a large percentage of the vote, and for non-traditional leaders, both made creditable showings. They themselves, by virtue of developing trade ties with the city, had turned into inside brokers, linking the country with the town.

3. Reinterpretation of National Issues by the Village

If village candidates made use of national political parties and were in turn made use of by the national political parties, so too did the local politicians attempt to take advantage of various national issues and the national parties' brokers or middlemen attempt to use national issues to affect local elections and to achieve their parties' ends.

In 1965 a wealthy Muslim ex-landlord, Torab Ali, of a village near Badarpur, began to incite people against Gafur, alleging that he was supporting the anti-government political group, the Awami League, which objected to the imposition of the Urdu language in Government papers and thus acted against the religion of Islam. Like most other ex-landlords of the country, Torab Ali was a Muslim Leaguer; he had been responsible for organizing the local Muslim League by recruiting members from the entire thana of Baidyar Bazar. The Chairman of Jampur Union, Karim, was also strongly identified with the Muslim League; this identification left the local opposition to Karim little choice as to what national party to support—the COP, which is composed of the Awami League, Krisak Sramik Dal and Nizam-E-Islam Dal. The argument of the Muslim League for Urdu was that since it was written in Arabic script and since Arabic was the language of the Prophet Muhammad and of the Holy Quran, any attempt to reduce Urdu influence was anti-Islamic. There was no Urdu-Bengali split in the village and the majority of the villagers seldom went to the mosque, privately ridiculing the Mollahs and Moulvis. Yet publicly opposing Islam in any way was sacrilegious, and knowledge of sacrilege was enough to incite the people to fight tooth and nail. That Gafur was supporting the COP was tantamount to sacrilege. Many people took sides against him. The Chowkidar and his people who had been humiliated in the Kabir vs. Husen Ali case added oil to the fire by siding with Torab Ali and opposing Gafur. (See supra p. 138.)

In the election campaign Gafur tried skillfully to convince his voters that he was not trying to help the cause of the anti-Islamic group by supporting the Awami League, and hence the COP, and that he was not underestimating the importance of Arabic. He was only trying to do something which was for the people's benefit. He explained that during the British rule everything was printed in English; and receipts people used to get from the tax collectors were quite frequently written to indicate something different from what should rightfully have been indicated. The poor villagers were often forced to pay the same taxes several times.[56] Gafur pleaded that if Urdu were substituted for English, the villagers would have to suffer in the same way. Memories of the old days were still alive in many minds. Yet the overseer's eloquence and the created gushthi split of "mirjafar" chowkidar proved to be more effective than Gafur's skillful attempt to convince the voters, and Karim's nominee, Imanuddin, won the election.

What can be noticed here is that an issue at the national level got changed as it was applied at the village level. The anti-Urdu politicking of Gafur was reinterpreted to the villagers by Torab Ali as anti-Islamic. Signing of the COP oath was also felt to be important at first (and Karim signed), but in their eventual voting few people really took much notice of whether the oath had been signed or not. Further, the central party support of particular village candidates was often based not on their agreement with the party's ideals, but on the party's desire that some other candidate had to be defeated.

So, too, where the national issue in 1965 concerned a choice between

Miss Fatimah Jinnah, and President Ayub Khan, the COP leaders in local public meetings denounced the government's policy (policy of Ayub Khan) as "step-motherly," and accused the government of favouring one region against the other. COP leaders showed why there should be discontent with the present set-up and urged the people to come out openly for Miss Fatimah Jinnah, as a means of showing this discontent.

The Badarpur candidates in the 1965 Union Council Elections, except for a few (Gafur, Zaman and Almas), did not at first come out openly in support of Miss Jinnah. But gradually, as the student community carried door-to-door propaganda in favour of Miss Jinnah, and stressed support for her candidacy as a way of expressing dissatisfaction, an opposition swing developed. This growing discontent should not be viewed as a reaction to any isolated set of events, but as having its roots in the society which in turn was influenced by the cultural forces of the country. A few individuals, like the chairman, Karim, and his followers, continued to support Ayub Khan. Village unrest against the Chairman could be expressed, and turned into an open conflict when student brokers provided means of expressing the discontent in a legitimate national political form.

In the Northern Constituency Zaman got unreserved support from the students because of his association with the COP. He signed an oath which guaranteed that he would support Miss Jinnah once he was elected (the COP local agents supplied the oath for signature to practically all the candidates who promised that they would support Miss Jinnah). Zaman's oath signing established his reputation with villagers as being in favour of change, and he thus became more popular than the sitting members, Kalu and Safaruddin Master, who were well-known for their pro-government views.

In the Southern Constituency, Karim saw how villagers perceived the oath-signing and changed his tone overnight, promising to support the COP. He also signed the oath to support Miss Jinnah, even though his lieutenants, Imanuddin and Kalu in the Central and Northern Constituencies, refused to sign. Similar changes of support were made in the rest of the villages of Jampur Union Council.

At the village level the fear of being treated as Bengalis by the Urdu-speaking element which dominated the Government and the army, simmered in the minds of emerging leaders such as Gafur, Zaman, and Almas who had direct contacts with the political leaders of the city. In some of their election pamphlets they not only listed the main national issues and local grievances, but also included their disapproval of local issues. For example, the Union Council had raised taxes on certain items, and the COP candidates tried to show that this was owing to the military dictatorship of President Ayub Khan who had no sympathy whatsoever for the welfare of the East Pakistani peasants.

Some of the speeches at village meetings dealt with national issues, but these speeches were generally made by those student political leaders (workers) who came from the urban areas. The local candidates always made supporting speeches after the students had started the meetings, but most of their election speeches concentrated on local problems, i.e., the school, mosque, sanitation, water, and roads. For although the villager votes for national parties and national candidates, the issues and arguments which influence his voting are the national issues reinterpreted in terms of village issues and groupings by the outside and the local brokers.

What we are leading up to is a discussion of the impact of outside political events on the village, of village reactions to outsiders, and of likely future reactions to outside changes. The most direct evidence of villager reactions is contained in a conversation which took place during one of the national elections (1954), when a group of Dacca University students came to Badarpur to canvass for a political party. A number of villagers were there, and an interesting picture was revealed in their conversation.

The first remark was directed towards the students by the village school teacher:[57]

> We are glad to see you good people in our village. You are the source of our joy and we feel inspired to live and wait for the good happy days.

The traditional head man responded:

> What have they come to do other than to collect votes? They are not interested in our welfare. Leaders promised so many things when we voted for them in the last election. These students came from the city and lured us with promises of a golden age. But once elected, they remembered nothing.

The school teacher then said:

> They have done a lot of things, built roads and mosques, renovated the school; we neither go to a mosque nor send our children to the school; we do not care how we use the roads. It is our fault our leaders cannot teach us and check us individually.

Next, a village boy studying at the college joined the discussion:

> Certainly they must do everything they promised. They secured our votes by promising that they would do this and that, but have done

nothing for us. Now we will have to make them do things they once promised to do.

A farmer who had been silent, said:

Nobody can do anything except *Allah* (God). What Allah has written in our *Nasib* (fate or luck) we must follow. See these students from the city; they have good meals and clean clothes every day. We work night and day, but don't even get enough rice to eat a day. *Allah* has written one kind of *Nasib* for us and another kind for them. Nobody can change it; it all depends upon one's *Nasib*.

The above conversation illustrates the point that dramatic differences in belief, form and practices exist within the superficially homogeneous peasant society. The so-called "changeless Indian villages" contain a number of opposing ideological segments. The first is represented by the village school teacher who has been schooled in the traditional religious values and also has been educated in the modern school system. This segment views Pakistan as a typical "Islamic State": ("they have done . . . children to school")—a kind of utopia, and also sees the existing political system in the country as close to a utopian ideal. To achieve a fully utopian state people such as the school teacher believe everyone should go to school. This group, therefore, favors conformity among the people; instead of taking a destructive attitude towards the existing government, people should look at its advantages and live a life which conforms to the political ideology of the country. Thus all criticism would be avoided. In an urban centre, the school teacher would be a Pan-Islamist and a member of a national party (the Muslim League), but in the village he appears simply as what we have seen in the chairman and others like him. The ideology of people of this type is based on the concept that Pakistan is a part and parcel of the "Islamic World," and that the people of Pakistan share greater affinity with other Muslim countries than with their Hindu neighbours.

The traditional village head man and the village farmer express a different outlook towards life. They represent a segment of the people that regards itself in a social context of "dominance-submission," resulting in a "sense of deprivation and frustration," which makes people indifferent (the village farmer) or hostile (the head man) towards life and the world. To such people life is full of anxiety and incurable helplessness. The world, to these people, has very little to offer; and if they have any ideology at all, it is the ideology of subordination, since they find themselves entangled in a mass of problems evident in every sphere of a life which they feel is too complicated.

The college student, on the other hand, is forceful in his rejection ("They must do everything they promised") and is determined to uphold his rights ("Now we still have to make them do the things that they once promised to do"). His love and concern for his country does not direct him toward any kind of aggressive destructiveness. People of this type want "social reintegration through a selective rejection, modification"; they are constructive in their approach and represent the middle class intellectuals of the urban centres. At the village level, Zaman, Gafur, and their followers represent this group.

These three types of villagers, as illustrated by their attitudes toward local issues, had their counterparts in the political and literary history of East Pakistan. In fact, these three trends of thought are reflections at a micro-level of the socio-political trends, discussed previously, of the country as a whole.

The third group, composed of middle-class intellectuals in the urban areas and represented by the educated students in the village, was ideologically in constant conflict with the government party in power, and as a result constantly seeked for reforms.[58] This group stressed its close and intimate links with the Bengali literature of both East and West Bengal, and at the same time tried to focus on the vast differences between it and the cultural elements infiltrating every day from West Pakistan. This group was one which:

1. took intense pride in the historical and literary glories of Bengal;
2. tried to perpetuate and promote a revival of Bengali culture in East Pakistan (which was affected by the constant diffusion of West Pakistani cultural elements);
3. was eager to make concessions to Hindus or to other minority groups in East Pakistan provided they showed allegiance exclusively to East Pakistan (thus the group hoped to weld East Pakistan into one strong "national" community, speaking one common language and proud of East Pakistani tradition);
4. was earnestly interested in social reform along secular lines.

In other words, its desire to forge nationhood in East Pakistan was coupled with an antipathy towards those who denied the claims of East Pakistan to be treated as a separate national entity.

The conversation stated above took place in 1954, immediately before the general election, when the Muslim League was totally defeated in East Pakistan (see supra chapter two, p. 28). This conversation can be compared with another conversation that took place fairly recently (in 1966). It is given below in the form of a case study:

Case 15: Fence Around the River

It was December 10, 1966, the middle of winter in Badarpur, corresponding to the Bengali lunar months of Poush and Magh. This is the season for the cultivation of spices and lentils, a relatively less tedious job than that of the cultivation of jute or paddy. Obviously, the farmers of the village have more time to gossip and work in a relatively more relaxed atmosphere.

I was invited by Karim to have lunch with him at his home just after the Juhar prayer (noon prayer). When I reached Karim's house, I found Dr. Gafur, Imanuddin, Azhar, and about ten other villagers from both the village and outside who had also been invited. Some of Karim's relatives from Burundi were there too, including Kalu. I did not expect Imanuddin and Kalu together, because it was Kalu who had disrupted Imanuddin's son Kemal's marriage with Zaman's daughter Tahera. However, later on I realized that both of them were invited by Karim and since all were related to each other (Karim, Kalu, and Imanuddin) they could not possibly refuse to accept the invitation without insulting the host. When we began to eat, Karim opened the conversation:

Karim:

> Before the next rainy season comes we would like to install a fence around the riverside so that no water hyachinth can enter the village and destroy our crops. I would appreciate it if you would all cooperate and recruit some voluntary labour from your own para.

A village farmer, cousin of Karim, though not from Badarpur, said immediately:

> When do we have time, Bhuiyan? We work on our land from morning to evening. There is no time left for any voluntary work.

Gafur:

> What is the government doing? If the government can give a contract to remove the water hyacinth so that S.D.O.'s boat can pass through, it can also provide some more money to put fences around the water.

Imanuddin:

> You want the government to pay to protect your land from the water hyacinth? I think it is our duty and we should do it.

Village Politics and National Issues

Azhar:

If we have to do everything then why do we have to pay taxes to the government? What benefit are we getting from the government except that the government increases the taxes every year?

Karim:

You do not pay taxes to the government to clean your "cowshed"; you have to clean it yourself.

Gafur:

It is not a question of cleaning one's own house; this is a task which will affect all of the village. Taxes are not paid to have individual work done, but to get advantages through government protection in times of national calamities and danger. I think it may be possible for us to make the government realize that this water hyacinth problem is a question of public protection; it is a question of saving the entire village from the danger of the water hyacinth, and it involves the future of the entire village.

Karim:

The government is maintaining your security. What would we have done if the government had not fought the Indians in the war?[59] What would have happened to all of us?

Azhar:

What could we have lost? What has this poor village that it can be afraid of losing? What is the use of such senseless protection, when we have nothing to lose?

Gafur:

That's not the point; the point is, we pay taxes to the government to build our roads and to clean them. This small river is the only "road" we have in the village. Now, we can rightfully claim that this river needs cleaning and to do it a fence will have to be erected around the land.

Karim:

You know the government cannot take such responsibilities for any particular village; what is the use of blaming the government?

Gafur:

Oh, I am certainly not blaming the government, nor am I suggesting that the government should take such responsibilities for all such difficulties of the village, but maybe it will. We can only find out after we have approached the government. Why don't we call the entire village on this issue and ask everyone to give their opinion. . . .

From the above conversation it is apparent that the three polar types of reaction to an issue still exist in the village. Karim, the Union Council Chairman is still supporting the Muslim League-dominated government even by evading issues that have been for the benefit of the villagers; Gafur, representing the democratic trends in the village, comes forward with constructive suggestions without making any attempt to create disruption in the village. The third group, which constitutes the majority of the villagers, is still in a stage of deprivation and frustration since the members feel that they have nothing in this world that they can lose.

CHAPTER EIGHT

Summary and Conclusion

This study has been concerned with village politics, in particular with political processes and change in a village of what was at the time East Pakistan, in order to show how they relate to the politics of the nation. Politics was defined as a process by which men set the conditions of their common alliances. An attempt was made to demonstrate that although change was not observable by the casual observer in contexts such as were found in East Pakistani villages, the rural-urban gap, the conflict between traditional and emergent leadership, clearly showed through. This may not be an entirely new idea, but it is certainly a matter of general theoretical importance and deserves emphasis.

The village community of Badarpur, although at a first glance deceptively simple, is actually highly complex and heterogeneous. It is not isolated but related to a larger society, in which the web of kinship links Badarpur to the neighbouring villages, and the intermediaries act as "broker" between the villages and the towns and cities. This refutes the concept of the "Changeless Indian Village" as a closed and self-sufficient system. Badarpur forms a part of the greater system, and the national political ideology casts its shadow even at the village level.

The question may be asked here to what extent the national political ideology directs or controls the village politics. The answer is that the village as such has very few direct connections if any at all. The individuals who control the village politics, the "brokers," are the ones who maintain contact with the national trends of politics. The ideational diversity and increased social distance created between East and West Pakistan was another barrier for the national political ideology to penetrate into the remote villages. Only a diluted form of national ideology was filtered down to the remote villages through the brokers. It has also been argued that "Islamic Society" means altogether different things to different people, and that although its saliency and paramountcy could not be denied in the question of survival, as a model for operational prescriptions for political life in the Pakistani system, it was nothing more than a viceregal system, shilly-shally and deficient.

The examples in this study show that although the nation directed ideology remained essentially alien to Badarpuris, there was a common "ideology" with other Bengalis which was different from the "national ideology" that conflicted with it. The ideologies to be found in the village resembled in many ways the ideologies discussed in previous chapters of the political and literary elites of Bengal since the early nineteenth century. The issues about which the villagers combine or argue differ markedly from those discussed by urban politicians, but the three polar types of reaction to any issue are the same—the creative use of traditional techniques and values; the passive acceptance of the status quo; the active seeking for change and novelty. The ideology successful in a given situation seems to be determined by the nature of the situation itself and not by the presence or absence of a particular ideology.

I

In order to answer the question of how typical Badarpur is of East Bengali villages, I have taken the structural organization of the village, placed it in the national setting, and have shown the typicality of the village in the greater context. Ecological background of the village has been depicted in much detail, showing the man-nature relationship which affects the villagers' way of life.

The family status still separates one village from another in social relations, as does para, gushthi, occupation or religious affiliation. These factors still provide to some extent the organizational frame for economic relations, political activities and interactions, and partly determine the structure of the village politics. Leaders of the village still use their kinship as an effective instrument for the achievement of personal success. Kinship, as a vehicle for manipulation, is as useful for a village leader as wealth is to an entrepreneur who has earned a fortune through trade. By playing kinship in inward and outward directions, a foresighted man can climb the social ladder faster and more effectively than others.

Village leaders also use sect loyalties to gain political support although there are structural factors which make it difficult and dangerous for a candidate to rely too much or too openly on such loyalties. In all except the central constituency, no one sect group comes anywhere near constituting a majority of the electorate, so that its support alone cannot win an election. Hence people try to gain additional power, for which there appears the most elastic demand, either by quarreling or appeasing, or by the use of material tokens of prestige through marriage negotiations. What has changed in this village is not only the dynamics by which political functions are processed, but the functions themselves.

II

What we have found in this study is roughly little more than the confirmation of one of the great truths of anthropology: "Structures change more slowly than functions, and often continue to be vessels in which very different wine is held." But we are still left with something which I have attempted to deal with under the heading of political processes.

Politics is too complex a human activity to lend itself to simple depiction or compendium. In a pluralistic structure like that of Badarpur, it must be legitimate for the members of a faith to organize for the protection of their interests against others and to obtain equal treatment, so long as that activity does not subvert the village interest. Whether the most effective organization for these purposes is a political party or a village faction is another matter and depends very much on the local political configuration. Beals and Siegel (1966:399) defined factionalism as an "overt conflict in a group which leads to increasing abandonment of cooperative activities." This definition suggests that factions may eventually "work themselves out" to the point where cooperative activity in the village has been abandoned. Such a conclusion does not fit well with the "life times" of factions in Badarpur as noted earlier in the Hanafis and Muhammadis. Consistent with Beals and Siegel (1966), in Badarpur factionalism is frequently connected with change in political structure; but factions, in the absence of conventional political divisions, perform necessary functions in organizing conflict.

III

Bailey has stated that in villages where the dominant caste is numerically large in relation to other castes, traditional panchayat members spend their energy largely in factional disputes. This statement can be interpreted to imply that the politically dominant caste group is usually the numerically dominant caste, and that there is much conflict between/within castes in this situation. In Badarpur, where factions are structured around gushthis, the numerically larger Gushthi B is not the politically dominant group. Rather Gushthi A is usually dominant.

There are two conditions which must be met before the smaller gushthi can become the dominant one. There must be a stable situation of factional coalition, similar to what Barth (1965:104) describes as a series of alliances of smaller corporate groups to form blocs. Secondly, the leader of the smaller gushthi must be able to mobilize the larger faction in matters which concern himself and his followers. He must also be able to resist its mobilization when this is not to his advantage. As Barth says (1965:125), "it is this outer sphere of his own bloc which holds the key to his success." In short, the group must have what Barth (p. 133) calls "individual captaincy," meaning a single leader for each group.

Although Gushthi A is smaller, it has the advantage of being more cohesive than the larger gushthi, and it also has what Barth calls "individual captaincy." Gushthi B's advantage in size is much reduced by increasing intra-factional dispute, in which opposing leaders within the same gushthi tend to split the votes (e.g. Latif and Gafur). This opposition within the group of the numerically larger gushthi leads to the political fission of such groups, and the alignments of the resulting two splinters in opposed blocs. The strength of the factions centered around Gushthi A is also increased by the manipulation of smaller factional groups, such as the faction led by Imanuddin of Gushthi C, for their support.

In addition, the traditional panchayat in Badarpur has hardly any function, either political or social. The Union Council organization is very much different from that of the traditional panchayat system. Hence, the traditional panchayat members in Badarpur, unlike their counterparts in Bailey's village, try to avoid politics, even factional politics.

Moreover, in Badarpur the politicking within factions polarizes around kinship groupings primarily, and only secondarily do the elected members of the Union Council spend their energy in the factional politics outside their kinship groupings. In other types of village factions these people, instead of trying to create more cleavages, help to resolve conflict.

IV

Nicholas, in his attempt to define a faction, has put forth five propositions. My data indicate that the factions in Badarpur do not fit his definition in at least two ways: the corporateness of the factional groups and the recruitment of faction members by leaders.

His first proposition, that factions are social conflict groups and that more than two factions can exist simultaneously is supported by the case studies reported in this book. In the case of the political marriage, for example, the conflict based on "scandal" about Zaman's daughter, was essentially between Gushthis A and C. The voters from Gushthi B supported the candidate from Gushthi A during the election, forming

Summary and Conclusion 159

a temporary coalition between Gushthis *A* and *B*. In this situation not only the opposing Gushthis *A* and *C* but also Gushthi *B* can be regarded as factions. Gushthis *A* and *B* together formed one side of this conflict, but their history of opposition makes them normally political rivals and therefore separate factions.

His second proposition is that the kind of conflict in which factions emerge is political. This proposition implies that in the case of Hafez Abul Basir vs. Karim, if the supporters of Basir and Karim can be regarded as factions, then the conflict centered around the appointment of the village Moulvi is also political. Since it entails disposal of power over resources such as the land around the Muhammadi mosque, and over the men who use it, the political nature of the conflict is consistent with Nicholas's definition of politics in terms of the use of public power, i.e. command over resources and control over men (Nicholas, 1965:14).

That members of factions are recruited on the basis of diverse principles, which is Nicholas's fifth proposition, is well supported by the data of this study. In addition to principles such as kinship and financial interest, there are principles of political marriage and playing up intergroup hostilities to increase faction membership, which operate, for example, in factions built on a structure of gushthis.

Nicholas's third proposition however, regarding the noncorporate nature of factions, is not clearly true for Badarpur. The members of Gushthis *A* and *B* have been rivals since the days of Rahim, who was the first man of Gushthi *A* to come to the village. Since Rahim, the leader of Gushthi *A* has always been the most powerful Muslim in the village. The members of Gushthi *B*, who were the earliest to settle in the village, have resented their subordination. Political conflict between these two gushthis can be seen in the case of grazing rights in the school yard, as well as in each election, where candidates from the gushthis frequently contest against each other. While the factions in these conflicts are not corporate groups (gushthis) themselves, they are built on a structure of corporate groups.

The second difference between my findings and those of Nicholas concerns the matter of recruiting support for faction leaders. The factions are indeed usually recruited by a leader, which is Nicholas's fourth proposition, but this leader may not always be the candidate himself. For example, in the case of Halim vs. Karim, the leaders of the faction supporting the candidate Halim were Zaman and Gafur. The candidate himself had little power to recruit supporters and was in fact a nonentity. Recruitment by Gafur and Zaman was largely based on gushthi membership; members of Halim's faction from Gushthi *A* were recruited to support a man from their own gushthi who promised less corrupted representation; members from Gushthis *B* and *C* were drawn to Halim by trusted spokesmen from their own gushthis, Gafur from Gushthi *B* and Zaman from Gushthi *C*. While factions are generally initiated by leaders, who initially recruit the members, in cases where the leader is not the candidate, the candidate may be recruited by faction members.

Of course, one could argue that Nicholas's proposition still holds true, that faction members are recruited by leaders. By selecting this particular candidate Halim, the faction, led by Gafur and Zaman, accepted the leadership of Halim who was thereupon authorized by the factional group to recruit and mobilize new members in support of the entire faction. In this way the structure of the faction was changed, and the recruitment of members by Halim was not inconsistent with Nicholas's proposition, since he was the new leader.

But I would argue that Halim did not in reality become the new leader of the faction. In reality, the candidacy of Halim and his role as a quasi-leader was manipulated by Gafur and Zaman in order to get a specific job done. The real leadership of the faction did not change and was still with Gafur and Zaman and not with Halim, although the latter became instrumental in recruiting and mobilizing new members from Gushthi *A* for the faction.

These two differences regarding the corporateness of factions and recruitment of faction members seem to be related parts of an interesting pattern. Whenever there are corporate groups which form the core of the grouping or otherwise form factions, a pattern can be seen in which the leader can remain in the background and at the same time can select a member to symbolize the group and to mobilize loyalty to corporate groups. Thus some of the functions that are usually performed by the leader may be taken over by a follower who himself is not a dynamic individual. In a situation with this sort of interest group, most of the actual politicking may be done behind the scene.

V

Three types of brokers function in Badarpur to link the village with the outside world, and to bring about change at the village level. The first type, required to meet the administration's demands for efficiency as well as the villagers' demands for patronage, is exemplified by Karim. The fact that he has been elected to the position of Union Council Chairman for more than thirty years, and that during this time he has always represented the Muslim League is a clear indication that he has not experienced the personal and institutional strain and

Summary and Conclusion 161

instability characteristic of Fallers' brokers; rather most of the time he has been effective in such things as getting new roads, getting government aid for the villagers and particularly in supporting his followers. Although Karim provides much patronage, mainly in the form of economic assistance, he does not encourage much change in traditional methods of farming for example, or in increased responsibility of the government for protection of the villagers. It was Zaman who initiated the Japanese method of paddy cultivation in the village, and it was Gafur who convinced the villagers that the school compound should be looked after by the entire village and not used for grazing cattle.

Traders and educated people of the village such as Zaman, Gafur, Azhar, and Almas, as cultural representatives of the national system, usually have little power or economic assistance to offer villagers. They are dependent on regional and national political figures for support to villagers. This type of village-residing cultural brokers does not necessarily cause change in the village. What the material in this book seems to show is that they get power when they contact the brokers of the third type. Both of these brokers are best understood in conceptual terms as polar complements; the political activities of each presupposes the presence of the other. Zaman, for example, by obtaining a contract to clear away the water hyacinth, was able to provide jobs for many villagers in exchange for their loyalty. This second type of broker also must rely on cross-cutting alliances and interfactional disputes to help him gain support. But the power gained is utilized to initiate cultural change, to make national traits known, and to relate the students' discussions of national goals to rural issues.

Brokers of the third type are the political party agents, students from the city, mass organization leaders, etc., who tend to be labelled as "outsiders," although they can get the support of other types of brokers to translate the national issues and make them relevant to villagers' way of life. These brokers exert their influence and power to help villagers in taking decisions as to which side they should vote for. This modification in the manner in which political contests occur in the village has been partly due to the political changes of universal suffrage and the seeking of political support by urban groups. The students constitute a regular source for village use in times of contest. Their talk about issues that concern the urban population, and the local candidates' translations of their arguments so as to relate them to rural issues, effected an association of rural and urban issues in the minds of the rural voters. Whereas thirty years previously the only national issues that had been relevant to the villagers were those concerning Muslim solidarity against Hindu landlords and the maintenance of religious purity, recent developments made the issues of East Pakistan against West Pakistan, of the Bengali language against Urdu, of guided democracy against elections vital to the local scene.

We have also seen that in this village factional conflicts do not impede decision making but rather help to implement or reject decisions. In the case of the new road construction, the rejection of the proposal was initiated by Zaman, supported by Gafur and finally, Karim's faction lost the case. On the other hand, the history of the creation of Hanafi and Muhammadi mosques in the village clearly indicates that it was factional dispute which was instrumental in creating these mosques. In the quarrel between Awal and the Trader, factional dispute did not stand in the way of the villagers uniting as a solid group behind Awal; in the case of the Hadudu game, no factional dispute disrupted village solidarity. A further example is the case of grazing rights in the schoolyard; because of factional dispute the villagers, influenced by Gafur, decided the entire village should be responsible for the school compound. Although brokers like Gafur are able to manipulate factional disputes to facilitate decision making and change, because loyalties to leaders fluctuate with individual gain, and positions taken by factions change with each issue, factions have not polarized to form political parties in Badarpur.

This idea of political parties is a novel one. In the earlier days one could easily align one's loyalties with one's gushthi and sect group; but now the villager is called upon to produce a new kind of loyalty, to a political party. Being in the middle of this tug-of-war, the villagers try to blend loyalties together. Social groupings in Badarpur still are not homogeneous in character, and still do not coalesce to form permanent political segments. The process described by Boissevain (1965) whereby transient factions within the village, by having consistent positions on a wide range of issues, develop into permanent political party groupings, has not progressed far in Badarpur.

Hence village politicking is a matter of individuals jockeying for support, using a multitude of ties through kinship, locality, religious sect, affinity, or personal friendship, and in relation to local issues. But this politicking occurs within a framework set by the village administrative structure which they can use in the outside world. On only a few issues are the intra-village disputes along the same line as the national disputes, yet village politicians do tend to polarize themselves in terms of national groupings if only for the support that national figures can give them. Only when national groupings can provide dramatic benefits for the local people (as well as for the politicians) will there emerge in the people the fixed adherence to national groupings that characterizes a modern structure.

Finally, what this study has shown is that increasing economic contacts with the world outside have opened up possibilities for new groups of people to become "brokers" or intermediaries between the villagers and the outside. The addition of new brokers to the village situation has meant that local political entrepreneurs have had to work harder to achieve majority support; and in doing so these local politicians have caused ordinary people to become politically involved in the village, and to learn about a wider range of issues.

In short, the wider political changes have opened up possibilities of communicating about national issues within the village context. Badarpur has become closer to the city. But politics within a changing village remain in many ways the same as always: politics is composed of small political units which are connected to the people by kinship, friendship, and sect lines. Therefore because of close contact with the populace, these "units" are under much pressure to conform to people's demands and to resist unwanted change.

Village politics is a matter of competitive struggles for influence and power on the village level. What has changed with economic development and political modernization is that those struggles have become clearer, more open, and subject to resolution by more objective means than was possible in the traditional society.

APPENDIX

A. Note on Non-English Words Used in the Study

All non-English words used in this study are explained either within parentheses following the word or in notes at the end of the book. A glossary of non-English words has also been included as Appendix II.

The use of "s" to indicate the plural form has been adopted for non-English words as well, despite the fact that in Bengali the system is different.

Most of the villagers use words in their everyday conversation that have their roots in Persian or in Arabic. A number of Turkish origin words are also widely used. But since these words have been incorporated in the Bengali vocabulary, no distinction has been made to differentiate them from otherwise Bengali words. Throughout the book, local dialect, rather than standard Bengali, has been used.

B. Glossary of Non-English Words

Allah
  Arabic word used by Muslims the world over to represent God.
Aman
  A type of paddy with several varieties according to size, colour, and taste of grain. Grown in relatively low land.
Ashar
  Name of a Bengali month; the beginning of the rainy season; the monsoon.
Aus
  A type of paddy grown in relatively raised land.

Awami
  Pertaining to people. Awami League may be translated as peoples' league.
Baithak
  Conference, a discussion session.
Baithak Khana
  Guest room (literally: meeting room), where discussions take place.
Bang
  The name of a people of Dravidian stock who were probably forced out of their original homeland by the Aryan expansion,

1000 B.C. (the word Bengal comes from Bang).
Bangalee
People who live in Bengal and speak Bengali.
Bara
Big.
Baraghar
Literal meaning: the big room where the big man (head of the family) lives.
Bari
House, dwelling.
Barsha
Rainy season, monsoon.
Basanta
Spring, a season.
Basanta Kal
The season of Spring.
Baul
Wandering minstrel.
Beel
Natural lake or pond (swamp).
Bhadralok
Gentlemen.
Bhaira
Wife's sister's husband.
Birca
A small plot of land adjacent to the dwelling house.
Boro
A kind of paddy.
Brahmaputra
Literal meaning: the Son of the God Brahma. Brahmaputra is the name of a river of East Pakistan (now Bangladesh).
Chasha
Farmer.
Chowkidar
The lowest ranking man representing the police at a village level.
Dal
Faction, group.
Daroga
Police Sub-Inspector.
Darvish
Wandering minstrel.

Dar-ul-Harab
Land of infidels.
Dakshin
South.
Diwali
Hindu festival of illumination.
Doa
Chant, prayer.
Durga
Hindu goddess, the goddess of strength and power. She is recognized by her ten arms.
Durga puza
The worship of the goddess Durga.
Fakir
Saint, the man who has renounced the world.
Ganges
Name of a river (known as **Ganga** in Bengali).
Geram
Vulgar form of gram, meaning a village.
Ghar
"Room," refers to a husband and wife living with their children.
Girhast
Son of a cultivator, farmer.
Gram
Village (usually pronounced as geram in Bangladesh villages).
Grishma
Summer, name of a season.
Grishma Kal
The season of summer.
Gushthi
"Kinsmen," parallels roughly what in anthropological literature refers to a clan.
Hadudu
Name of a local game.
Hambali
A sect in Islam (the followers of Imam Ahmad-Bin-Hambal).
Hanafi
Name of a Muslim sect (the followers of Imam Abu Hanifa).

Hartal
Strike; revolt; demonstration expressing disagreement.
Hat
A village market.
Hemanta
Name of a season (corresponds to autumn).
Hemanta Kal
The season of autumn.
Hindi
The National language of India.
Hindu
Name of a religion.
Hookka
A smoking implement.
Idd
Muslim festival that parallels Christmas of the Christians or Durga puza of the Hindus.
Idd-ul-Azha
Name of an Idd day; also known as Idd-uz-Zoha.
Idd-ul-Fitr
Muslim festival, name of an Idd day.
Idd-uz-Zoha
Muslim festival, name of an Idd day, also known as Idd-ul-Azha.
Iftar
Breaking of the fast during the month of Ramadan.
Imam
Man who leads prayer, priest.
Jaina
An Indian religion preached by Mahavira.
Jajmani
Patronage, adjective describing the system of economic changes characteristic of rural India.
Jalua
Fisherman caste.
Jalu Para
Enclave of the fishermen.
Kani
Approximately 2/7 of an acre; a Bengali unit of measurement of land.

Kabiraj
Medicine man, village doctor of traditional teaching.
Khalifa
The Head of the State (in the local dialect Khalifa also refers to a tailor).
Khana
Feast.
Khana
Home, house.
Khandan
Lineage.
Kharam
Wooden-made slipper.
Kosha
A type of country boat.
Krisak
Farmer.
Lakshmi
Name of Hindu goddess of wealth.
Lakshmi puza
Worship of the goddess of wealth.
Lathial
Leader of the guards.
Lungi
Loin cloth tied around the waist which drapes down like a skirt.
Mach
Fish.
Machli
Hindi equivalent of Bengali Mach.
Machli Khor
Fish eater.
Machli Khor Bengalee
Fish eating Bengali.
Mahabharata
Hindu religious epic, probably written or compiled by a mythical Veda Vyas around 1,000 B.C.
Maiz
Central.
Maiz Para
Central enclave.
Majhab
Sect (a vulgar form of Mujhab).
Majhi
Boatman, one who rows a boat.

Majlish
Meeting, conference.
Matbar
An elderly person who has been accepted by the villagers as a leader.
Maulana
A Muslim religious scholar.
Meghna
Name of a river.
Mehr (Mohar)
The sum of money the bridegroom or his family agrees to pay the bride under specified conditions.
Milad
Religious discussion.
Mir Zafar
An independent Sultan (ruler) of Bengal who betrayed Nawab Sirajuddoullah. (In Bengal the word Mir Zafar is synonymous with treacherous or betrayer.)
Moulvi
Man who leads the prayer in a mosque, priest.
Mujhab
Sect.
Mullah
Religious scholar.
Munshi
Religious teacher.
Mussalman
One who believes in Islam.
Nama
Low, a vulgar form of nimna.
Nama Para
Low enclave.
Nasib
Fate, luck, nemesis.
Nawab
King, ruler.
Nizam-E-Islam
Name of a political party (literal meaning: Islamic Kingdom).
Paik
Guard.
Pala
A Hindu dynasty of kings who once ruled in Bengal.
Panchayat
Traditional decision-making group forming the village administration.
Para
Enclave, sector.
Paribar
"Group of houses" where all the members are agnatically related.
Pathan
A Muslim dynasty of emperors who ruled India.
Pulau
A kind of fried-boiled rice served in ceremonies and in festivals.
Puza
Worship.
Quran
The holy Book of the Muslims.
Ramadan
Name of a month during which all Muslims are to fast from sunrise to sunset.
Rasul
Messenger, the prophet.
Rasuli-Mehr
Tradition holds that when Muhammad's daughter Fatimah married Ali, the bridegroom pledged 32 rupees or about $5.00. Emulation of the prophet and his family has continued as a religious tradition among the Muslims. This is known as Rasuli-Mehr.
Rashtrya
Pertaining to the state.
Ryot
Subject.
Sab-E-Barat
Muslim festival coinciding with the birthday of the Prophet Muhammad.
Sadhu
Hermit, saint.
Safi
Muslim sect (followers of Imam Ahmad-Bin-Safi).
Sangha
Organization.

Sanskrit
The classical language of India.
Sarat
Name of a season in Bengali (autumn).
Sarat Kal
The season of Sarat (autumn).
Sawal
Name of an Arabic month.
Sena
Hindu dynasty of rulers who used to rule Bengal.
Sevak
Servant.
Shalish
Meeting where disputes are settled.
Shariat
Religious teachings and injunctions.
Siah
Muslim sect (followers of Hajrat Ali).
Sit
Winter, name of a Bengali season.
Sit Kal
The season of Sit.
Sramic
Labourer.
Sunna
Religious ethics (Islamic).
Sunni
Name of a Muslim sect.
Tabiz
Talisman.
Talukdar
Petty landlord.
Tamuddun
Culture.
Tamuddun Majlish
Cultural congregation.
Tan
Raised.
Tan zami
Raised land.
Thana
Police station.
Ulama
Religious scholar.
Urdu
Name of a language (the state language of Pakistan).
Usar
Barren.
Uttar
North.
Varsha
Rainy season.
Veda
Hindu religious book.
Zami
Land.
Zamiat-E-Ulama-E-Hind
Congregation of the religious scholars of India.
Zamiat-E-Ulama-E-Islam
Congregation of the religious scholars of Islam.
Zamindar
Landlord.
Zin
A supernatural being created by fire and believed in by Muslims.

Notes

1. "Usually the village had a council, known as Panchayat, which governed it. It functioned inside the village no matter what government was in power. Traditionally, the panchayat consisted of five of the most respected people of the village, and a head man who frequently represented the government. In some localities, the village was governed by committees chosen by lot or operated under a form of constitutional government; in others, all households actively participated in the decision-making process." See: Paul Thomas Welty (1966), *The Asians: Their Heritage and Destiny*.
2. *Gushthi* is not strictly a territorial unit because some of its members may live in other locations. However, most members live in the location of their own gushthi. For definition of the term see Chapter Four.
3. That Bengal was to be divided for administrative purposes was the British view. But the Hindus protested vigorously until the Government was compelled to unite the two sectors again. According to Humayan Kabir (once India's Central Minister for Education) in his *Green and Gold* (1958:10) "The partition of Bengal in 1905 has been described as the beginning of mass political agitation in India. The annulment of that partition in 1912 was the first great success of the Indian nationalist movement."
4. For details see: Ahmad, K. (1967). Kamruddin Ahmad, former ambassador for Pakistan in Burma, has given a lucid picture on this topic in his book *The Social History of East Pakistan*.
5. The other jute producing country in the world is India. But the amount of jute produced in India is far below the requirement of the country. East Pakistan used to export jute even to India before the war between the two countries in 1965. Kamruddin Ahmad writes (1967:96) "East Pakistan grows jute which still provides more than half of Pakistan's export, and it was jute which saved Pakistan when it was collapsing after independence. The Korean war came as a great blessing and due to a boom in jute export, Pakistan earned a fantastic amount of foreign exchange during the Korean war."
6. Although this view of Aryan penetration in Bengal is controversial, the majority of the scholars are in consensus with Shahidullah (1963).
7. Legend has it that sixteen Pathan horsemen conquered Bengal. This would have been impossible unless they found widespread local support. What happened is that there was a revolt of the people against the ruling dynasty as soon as its power was challenged by foreign invaders.
8. Legend says that Emperor Jahangir (1605–1627) permitted the British traders to run their business without any tax out of gratitude to an English doctor who cured his daughter from a deadly disease.
9. In the village Badarpur, "Mirjafar" is freely used to indicate that somebody did not keep his promise or did not perform his obligations. This is

equally true in the city of Dacca. Even people who are not familiar with the historical incident know and use this word in the same context.

10. "The Mutiny" of 1857 has always been recorded in history as "the Sepoy Mutiny of 1857," but since partition of 1947, scholars view the incident as India's First War of Independence. In 1957 there was a symposium at the University of Dacca in East Pakistan to celebrate the centenary of this First War of Independence. Malik Salah-ud-din, however, in *Mutiny, Revolution or Muslim Rebellion: British Public Reactions Towards the Crisis of 1857* (unpublished Ph.D. thesis, McGill University, 1966), shows that it was a mutiny on the part of the British and not on the part of the Sepoys. Britons were permitted to trade in India (see note 8 on p. 175) but defiance of the (Indian) government constituted an act of mutiny and the sepoys were ordered (by the Indian government) to subdue the British. The word "crisis" which I use will always apply whatever the truth be in the final analysis.

11. Bankim and Modhusudan laid the foundation for Modern Bengali literature and enabled the followers to have a firm footing. For details see: *Bangla Goddya Shahityer Itihas* by Monomohan Ghosh, Calcutta, 1952. See also *Bangla Shahityer Itibritto* (1954) by Muhammad Abdul Hai and Syed Ali Ahsan, Dacca University Press.

12. A universal characteristic of the "pre-literate" societies of the world is that they belong to the land on which they live, and that the land does not belong to them. This might explain the reason for the minimum number of immigrants in developed areas from these "preliterate" societies. Villagers hardly ever sell their land if they can avoid doing so.

13. Even after the establishment of Fort Williams College in 1801, the Muslims of Bengal did not participate in western education and for a long time remained confined to the traditional education through Persian and Arabic. The Hindus on the other hand accepted western education immediately and enrolled in the colleges.

14. With the spread of Western education, the Indian banks and insurance corporations soon came under Hindu control together with all other chief industries. In finances and big business the supremacy of the Hindus amounted to a monopoly.

15. The history of the Muslim League in many respects is the history of the Muslim Renaissance in the subcontinent. Its creation was the product of the nation's awakening which was stimulated by the western institutions established by the British Government itself. For details see: Sayeed, K. B. (1960: 191–240).

16. The "Khelafat Party" was not a part of the Muslim League but rather a separate political organization under the Ali Brothers. This party grew up following the first Great War with an objective to reinstate the Khalifa of Turkey. Hence, this was related to the Pan-Islamic movement, whereas the objectives of the Muslim League were mainly to solve the problems of the Indian Muslims.

17. At this time, Mahatma Gandhi was organizing his non-cooperation movements and he stepped forward as Khelafat champion in order to unify the two communities against the British. Muhammad Ali and his brother Sawakat Ali, leaders of the Khelafat movement, proclaimed a Hindu-Muslim entente and the joint forces toured India in demonstrations meant by Gandhi to be non-violent and to consist of protest by *hartal* (a sort of strike). How-

Notes 173

ever, disorders erupted and the movement became increasingly marred by incidents of bloodshed and force. These bloody outbreaks marked the termination of the Hindu-Muslim entente, and the Muslim League announced withdrawal from the non-cooperation campaign of Congress. The last big *hartals* in East Pakistan were in 1952 (in connection with the State Language Movement) and in 1970 (against the Yahia regime).

18. The Treaty of Sevres was signed between the allied and the Turkish governments on August 10, 1920. However, it was not ratified and was later superseded by the Treaty of Lausanne, on July 24, 1923. Lloyd George clearly stated in 1918 that the Allies would not deprive Turkey of her capital or any lands in Asia Minor or Greece. Yet, at the end of the War, the Greeks, who had fought with the British, attacked Turkey as though in a campaign of annihilation. If Turkey were defeated the Holy places which the Prophet had bidden Muslims to preserve would be placed under non-Muslim control; the Sultan of Turkey, Commander of the Faithful and the successor and *Khalifa* of the Prophet, would be deprived of the bulk of his territory.

19. The *Krisak Praja Samiti* renamed as *Krisak Sramik Dal* was an indigenous organization mainly confined to the province of Bengal. Its leader, A. K. Fazlul Huq was the most popular of the Muslim politicians that Bengal produced. The objectives of the Krisak Praja Samiti were to improve the social life of the peasants and labourers of the country, the majority of whom were Muslims. Thus the fundamental ideals of the Krisak Praja Samiti did not differ from those of the Muslim League. In fact in 1940, it was A. K. Fazlul Huq who was first to bring forward the Pakistan Resolution in the Annual Meeting of the All India Muslim League, and urged, together with Sir Sikandar Hayat Khan of the Punjab and the Chief Minister of Assam, the Muslims of the subcontinent to join the Muslim League in the fight for independence. He favoured his Krisak Praja Samiti at the provincial level, and at the National (all India) level, the Muslim League. Because of the personal conflict with Jinnah (about joining India's defense committee), the two leaders took different sides and Huq was then forced to work against the Muslim League.

20. Muhammad Ali Jinnah was honoured as Quaid-i-Azam (The Great Leader). Pakistan realized that the new nation stood as his monument.

21. The issue of the State language was a very touchy one for the Bengalis. Even within the Muslim League Abul Hashem, a socialist and general secretary of the Bengal provincial Muslim League, was waging a battle inside the Provincial League against the group led by the Nawab of Dacca and Khwaja Nazimuddin, and against the Urdu-Bengali split prior to the formation of Pakistan. But no such conflict could take any serious shape, for as Jinnah once said: "We shall have time to quarrel ourselves and we shall have time when these differences will have to be settled, when wrongs and injuries will have to be remedied. We shall have time for a domestic programme and policies..." See: Ahmad, J. ed. (1947:393).

22. Liaquat Ali Khan was the Secretary General of the Muslim League and later on the first Prime Minister of the country.

23. Mafizuddin Ahmed, Minister for Relief and Rehabilitation in East Bengal, speaking on the sales tax bill in the Central Legislature, said, "East Bengal is almost on the verge of collapse and unless this tax is returned, unless a fair reallocation of the revenues is made, Sir, I find darkness and dark-

ness." See: *Constituent Assembly (Legislature) of Pakistan Debates,* Government of Pakistan 2nd April, 1951, Vol. I:12:753.

24. In fact, the Muslim League in East Pakistan died earlier. In the 1954 general elections (this was the first general election after 1947) the Muslim League Party was totally defeated by the Awami Muslim League. But the seed of this defeat was sown in 1949, when one Mr. Shamsul Huq defeated a Muslim League candidate in a by-election in Tangail Sub-Division; the Awami Muslim League then was formed at Dacca with Maulana Bhashani as President and Mr. Shamsul Huq as its founding General Secretary. The present Prime Minister, Sheikh Mujibar Rahman was an Assistant Secretary of the organization.

25. For details see Chapter V.

26. The Combined Opposition Party, popularly known as COP, was formed in 1964 between Awami Muslim League, Krisak Sramik Party and Nizam-E-Islam.

27. On March 26, 1972 the Prime Minister of Bangladesh announced in a radio broadcast the raising of all subdivisions of Bangladesh to the status of districts. There are 19 districts and 51 subdivisions in Bangladesh today (1972).

28. *Nama Para* is isolated from the rest (see map of the village).

29. During the communal disturbances of 1964 the Muslims of Badarpur formed an organization to protect their Hindu neighbours. Dr. Gafur and Halim took the initiative and a volunteer group was formed to guard the Hindu families every night in a group. Due to this care on the part of the villagers and their concern about their Hindu neighbours, Badarpur remained the only village in the whole area without any communal trouble.

30. Although such an attitude has its roots earlier, it actually polarized during the 20's of the century when Gandhi's non-cooperation movement merged with the Ali Brothers' Khelafat movement.

31. Dacca National Medical School is an institution founded by the followers of Gandhi during the time of his non-cooperation movements. Gandhi called the then Indians to boycott all western institutions and things. As a result western institutions soon became deserted and political leaders tried to organize corresponding institutions in the country. Dacca Mitford Medical School (now, Sir Salimullah Medical College) was already there. The National Medical School was founded as an alternative where students could get training in medicine. The school is still there although it is in dilapidated condition.

32. This system entitles a girl to have one-half the amount of property her brother receives from their father. She will also get half of the amount of property her son will receive from her husband, thus bringing her own property theoretically at least (assuming that her husband and father had the same amount of property) to equal that of her own son and brother. This is why Islam claims that it gives equal rights to its men and women.

33. Idd-ul-Azha means celebration of the sacrifice. It is celebrated on the tenth day of the Arabic month *Zulhadj*. The Muslims from all over the world on this day congregate in the sacred field of Arafat and pray to God for resurrection. This day has legendary connections with the mythical prophet Abraham.

34. A Muslim festival observed by all the Muslims of the world. This is the birthday of the prophet Muhammad. Muslims will pray, visit their friends and kin and distribute sweets this day.

35. Diwali is essentially a Hindu festival and is observed by all the Hindus of India and Pakistan. This is also the first day of the Bengali year.

36. Idd-ul-Fitr (*Idd* means happiness, joy; *Fitr* means to control). On the first day of the Muslim month, *Sawal*, Muslims all over the world celebrate this day. The month before Sawal is the month of *Ramadan* when they fast for 30 days. After Ramadan, on the day of Idd-ul-Fitr, they congregate for a prayer, and following the congregational prayer visit friends and relatives, distribute food and sweets, dress in their best and rejoice together.

37. Durga Puza is more or less a universal festival throughout the subcontinent of India and Pakistan. Although it is essentially a Hindu religious festival, I have seen Muslims participate in it even after the division of India when the tension between these two religious groups had reached its climax.

38. Baul is the term given to wandering minstrels who have denounced all forms of earthly religion and who survive on alms from people for their singing. They constitute a community. However, not all the bauls have denounced religion totally; some of them claim to follow a definite religious path allegedly directed by Islam.

39. These "Muslim Bauls" are known as Darvishes. One of the most renowned of Muslim Bauls was Lalon Shah. All of their songs concern spiritual betterment of humanity. In these songs the idle rich, the depraved and the erring are all solemnly admonished and the impermanence of earthly possessions is constantly pointed out. The positive aspect to their belief is that salvation lies in the ceaseless exploration of the Ultimate Being and in complete dependence on Him.

40. The usage in the village of this originally Persian word "Khandan" varies. Sometimes it distinguishes the members of one paribar, and sometimes it includes all the members of the gushthi.

41. Although divorce is not frequent in this village, and is much lower than the average rate of divorce in East Pakistan which is 12% (Alam, 1966:75), a Muslim in East Pakistan could until recently divorce his wives by saying "divorce, divorce, divorce" (talak, talak, talak), three times to his wife in presence of a witness. This was changed in 1961 by the *Muslim Family Ordinance*.

42. In the kinship chart, however, only persons living in Badarpur are indicated. Relatives living outside are so numerous and scattered over such distant places that it was virtually impossible to trace them. Moreover, people of Badarpur only vaguely knew that some of their relatives lived in different villages, and in many cases they were not even sure of it.

43. Majhabs (Mu'jhab) are the different schools of thought in Islam mainly developed due to the breach of unity in Islam. The first school to take definite form was the Hanafite, founded by Abu Hanifa (767 A.D.). He used few traditions, and preferred to go back to the Quran, and extract from it by reasoning the ruling which fitted his ideas. The second school of thought, the Malikite, was founded by Malik Ibn Anas, who used traditions much more generally than did Abu Hanifa. The third school of thought was founded by Ash-Shafi who laid great stress on tradition, but gave to the principle of agreement its full rights. The fourth, the Hambalite school, was founded by schol-

ars of Ahmad Ibn Hambal after his death in 885 A.D. In Badarpur there are no people following this school of thought.

44. See: *Marriage and Family Law: Government of Pakistan,* Pakistan Government Press, Karachi, 1961. According to this law no Pakistani national can take a second spouse unless the first one is incapable of bearing children, is mentally insane or gives permission willingly for a second spouse because of health reasons which are backed by medical examinations. By this law women also gained the power of divorce for reasons such as cruelty and negligence.

45. Mehr is the sum of money the bridegroom or his family agrees to pay the bride under specific conditions. Tradition holds that when Muhammad's daughter Fatimah married, Ali, the bridegroom, pledged 32 rupees or about $5.00. Emulation of the Prophet and his family has continued as a religious tradition among the Muslims.

46. After the death of Muhammad, a number of saints tried to reform Islam. Imam Abu Hanifa, Imam Malik Ibn Anas, Imam Ash-Shafi and Imam Ahmad Ibn Hambal are to be mentioned first. A good many Pir and Awalias (saints) have their own followers. The number of these saints became so great that a group of Muslims virtually became impatient, refused to follow these middlemen (saints) and decided to follow the Prophet of Islam (Muhammad) only. These people are known as Muhammadi.

47. The battle of Siffin (657) between Hairat (holy) Ali and Hairat Mu'awiya was the occasion of the first breach in the unity of Islam, and the results are to be seen to this day. The most important sectarian divisions in Islam, Sunnites, Shiite, and Khawaniz have their origins in divergent theories about the office of the Caliph, the head of the Muslim community, the successor to the Prophet.

48. The injunction laid down in the *Holy Quran* relating to fasting in the month of Ramadan, runs as follows: "The month of Ramadan is that in which the Quran was revealed, a guidance to men and clear proofs of the guidance and the distinction; therefore, whoever of you witnesses the coming of this month, he shall fast therein." (2:185)—*The Religion of Islam,* pp. 485-496, by Maulana Muhammad Ali (1936)—Published by the Ahmadiyya Anjuman Isha at Islam, Lahore. However, the actual appearance of the moon may be established by the evidence of a single man if he be trustworthy. It is related that on a certain occasion the people of Madina were doubtful about the appearance of the new moon of Ramadan and they had decided not to fast. When a man came from the desert and gave evidence that he had seen the moon, the Holy Prophet accepted his evidence and directed the people to fast.

49. According to the Muslims of the village (as well as to the Muslims all over the subcontinent) God created man and zin as two distinct groups. Like man, zins will also have to face a trial after death where evaluations will be made of all of their deeds.

50. Finally, I explained to a girl student from the Department of Sociology, Dacca University, what I wanted to know. She interviewed the female patients of Idris Kabiraj, but could not get anything out of them to give me a better understanding of these zin (which I have never seen) or of the type of suffering these patients go through. This phenomenon of the zin victim in the vil-

lage is not confined to Badarpur. I have visited several other villages and did not find a single one where there was not any zin victim. When I discussed this problem with the educated class, particularly at the university teachers' club, the unanimous opinion was that it is all a result of psychological trouble and superstition.

51. Webster's Dictionary (1950) defines jajman as "a person by whom a Brahman is hired to perform religious services, hence a patron, client." The word is derived from the Sanskrit yajmana, the present participle of yaj, to sacrifice. The term ultimately came to be used for anyone in the relationship of an employee. The family or family head served by an individual is known as his jajman.

52. The Permanent Settlement Act of 1793 was responsible for the Zamindari system in the country. Until 1871 any Zamindar could take away land from his subjects with or without any reason. According to the act of 1871, the Zamindar could no longer appropriate land from a peasant who paid his taxes.

53. In the elections of East Pakistan it is not necessary that a candidate be a resident of the constituency from which he is seeking votes. A Zamindar's relative living in a city or elsewhere could easily seek election on the Zamindar's ticket from his Zamindari, hence the people more than frequently did not even know the man they were voting for.

54. "Hafez" means one who has memorized the whole of the *Holy Quran*. The Prophet Muhammad asked Muslims (a few) to memorize the Holy Quran so that even if the Quran were destroyed by enemies, it could be rewritten by the people who had memorized it, thus keeping its contents unchanged. This is why the Quran, unlike some other religious scriptures, has only one version throughout the world.

55. "Hadudu" is a local game, which can be played between two teams of any number, normally varying from four to nine on each side. One player crosses the center line and touches a player of the other side in a single breath and tries to come back to his own side, while the opponent group as a body will try to keep him on their side, forcibly, until he can no longer hold his breath.

56. In fact during the British rule all the official papers were written in English together with equivalent translations in local provincial languages. Hence, in Bengal, all the official papers during the British rule used to appear in both English and Bengali. It is to be noted that the Britishers divided India into several provinces mainly on a linguistic basis. This is one of the main reasons why during the Independence in 1947 both the provinces of Punjab and Bengal had to be divided again on the basis of religion. (There are Punjabi-speaking Muslims and Sikhs—and Bengali-speaking Hindus and Muslims.) The villagers of Badarpur were at a disadvantage during the British rule because they could neither read nor write even Bengali, to say nothing of English.

57. This school teacher was Kafiluddin, who in 1956 was nominated as a Union Board member on the recommendations of Karim, and who created a split in Gushthi *B*, by siding with Karim against Gafur.

58. Under the regime in power all the ex-Awami Muslim League leaders have been banned from participating in any election; students have been

directed not to get involved in practical politics; newspapers are advised not to print news that might go against the Government; and the office of the Daily Ittefaq (the most widely circulated Bengali daily and the voice of the Awami Muslim League) has been locked by the security police for an indefinite period.

59. Refers to 1965 India-Pakistan War.

References Cited

Ahmad, K.
(1967) *The Social History of East Pakistan*, Dacca.
(1970) *The Social History of Bengal*, Dacca.
Bailey, F. G.
(1957) *Caste and Economic Frontier; a Village in Highland Orissa*. Manchester University Press, Manchester.
(1960) *Tribe, Caste, and Nation: A Study of Political Activity and Political Change in Highland Orissa*. Manchester University Press, Manchester.
(1963) "Politics and Society in Contemporary Orissa." In C. H. Phillips ed., *Politics and Society in India*. Frederick A. Praeger, New York.
(1965) "Decisions by Consensus in Councils and Committees: with Special Reference to Village and Local Government in India" in *Political Systems and the Distribution of Power*. ASA Monogram No. 2 Tavistock.
Barth, F.
(1965) *Political Leadership Among Swat Pathans*, London School of Economics Monograph on Social Anthropology No. 19. London.
Beals, A. R. and Siegel, B. J.
(1966) *Divisiveness and Social Conflict*. Stanford University Press, Stanford.
Bentley, A. F.
(1949) *The Process of Government*. Principia Press, Bloomington, Indiana.
Boissenvain, J.
(1965) *Saints and Fireworks: Religion and Politics in Rural Malta*. The Athlone Press, New York.
Bose, N. S.
(1960) *The Indian Awakening and Bengal*. Firma K. L. Mukhopadhyaya, Calcutta.
Campbell, R. D.
(1963) *Pakistan: Emerging Democracy*. D. Van Nostrand Co., Princeton.
Coser, L. A.
(1956) *The Functions of Social Conflict*. Free Press. Glencoe, Illinois.
Dhillon, H.
(1955) "Leaders and Groups in South Indian Village." Planning Commission, Program Evaluation, Organization. Government of India, Delhi.
Easton, D.
(1953) *The Political System*. Knopf, New York.
Fallers, L. A.
(1956) *Bantu Bureaucracy*. W. Haffer and Sons, Cambridge.
Frankenberg, R.
(1957) *Village on the Border*. Cohen and West, London.
Geertz, C.
(1963) *Peddlers and Princes: Social Change and Economic Modernization in Two Indonesian Towns*. University of Chicago Press, Chicago.

Gluckman, M.
(1955) *Custom and Conflict in Africa.* Blackwell, Oxford.
Gopal, R.
(1959) *Indian Muslims, a Political History.* Asia Publishing House, Calcutta.
Government of Pakistan
(1951) *Pakistan Census.* Government of Pakistan, Karachi.
(1951) *Constituent Assembly (Legislature) of Pakistan Debates.* March 19, 1956. Vol. I:12:753.
(1956) *Constituent Assembly (Legislature) of Pakistan Debates.* April 2nd, 1951, Vol. I:4:216.
(1961) *Marriage and Family Law.* Government Press, Karachi.
(1961) *Pakistan Census.* Government of Pakistan, Karachi.
(1963) "Statistical Section" of *The Economic Survey of Pakistan Bulletin,* Karachi.
Hai, M. A. and Ahsan, S. A.
(1954) *Bangla Shahityer Itibritto.* Dacca University Press, Dacca.
Islam, A. K. M. Aminul
(1955) *Jasim-Uddin: Kavi-O-Kavya.* Eden Press, Dacca.
(1959) *Bangla Shahitye Muslim Kavi-O-Kavya.* The Book Stall, New Market, Dacca.
Kabir, H. (ed.)
(1958) *Green and Gold: Stories and Poems from Bengal.* Chapman and Hall, London (Associate editors: T. Bannerjee and P. Mitra).
Lasswell, H.
(1931) "Faction." *Encyclopedia of the Social Sciences.* Vol. V:49–51. The Macmillan Company, New York.
Mansur, U.
(1959) *Haramani.* Dacca University Press, Dacca.
McCarthy, F. E.
(1967) *Bengali Village Women Mediators Between Tradition and Modernity.* Unpublished M.A. Thesis, Soc. Dept., Michigan State University, Lansing, Michigan.
Merton, R. K.
(1964) *Social Theory and Social Structure.* The Free Press, Glencoe, Illinois.
Murdock, G. P.
(1965) *Social Structure.* A Free Press Paperback, The Macmillan Co., New York.
O'Malley, L. S. S.
(1934) *India's Social Heritage.* Clarendon Press, Oxford.
Orenstein, H.
(1965) *Gaon: Conflict and Cohesion in An Indian Village.* Princeton University Press, Princeton, New Jersey.
Rasiduzzaman, M.
(1966) *Politics and Administration in the Local Councils: A Study of Union and District Councils in East Pakistan.* Oxford University Press.
(1966) "Election Politics in Pakistan Villages" in *Commonwealth Political Studies,* November, 1966, London.

Redfield, R.
(1953) *The Primitive World and Its Transformation.* Cornell University Press, Ithaca, New York.

Salah-ud-din, M.
(1966) *Mutiny, Revolution or Muslim Rebellion: British Public Reaction Towards the Crisis of 1857.* Unpublished Ph.D. thesis, History Department, McGill University, Montreal.

Salisbury, R. F.
(1962) *From Stone to Steel.* Melbourne University Press on Behalf of Australian National University, Melbourne.
(1964) "Despotism and Australian Administration in the New Guinea Highlands." *American Anthropologist,* Vol. 66:4 Part 2. 1:235–239.

Sayeed, K. B.
(1960) *Pakistan: the Formative Phase.* Institute of Pacific Relations, New York.

Shahidullah, M.
(1953) *Bangla Bhashar Itibritto.* Renaissance Publications, Dacca.
(1963) *The Traditional Culture in East Pakistan: A UNESCO Survey.* Dacca University Press, Dacca.

Smith, W. C.
(1947) *Modern Islam in India: A Social Analysis.* Ripon Printing Press, Lahore.

Swartz, M.; Turner, N.; and Tuden, A. (ed.)
(1966) *Political Anthropology.* Aldine Publishing Co., Chicago.

Turner, V. W.
(1957) *Schism and Continuity in African Society.* Manchester University Press, Manchester.

Van Velsen, J. A.
(1964) *The Politics of Kinship.* Manchester University Press, Manchester.
(1967) "The Extended-case Method and Situational Analysis" in Epstein, A. L. (ed.). *The Craft of Social Anthropology,* Social Science Paperbacks No. 20. Tavistock, London.

Voget, F. W.
(1956) "American Indians in Transition, Reformation and Accommodation," *American Anthropologist,* Vol. 58:2:249–263.

Webster, N.
(1950) *Webster's New Collegiate Dictionary.* New York.

Wilber, D. N.
(1964) *Pakistan: Yesterday and Today.* Holt, Rinehart and Winston, New York.

Wolf, E.
(1956) "Aspects of Group Relations in a Complex Society: Mexico." *American Anthropologist,* 58:10:56–1078.

Wolf, K. H. and Bendix, R.
(1964) "Continuities in the Theory of Reference Groups and Social Structure." In *Social Theory and Social Structure* by Merton, R. K. (1964), Free Press, Glencoe, Illinois.

General Bibliography

Ahmad, A.
(1964) *Studies in Islamic culture in the Indian environment.* Oxford: Clarendon Press.
(1967) *Islamic modernism in India and Pakistan (1857–1964).* London: Oxford University Press.

Ahmad, I.
(1965) "Social stratification among Muslims." *The Economic Weekly* 1:159–167.

Ahmad, J.
(1947) *Some recent speeches and writings of Mr. Jinnah.* Vol. II, Ashraf, Lahore.

Ahmad, N.
(1956) "The patterns of rural settlements in East Pakistan." Geographical Review, July, Vol. 46:388–398.

Ahmed, M.
(1971) *Bangladesh: contemporary events and documents.* External Publicity Division, People's Republic of Bangladesh, Mujibnagar.

Aiyappan, A.
(1965) *Social revolution in a Kerala village: a study in cultural change.* Bombay: Asia Publishing House.

Ali, M. M.
(1936) *The religion of Islam.* At Islam, Lahore, Ahmadiyya Anjuman Isha.

Ali, T.
(1971) *Pakistan: military rule or people's power?* Delhi: Vikas Publications.

Ansari, Ghaus
(1955) "Muslim marriage in India." *Wiener Volkerkundliche Mitteilungen* 3:191–206.
(1960) "Muslim caste in Uttar Pradesh: a study of culture contact." *The Eastern Anthropologist* (special number) 13:5–80.

Atal, Y.
(1963) "Short-lived alliances as an aspect of factionalism in an Indian village." *The Journal of Social Sciences* (Agra) 3:65–75.

Ayoob, M., et al.
(1971) *Bangladesh—a struggle for nationhood.* Delhi: Vikas Publications.

Bacon, E. E. (ed.)
(1956) *India sociological background: an area handbook.* New Haven: The Human Relations Area Files.

Baden-Powell, B. H.
(1896) *The Indian village community.* London: Longmans, Green and Co. (Reprinted by HRAF Press: New Haven, 1957.)

Bailey, F. G.
- (1960) *Tribe, caste and nation: a study of political activity and political change in highland Orissa.* Manchester: Manchester University Press.
- (1961) " 'Tribe' and 'caste' in India." *Contributions to Indian Sociology* 4:107–124.
- (1963) *Politics and social change: Orissa in 1959.* Berkeley: University of California Press.

Banerjee, D. N.
- (1969) *East Pakistan: a case study in Muslim politics.* Delhi: Vikas Publications.

Barth, F.
- (1960) "The system of social stratification in Swat, North Pakistan." In *Aspects of caste in South India, Ceylon and Northwest Pakistan,* E. R. Leach, editor, pp. 113–146. Cambridge Papers in Social Anthropology, No. 2. Cambridge: Cambridge University Press.

Basham, A. L.
- (1954) *The wonder that was India.* London: Sidgwick and Jackson.

Basu, T. K.
- (1962) *The Bengal peasant from time to time.* London and Bombay: Asia Publishing House.

Beals, A.
- (1962) *Gopalur: A South Indian village.* New York: Holt, Rinehart and Winston.
- (1964) "Conflict and interlocal festivals in a South Indian region." *The Journal of Asian Studies* 23:95–113.

Beech, M. J.; Bertocci, P. J.; and Corwin, L. A.
- (1966) "Introducing the East Bengal village." In *Inside the East Pakistan village. (Asian studies papers. Reprint series, 2.)* East Lansing: Michigan State University.

Berreman, G. D.
- (1960a) "Caste in India and the United States." *American Journal of Sociology* 6: 120–127.
- (1962b) "Caste and economy in the Himalayas." *Economic Development and Cultural Change,* 10:386–394.
- (1962d) "Village exogamy in northernmost India." *Southwestern Journal of Anthropology,* 18:55–58.

Bertocci, Peter J.
- (1970) *Elusive villages: social structure and community organization in rural East Pakistan.* Unpublished Ph.D. dissertation, Michigan State University.

Bharati, A.
- (1961) *The ochre robe.* London: Allen and Unwin.

Bhattacharya, J. N.
- (1896) *Hindu castes and sects.* Calcutta: Thacker, Spink and Co.

Bose, N. K.
- (1951) "Caste in India." *Man in India* 31:107–123.
- (1954) "Who are the backward classes?" *Man in India* 34:89–98.
- (1958a) "East and west in Bengal." *Man in India* 38:157–175.

(1958b) "Some aspects of caste in Bengal." *Man in India* 38:73–97.
Bose, N. K. and Sinha, S.
(1961) *Peasant life in India: a study in unity and diversity.* Anthropological Survey of Indian Memoirs No. 8.
Burling, R.
(1960) "An incipient caste organization in the Garo Hills." *Man in India* 40:283–299.
Callard, K. B.
(1957) *Pakistan: a political study.* New York: Macmillan.
Cambridge University Press
(1953) *Cambridge history of ancient India.* (Various selections, none ancient.) Cambridge: Cambridge University Press.
Carstairs, G. M.
(1957) *The twice born: a study of a community of high caste Hindus.* London: The Hogarth Press.
Chauhan, B. R.
(1960) "An Indian village: some questions." *Man in India* 40:116–127.
Cohn, B. S.
(1961d) "The pasts of an Indian village." *Comparative Studies in Society and History* 3:241–249.
(1962) "Review of M. Marriott, 'Caste ranking and community structure in five regions of India and Pakistan.'" *Journal of the American Oriental Society* 82:425–430.
Cohn, B. S. and McKim, M.
(1958) "Networks and centres in the integration of Indian civilisation." *Journal of Social Research* (Ranchi) 1:1–9.
Datta-Majumder, N.
(1956) *The Santal: a study in culture change.* Department of Anthropology, Government of India. Memoir No. 2.
Davis, K.
(1951) *The population of India and Pakistan.* Princeton: Princeton University Press.
Derrett, J. D. M.
(1960) "Law and the predicament of the Hindu joint family." *The Economic Weekly* 12:305–311.
Desai, I. P.
(1956) "The joint family in India: an analysis." *Sociological Bulletin* 5:144–156.
Dhillon, H. S.
(1955) *Leadership and groups in a South Indian village.* Planning Commission, Programme Evaluation Organisation. New Delhi: Government of India. P.E.O. Publication No. 9.
Drekmeier, C.
(1962) *Kingship and community in early India.* Stanford: Stanford University Press.
Dube, S. C.
(1955a) "A Deccan village." In *India's villages*, pp. 180–192. Calcutta: West Bengal Government Press. (Second edition, 1960, M. N. Srinivas, editor, pp. 202–215. London: Asia Publishing House.)

(1955b) *Indian village.* Ithaca, New York: Cornell University Press.
(1958) *India's changing villages.* Ithaca, New York: Cornell University Press.

Dumont, L.
(1957a) *Hierarchy and marriage alliance in South Indian kinship.* Occasional Papers of the Royal Anthropological Institute, No. 12. London: Royal Anthropological Institute.
(1967) "Caste: a phenomenon of social structure or an aspect of Indian culture?" In *Caste and race, comparative approaches,* A. de Reuck and J. Knight, editors, pp. 28–38. London: J. and A. Churchill.

Dumont, L. and D. Pocock
(1957c) "Kinship." *Contributions to Indian Sociology* 1:43–64.

Eglar, Z.
(1960) *A Punjabi village in Pakistan.* New York: Columbia University Press.

Ellickson, J.
(1972) *A Believer Among Believers: The Religious Beliefs, Practices, and Meanings in Bangladesh.* Unpublished Ph.D. thesis, Dept. of Anthropology, Michigan State University.

Epstein, T. S.
(1959) *Economic development and social change in South India.* Manchester University Press; New York: The Humanities Press.

Fortes, M.
(1958) "Introduction. In the developmental cycle in domestic groups," pp. 1–14. *Cambridge Papers in Social Anthropology, No. 1.* Cambridge: University Press.

Fox, R. G.
(1967) "Resiliency and culture in the Indian caste system: the Umar of U.P." *The Journal of Asian Studies* 26:575–587.

Freed, S. A.
(1963) "Fictive leadership in an Indian village." *Ethnology* 2:83–103.

Geertz, C.
(1960) "The Javanese kikaji: the changing role of a cultural broker." *Comparative Studies in Society and History* 2:228–249.

Ghosh, M. M.
(1952) *Bangla Goddya Shahityer Itihas.* Calcutta: Calcutta University.

Ghurye, G. S.
(1953) *Indian sadhus.* Bombay: The Popular Book Depot.

Gideon, H.
(1962) "A baby is born in the Punjab." *American Anthropologist* 64:1220–1234.

Gore, M. S.
(1961) "The husband-wife and the mother-son relationships." *Sociological Bulletin* 11:91–102.
(1965) "The traditional Indian family." In *Comparative family systems,* M. F. Nimkoff, editor, pp. 209–231. Boston: Houghton Mifflin.

Gough, E. K.
(1955) "The social structure of a Tanjore village." In *Village India,* M. Marriott, editor, pp. 36–52. Chicago: University of Chicago Press.

(1960) "Caste in a Tanjore village." In *Aspects of caste in South India, Ceylon, and North-West Pakistan,* E. R. Leach, editor, pp. 11–60. *Cambridge Papers in Social Anthropology,* No. 2. Cambridge: Cambridge University Press.
(1961) "Nayar: Central Kerala." In *Matrilineal kinship,* David M. Schneider and Kathleen Gough, editors, pp. 415–442. Berkeley and Los Angeles: University of California Press.
(1963) "Indian nationalism and ethnic freedom." In *The Concept of freedom in Anthropology,* David Bidney, editor, pp. 170–207. The Hague: Mouton.

Gould, H. A.
(1958) "The Hindu jajmani system: a case of economic particularism." *Southwestern Journal of Anthropology* 14:428–437.
(1965a) "Lucknow rickshawallas: the social organization of an occupational category." *International Journal of Comparative Sociology* 6:24–47.
(1965b) "True structural change and the time dimension in the North Indian kinship system." In *Studies on Asia,* 1965, R. K. Sakai, editor, pp. 179–192. Lincoln: University of Nebraska Press.

Guha, U.
(1965) "Caste among rural Bengali Muslims." *Man in India* 45:167–169.

Gumperz, John J. and C. M. Naim
(1964) "Religion and social communication in village North India." *The Journal of Asian Studies* 23:89–97.

Gupta, D. C.
(1970) *Indian national movement.* Delhi, India: Vikas Publications.

Gupta, T. R.
(1961) "Rural family status and migration: study of a Punjab village." *The Economic Weekly* 13:1597–1603.

Hai, M. A.
(1963) *Bangal bhasha-o-shahitya.* Dacca: Dacca University Press.

Harper, E. B.
(1959a) "A Hindu village pantheon." *Southwestern Journal of Anthropology* 15:277–234.
(1959b) "Two systems of economic exchange in village India." *American Anthropologist* 61:760–778.

Harper, E. B. and Harper, L. G.
(1959) "Political organization in a Karnataka village." In *Leadership and political institutions in India,* Richard L. Park and Irene Tinker, editors, pp. 453–469. Princeton: Princeton University Press.

Harrison, S. S.
(1965) *India: the most dangerous decades.* Princeton: Princeton University Press.

Hsu, F. L. K.
(1963) *Clan, caste, club.* Princeton: D. Van Nostrand Company.

Huq, M. E.
(1957) *Muslim Bangala Shahitya.* Dacca: Bengali Academy.

Hussain, M.
(1955) *East Pakistan: a cultural survey.* Lahore: Pakistan Center.

Hutton, J. H.
(1941) "Primitive tribes." In *Modern India and the West*, L. S. S. O'Malley, editor, pp. 417–444. London: Oxford University Press.

Islam, A. K. M. Aminul
(1968) "Anthropologists' Model for the Study of Social Change." In *Pakistan Sociological Perspectives*, the Punjab University Press.
(1969) "Reconstruction of Certain Cultural Patterns of Prehistoric Pakistan" in *Anthropological Quarterly*, Vol. 42:1:16–23, Washington, D. C.

Hutton, J. H.
(1961) *Caste in India: its nature, function and origin*. Third edition. Bombay: Oxford University Press.

Ikram, S. M.
(1963) *Muslim civilization in India*. New York: Columbia University Press.

Ishwaran, K.
(1966) *Tradition and economy in village India*. New York: Humanities Press Inc.

Izmirlian, H. Jr.
(1964) *Caste, kin and politics in a Punjab village*. Doctoral dissertation, University of California, Berkeley.

Kapadia, K. M.
(1947) *Hindu kinship: an important chapter in Hindu social history*. Bombay: The Popular Book Depot.
(1959) "The family in transition." *Sociological Bulletin* 8:68–99.
(1966) *Marriage and family in India*. Third edition. Bombay: Oxford University Press.

Kabir, H.
(1958) *Green and gold: stories and poems from Bengal*. (Associate editors: T. Bannerjee and P. Mitra.) London: Chapman and Hall.

Karim, A. K. N.
(1956) *Changing society in India and Pakistan*. Dacca: Oxford University Press.

Karve, I.
(1953) *Kinship organization in India*. Poona, Deccan College Monograph Series, No. 11. Poona: Deccan College.
(1958) *The Indian village*. Bulletin of the Deccan College 18:73–106.
(1965) *Kinship organization in India*. Second revised edition. Bombay: Asia Publishing House.

Khan, A. K.
(1951) *Constituent Assembly* (legislature) *of Pakistan debates*. Karachi: March, 1956.

Khan, A. R.
(1956) *Constituent Assembly* (legislature) *of Pakistan debates*. Karachi: March, 1956.

Kolenda, P. M.
(1968) "Region, caste, and family structure: a comparative study of the Indian 'joint' family." In *Structure and change in Indian society*, M. Singer and B. S. Cohn, editors. Chicago: Aldine Publishing Company.

Kothari, R. and Rishikesh, M.
(1965) "Caste and secularism in India: case study of a caste federation." *The Journal of Asian Studies* 25:33–50.

Kudryavtsev, M. K.
(1964) "On the role of Jats in North India's ethnic history." *Journal of Social Research* (Ranchi) 7:126–135.

Kulp, D. H.
(1925) *Country life in South China: the sociology of familism.* Bureau of Publications, Teachers College, Columbia University, New York.

Laswell, H.
(1958) *Politics: Who Gets What, When, How.* New York: Meridian Books.

Lewis, O. and Barnouw, V.
(1956) "Caste and the jajmani system in a North Indian village." *Scientific Monthly* 83:66–81.

Linck, O. F.
(1959) *A Passage Through Pakistan.* Detroit: Wayne State University Press.

Majumdar, M.
(1948) *Sree Modhusudan.* Calcutta: Bishva Bharati Publications.

Malaviya, H. D.
(1956) *Village panchayats in India.* New Delhi: Economic and Political Research Dept., All India Congress Committee.

Malik, H.
(1963) *Moslem Nationalism in India and Pakistan,* Washington, D. C.

Mandelbaum, D. G.
(1947) "Hindu-Moslem conflict in India." *The Middle East Journal* 1:369–385.
(1948) "The family in India." *Southwestern Journal of Anthropology* 4:123–139.
(1956) "The Kotas in their social setting." In *Introduction to the civilization of India.* Milton Singer, editor. Chicago: University of Chicago Press.
(1964) "Introduction: process and structure in South Asian religion." In *Religion in South Asia,* Edward B. Harper, editor, pp. 5–20. Seattle: University of Washington Press. (Also published in *The Journal of Asian Studies* 23:5–20.)

Marriott, M.
(1955) "Little communities in an indigenous civilization." In *Village India,* Marriott, editor, pp. 171–222. Chicago: University of Chicago Press.

Mathur, K. S.
(1958) "The Indian village: is it structural unity?" *Journal of Social Research* (Ranchi) 1:50–53.

Mencher, J.
(1965) The Nayars of South Malabar. In *Comparative Family Systems,* M. F. Nimkoff, editor, pp. 163–191. Boston: Houghton Mifflin.

Mencher, J. and Goldberg, H.
(1967) *Kinship and marriage regulations among the Namboodiri Brahmins of Kerala.* Man n.s. 2:87–106.

Morris-Jones, W. H.
(1967) *The government and politics of India.* Anchor Books edition. New York: Doubleday and Co.

Nadel, S. F.
(1954) "Caste and government in primitive society." *Journal of the Anthropological Society of Bombay*, pp. 9–22.
Nair, K.
(1963) *Blossoms in the dust*. New York: Frederick A. Praeger.
Nath, V.
(1961) "The village and the community." In *India's Urban Future*, Roy Turner, editor, pp. 139–154. Berkeley and Los Angeles: University of California Press.
Nicholas, R.
(1961) "Caste and government in primitive society." *Journal of the Anthropological Society of Bombay*, pp. 9–22.
(1968) "Structures of Politics in the Villages of Southern Asia." In *Structure and Change in Indian Society*. Edited by Singer, M. Cohn, B. S. (1968), Aldine Pub. Co., Chicago.
(1962) "Villages of the Bengal Delta: a study of ecology and peasant society." Doctoral dissertation, University of Chicago.
(1963) "Ecology and village structure in deltaic West Bengal." *The Economic Weekly* 15:1185–1196.
(1966) *Segmentary factional political systems*. In Political Anthropology, M. S. Swartz, V. W. Turner, and A. Tunden, editors, pp. 49–59. Chicago: Aldine Publishing Co.
O'Malley, L. S. S.
(1934) *India's social heritage*. Oxford: Clarendon Press.
Opler, M. E.
(1956) "The extensions of an Indian village." In *The Indian village: a symposium*. The Journal of Asian Studies 16:5–10.
Orenstein, H.
(1959) "Leadership and caste in a Bombay village." In *Leadership and political institutions in India*, Richard L. Park and Irene Tinker, editors, pp. 415–426. Princeton: Princeton University Press.
(1965) "The structure of Hindu caste values: a preliminary study of hierarchy and ritual defilement." *Ethnology* 4:1–15.
Pakistan Embassy
(1969) *On the Hot Line: Pakistan's Economic Growth*. Washington, D. C.
Piggot, S.
(1954) *Prehistoric India*. Harmonsworth: Penguin Books.
Pradhan, M. C.
(1965) "The Jats of Northern India: their traditional political system." The Economic Weekly 17:1821–1824, 1855–1864.
Rasiduzzaman, M.
(1971) "Dynamics of Regionalism in East Pakistan." Paper presented at the Columbia University National Seminar on Pakistan, April 1971.
(1972) "Leadership, Organization, Strategies and Tactics of the Bangladesh Movement"–in *Asian Survey* vol. xii: 3:185–200.
Rawlinson, A. H.
(1948) *The British Achievement in India*. William Hodge and Co., London.
Retzlaff, R. H.
(1962) *Village government in India*. London: Asia Publishing House.

General Bibliography

Ross, A. D.
(1961) *The Hindu family in its urban setting.* Toronto: University of Toronto Press.
Roy, S. C.
(1934) "Caste, race and religion in India: inadequacies of the current theories of caste." *Man in India* 14:75–220.
Rudolph, L. E. and S. H. Rudolph
(1960) "The political role of India's caste association." *Pacific Affairs* 33: 5–22.
(1967) *The modernity of tradition: political development in India.* Chicago: University of Chicago Press.
Sachchidananda
(1965) *Profiles of tribal culture in Bihar.* Calcutta: Firma K. L. Mukhopadhyay.
Sankalia, H. D.
(1962) *Indian Archaeology Today,* New York.
Saraswati, T. S. S.
(1953) *Unish Sataker Pathick.* Calcutta: Bengal Printers.
Sarker, J. (ed.)
(1948) *History of Bengal.* Dacca: Dacca University Press.
Sarma, J.
(1955) "A village in West Bengal." In *India's Villages,* pp. 161–179, West Bengal Government Press.
Shah, A. M.
(1959) "Social anthropology and the study of historical societies." *The Economic Weekly* 11:953–962.
Shahani, Savitri
(1961) "The joint family: a case study." *The Economic Weekly* 13:1823–1828.
Singer, M.
(1956) Introduction. In "The Indian village: a symposium." *The Journal of Asian Studies* 16:3–5.
(1964) *The social organization of Indian civilization.* Diogenes, Winter issue 1964, pp. 84–119.
(1968) "The Indian joint family in modern industry." In *Structure and change in Indian society,* Milton Singer and Bernard S. Cohn, editors, pp. 423–452. Chicago: Aldine Publishing Co.
Singh, R. D.
(1956) "The Unity of an Indian village." In "The Indian village: a symposium." *The Journal of Asian Studies* 16:10–19.
Singh, Y.
(1959) "Group status of factions in rural community." *Journal of Social Sciences* 2:57–67.
Smith, R. M.
(1962) "Tradition and Modernization in India." *University of Toronto Quarterly,* Vol. XXI:2:337–391. Toronto.
Smith, W. C.
(1957) *Islam in Modern History.* Princeton: Princeton University Press.
Spate, O. H. K.
(1954) *India and Pakistan: a general and regional geography.* New York: E. P. Dutton.

Srinivas, M. N.
(1955) "The social structure of a Mysore village." In *India's villages*, pp. 15–32. Calcutta: West Bengal Government Press.
(1962) *Caste in modern India and other essays*. Bombay: Asia Publishing House.
(1966) *Social change in modern India*. Berkeley and Los Angeles: University of California Press.

Srinivas, M. N. and A. Béteille
(1964) "Networks in Indian social structure." *Man* 64:165–168.

Stephens, W. N.
(1963) *The Family in Cross-Cultural Perspective*. New York: Holt, Rinehart, and Winston.

Symonds, R.
(1950) *The Making of Pakistan*. London: Faber and Faber Ltd.

Tinker, H.
(1963) *India and Pakistan: a Political Analysis*. New York: Frederick A. Praeger.

Trivedi, R. K.
(1965) "Fairs and festivals: Gujarat." *Census of India, 1961*, Vol. 5, part 7-B.

Weber, M.
(1958) *The Religion of India*. Glencoe, Illinois: The Free Press.

Wheeler, M.
(1953) *The Cambridge history of India*. Supplementary vol.: the Indus civilization. Cambridge University Press.

Wilcox, W. A.
(1963) *Pakistan: the Consolidation of a Nation*. New York: Columbia University Press.

Wiser, W. H.
(1963) *The Hindu jajmani system: a socio-economic system inter-relating members of a Hindu village community in service*. Lucknow: Lucknow Publishing House.

Wiser, W. H. and C. V. Wiser
(1963) *Behind mud walls*. Berkeley and Los Angeles: University of California Press.

Wolf, E. R.
(1966) "Kinship, friendship and patron-client relations in complex societies." In *The Social Anthropology of Complex Societies*, Michael Banton, editor. London: Tavistock Publications.

Woodruff, P.
(1964) *The Men Who Ruled India*. Vol 2. New York: Schocken Paperback edition.

Zaidi, S. M. H.
(1970) *The Village Culture in Transition; a study of East Pakistan rural society*. Honolulu: East-West Press.

EPILOGUE, 1987

Sixteen long years have gone by since Liberation (December 16, 1971), and the People's Republic of Bangladesh still faces a formidable array of ideological conflicts. On the one hand, it strives for an effective sense of national identity; on the other, the confluence of different ideologies creates an unending melee in the political arena.

Soon after Liberation, the Head of State and "Founder" of Bangladesh, Sheikh Mujibar Rahman, was killed in a coup. Those members of his family then present in Bangladesh were massacred. The coup leaders installed one Mustaq Ahmed as the president of the country in 1975. Within a few months, General Ziaur Rahman ousted Mustaq Ahmed, declared martial law, and subsequently installed himself as President.

During the period when General Ziaur Rahman reigned (1975-1981), it is said by the Bengalis that there were more than a dozen unsuccessful coups in Bangladesh. Finally, in another coup, General Rahman was killed, and General H.M. Ershad installed himself, first, as a Chief Martial Law Administrator and then as President of Bangladesh.

In addition to counting some two dozen identifiable political parties[1] and their student counterparts, the government is also facing the problem of deciding whether the people of Bangladesh should move in a religious or a secular direction. Ideological conflicts clearly indicate that there is an inadequacy in the decision-making process which, in turn, is inhibiting desired cohesion and, thus, hampering developmental changes in the country.

This is documented in many sources. For instance, *The Chronicle of Higher Education* (23 February 1983:20) writes:

> The military government of Bangladesh closed the University of Dhaka last week following violent anti-government protests during which at least three people were killed and more than 200 injured....
>
> Eyewitnesses told reporters that police and paramilitary forces had fired tear gas and sprayed boiling water at the students. About 50 policemen were injured....
>
> In addition to opposing martial law, the students were protesting a new policy making the teaching of Arabic compulsory in elementary schools.... Critics of the Arabic requirement have charged that the government wants to turn Bangladesh into an Islamic state.

Let us briefly consider some of the relevant background to this student unrest and the symptoms of deeper problems. On Tuesday, December 28, 1982, the Chief Martial Law Administrator, Lt. General H.M. Ershad, said in Dhaka:

> The present-day complicated problems could be solved by implementing the dynamic principles of Islam. If we can reflect the ideals of Islam in every sphere of our national life, only then we shall be able to fulfill the dreams and the hopes and aspirations of the people by achieving overall development of the country *(Bangladesh Observer,* 30 December 1982).

Only a day earlier, on the 27th of December, General Ershad had said:

> Bangladesh is the second biggest Muslim State in the world. Hazrat Muhammad (SM) is enshrined in the heart of every person in this country. They want the establishment of a happy, contented society following the ideals of the Prophet. We have embarked on building a new Bangladesh eliminating poverty, exploitation, disparity and corruption to materialize the hopes and aspirations of the masses *(Bangladesh Times,* 28 December 1982).

At first sight, these two statements by the Head of State constituted hopeful news, particularly to those Bengalis who are sensitive to ideological nuances. Bangladesh, however, follows a unique brand of nationalism which is different from any other nationalist movement we have seen around the world. In other countries, the national boundary usually coincides with the political boundary. In Bangladesh, through their courage and fortitude, Bengalis have carved out a new political boundary which corresponds to their own brand of nationalism. During the initial stages of the Liberation Movement, the focus was on the linguistic boundary alone, obliterating other cultural factors such as religion, values, ethos, etc. This quixotic detachment from social reality placed the Bengali people in a precarious position in post-Independence days.

During the Liberation Movement, this detachment helped the leaders bring the diverse elements together, but the fact remains that these diverse factors cannot be obliterated completely from the people's idea of a nation. Hence, conflict is inevitable. It is rather tragic that most democratic liberation movements (Islam, 1978:91) which have occurred on the subcontinent have resulted in autocratic governments where only a handful of persons play the role of decision makers, ignoring the masses.

On the other hand, in a country where eighty percent of the people are Muslims, fervor for Islamic fundamentalism is also deep-rooted; thus it could be anticipated that the secular liberation movement is bound to collide with Islamic fundamentalists. When General Ershad came to power, the conflict surfaced; even during Ziaur Rahman's regime, it was simmering.

There are several ideas which are evident in the General's speech. First, there are "complicated problems" in Bangladesh which can be solved "by implementing the dynamic principles of Islam," and, second, although "Bangladesh is the second biggest Muslim State in the world," the General has embarked on "building a new Bangladesh." If Islam can solve the problems of Bangladesh, and if Bangladesh is the second largest Muslim State in the world, why does he have to build a new Bangladesh? What is the correlation?

In semantics, we say that meaningless sounds are called "noise." For example, baby talk is noise because the sounds have little correlation with each other or with reality. Similarly, the thought of solving a country's problems by instituting an Islamic regime and, in the process, exerting or making a new country has little correlation with the reality of Bangladesh. Such unrelated utterances are just "noise."

The statements that Bangladesh is the second largest Muslim State in the world, that Hazrat Muhammad (SM) is enshrined in the hearts of every Muslim may be viewed as bits and pieces of knowledge, but they do not constitute understanding. A child specialist, a pediatrician, knows a child, but a mother, even though illiterate, knows a particular child better. The doctor has bits and pieces of knowledge about the child, no doubt, but the mother has *understanding* about the child because she is closest to the child though furthest from "knowledge."

We all know that a Rockefeller or a Henry Ford can write a cheque for two million dollars. I also can write a cheque for two million dollars, because I have a chequebook and know how to write and sign. This is all knowledge, but merely possessing a chequebook, and knowing how to sign a cheque, without having any money in the bank (which is understanding) does not allow me to write a cheque.

So, most of the public speeches, seminars, workshops, and prophecy by pulpit orators, whether by the Chief Martial Law Administrator or any other political leader of present-day Bangladesh, about "eliminating poverty, exploitation, disparity and corruption to materialize the hopes and aspirations of the masses" is full of noise and very little understanding.

A military general can neither know about the quality of the problems Bangladesh has nor claim to have mastered the technique to remedy a political disease. A general who was out of the country during the Liberation War,[2] who did not live in the country during the days of the ideological shift that the populace of Bangladesh went through, is indeed remote from reality.

"Noise" should be avoided as far as prestige may allow; words should be used as far as one's understanding goes, for it is only then that "plans" will have a semblance of reality. People of the world, particularly of Bangladesh, know what happened in this marshy land of ninety million people during the last ten months of 1971.[3]

There is, however, always a fear, the fear of mediocrity. Mediocrity loves mediocrity. That is why a country or, for that matter, a government of mediocre intelligence has to keep up a show. It is very difficult to release oneself from the fetters of false consciousness, but there is no alternative. The country must rise above this in order to prosper.

Words are symbols for reality. If what is being spoken about does not exist in reality, the symbols are only so much noise. In the above cited case, excluding the phrase "second biggest Muslim State," the rest is noise.

Looking at the other end of the spectrum, we encounter a different type of problem. Throughout the War of Liberation, the crystallization of Bengali nationhood took place when Bengali national leaders of the period preached to the populace to avoid anything "Islamic," hence "Pakistani." These were "foreign ideologies," counter to "Bengali ideologies," hence to be avoided at any cost. Bengali leaders, however, did not attack "Islam" directly, although they reminded people that "Allah is Rabbul Alamin" and not "Rabbul Muslemin"; thus, Islam should be avoided as a "foreign ideology."[4] The phrase *foreign ideology* has popular colour in the parlance of present-day Bangladesh. Currently, this phrase is used by many persons on numerous occasions. The rich and poor alike use this phrase. The central theme of many a person's speech is that foreign ideology should be given up.[5] They hold that "no country can prosper by accepting foreign ideology. It is like seeds of poison and should not be allowed to persist in our society."

Now, the matter for reflection is: what is foreign and what is ideology? Foreign means that which is from outside, and ideology means collected results of human thought and action. It is interesting to note that the collected results of human thought and action have always influenced civilization; this knows no national boundary. The torch of truth lit in a corner of the world has from time immemorial lighted the universe. Buddhism, born in India, was certainly "foreign" to the Chinese. Islam, born in Arabia, was "foreign" to Bangladesh and Ayatollah's Iran. Christianity, born in Jerusalem, was definitely "foreign" to the Anglo-Saxons and the Romans, and so on.

Moreover, the great sweep of the Renaissance and the Reformation, which crumbled the old values of the Middle Ages in Europe, was certainly foreign to England, but does that mean that these religions and cultural ideologies were rejected as "foreign" ideologies? Science has broken the barriers and frontiers of nations. It has earned the torch of truth everywhere.

The ideas of Liberty, Fraternity, Equality, born in France during the days of revolution, were definitely foreign to any other country of the world. For that matter, so were the ideas of Socrates, Aristotle, Plato, and Galileo. But would anyone say that these ideologies are "foreign" and, as such, should be given up? In fact, the results of their thinking have become truth and, as such, are all-pervasive.

Again, how do the Bengalis define "foreign" in the context of modern political changes? Before 1947, the whole of India was the homeland. Bengalis used to boast of being Indian. India was not a foreign land. After August 14, 1947, India became a "foreign" country, and Bengalis became Pakistanis. Then again, in 1971, both India and Pakistan became "foreign" to the people of Bangladesh. Today, anything Indian or Pakistani is "foreign," and who knows what will happen in years to come. Hence, in the changing concepts of independence, the term *foreign ideology* is a misnomer.

General Ershad and some others in the group tend to think of Bangladesh as a Muslim country whose people have a highly developed Islamic consciousness and, for that reason, a society with a high degree of homogeneity and solidarity. They believe that South Asia is no longer the primary arena as far as Bangladesh is concerned. To them, Bangladesh is more a part of the Middle East and must, therefore, be concerned with affairs of that region. Its diplomacy and international activity should be directed toward brotherly nations, the wealthy and influential Arab World; links with Arab countries could give Bangladesh the kind of weight in international affairs which it cannot ever hope to get on its own. In reality, today's Bangladesh is a country in which active and competing ethnic identities have emerged. Given the present demographic situation[6] and political setup, these ethnic identities are likely to create greater stress and strain in Bangladesh society and in the State than ever before.

When a large section of a country's population regards the existing political system as "inappropriate," then the country faces a political crisis of a fundamental kind. In such a situation, there is inevitably a debate on the type of polity the country should have. This is precisely what is happening in Bangladesh today. The group or groups who tend to take the easy way out by agreeing to describe it as an "Islamic State" but without any effort at spelling out the implications of this nomenclature for the way the state is to be organized, might do well to remember what Naipal (1981:346) said about Indonesia, which may be paraphrased to apply to Bangladesh:

> Islam did not come to *Bangladesh* [emphasis mine] as a civilization; rather, it came only as a faith, or a complement to the old faiths. It used what was already there.

The present regime is clearly attempting to play upon Islamic sentiments and thereby to generate support and credibility. Meanwhile, opponents of the Islamization programme are trying to label the attempt as gimmickry, as political pyrotechnics by the regime to divert public attention from the real issues so that the public resentment against the regime does not grow any deeper.

In conclusion, I would say that the Bengali Muslims who numerically dominate Bangladesh appear to have a predilection to unreal goals and ethical visions. Because of such a psychic make-up, they have rarely had a sense of success and satisfaction even when they have had achievements to their credit. This is precisely what happened after Bangladesh was established. Instead of a feeling of satisfaction, security and self-confidence for having gained a separate homeland, a fresh feeling of inadequacy and grievance followed the creation of Bangladesh. Values and attitudes do change, but this change has a rhythm of its own which must be honoured. The identification of this rhythm and the consequent modes of direction are lacking in Bangladesh today.

ENDNOTES

[1] Casual reading of any Bangladesh newspaper will confirm this assertion. *Holiday* (a weekly newspaper), 26 February 1983, mentioned the following parties in one of its articles: J.S.D. (Jatya Samajtantri Dal), Workers' Party, Sramik-Krisak-Samajbadi Dal, Bangladesher Samajtantrik Dal, Samyabadi dal-Faction I, Samyabadi dal-Faction II, Bangladesh Muzdur Party led by Abul Basar, C.P.B., N.A.P.(M), N.A.P.(H), Ekota Party, Awami League(H), Awami League (Farid), Gono Azadi League, Awami League, Democratic League, Gana Sanskriti Parishad, Bangladesh Muslim League, Janata Party, Bangladesh Government Party. In the 1986 elections, more than fifty registered political parties participated.
[2] During the "Liberation War" (March-December, 1971), General Ershad (then a colonel) was in West Pakistan and did not or could not participate in the War.
[3] For details, see Bangladesh Association, 1971; Islam, 1973, 1978.
[4] Bengali national leaders at that time consisted mostly of members of the Awami League, a political party advocating secularism as opposed to the Islamic Fundamentalism preached by West Pakistani rulers.
[5] Even the Pro-Moscow and Pro-China groups, two Communist parties of Bangladesh, do not hesitate to urge people to avoid foreign ideology while they preach their own brand of communism.
[6] There is a movement in the Chittagong-Hill-Tract region whereby tribal people are coalescing around a desire for a separate independent state. Even a group of Sylheties in Bangladesh are clamouring for secession.

REFERENCES CITED

Newspapers
Bangladesh Observer (30 December 1982) — English daily from Dhaka, Bangladesh.
Bangladesh Times (25 December 1982) — English daily from Dhaka, Bangladesh.
Chronicle of Higher Education (3 February 1983) — Weekly news on education from Washington, D.C.
Holiday (26 February 1983) — English weekly from Dhaka, Bangladesh.
Dayton Journal Herald (1 April 1983) — Dayton, Ohio daily.

Books and Articles
Bangladesh Association. 1971. *The Case for Bangladesh*. Washington, D.C.
Dil, Shaheen F. 1980. "The Myth of Islamic Resurgence in South Asia." *Current History* 78, No. 856.
Fazlur, Rahman. 1979. *Islam*. Chicago: Chicago University Press, 68.
Islam, A.K.M. Aminul. 1973. "Bangladesh in Transition, Reformation and Accommodation." Southasian Scenes Occasional Paper 21. Ann Arbor: Michigan State University Press, Asian Studies Center.
Islam, A.K.M. Aminul. 1978. *Victorious Victims*. Cambridge: G.K. Hall.
Naipal, V.S. 1981. *In the Land of the Believers*. New York: Harper and Row, 346.

Also Available from Waveland Press, Inc.

Aschenbrenner, *Lifelines: Black Families in Chicago*
Barrett, *Benabarre: The Modernization of a Spanish Village*
Barth, *Nomads of South Persia: The Basseri Tribe of the Khamseh Confederacy*
Bascom, *The Yoruba of Southwestern Nigeria*
Basso, *The Cibecue Apache*
Bastien, *Mountain of the Condor: Metaphor and Ritual in an Andean Ayllu*
Bauman, *Verbal Art as Performance*
Beidelman, *The Kaguru: A Matrilineal People of East Africa*
Bernard-Pelto, *Technology and Social Change, Second Edition*
Cazden, et al., *Functions of Language in the Classroom*
Chinas, *The Isthmus Zapotecs: Women's Roles in Cultural Context*
Cohen, *The Kanuri of Bornu*
Crane-Angrosino, *Field Projects in Anthropology: A Student Handbook, Second Edition*
Davidson, *Chicano Prisoners: The Key to San Quentin*
Deng, *The Dinka of the Sudan*
de Rios, *Visionary Vine: Hallucinogenic Healing in the Peruvian Amazon*
Downs, *The Navajo*
Dozier, *The Pueblo Indians of North America*
Dwyer, *Moroccan Dialogues: Anthropology in Question*
Ekvall, *Fields on the Hoof: Nexus of Tibetan Nomadic Pastoralism*
Fakhouri, *Kafr el-Elow: Continuity and Change of an Egyptian Community, Second Edition*
Faron, *The Mapuche Indians of Chile*
Farrer, *Women and Folklore: Images and Genres*
Fraser, *Fishermen of South Thailand: The Malay Villagers*
Freeman, *Scarcity and Opportunity in an Indian Village*
Friedl, *Women and Men: An Anthropologist's View*
Gamst, *The Qemant: A Pagan Hebraic Peasantry of Ethiopia*
Garbarino, *Big Cypress: A Changing Seminole Community*
Garbarino, *Sociocultural Theory in Anthropology: A Short History*
Gmelch, *The Irish Tinkers: The Urbanization of an Itinerant People, Second Edition*
Gmelch-Zenner, *Urban Life: Readings in Urban Anthropology, 2/E*
Guld, *St. Pascal: Changing Leadership and Social Organization in a Quebec Town*
Gossen, *Chamulas in the World of the Sun: Time and Space in a Maya Oral Tradition*
Halpern-Halpern, *A Serbian Village in Historical Perspective*
Hanson, *Rapan Lifeways: Society and History on a Polynesian Island*
Harris, *Casting Out Anger: Religion Among the Taita of Kenya*
Holmberg, *Nomads of the Long Bow: The Siriono of Eastern Bolivia*
Holmes-Schneider, *Anthropology: An Introduction, Fourth Edition*
Isbell, *To Defend Ourselves: Ecology and Ritual in an Andean Village*
Islam, *A Bangladesh Village: Political Conflict and Cohesion*
Jacobs, *Fun City: An Ethnographic Study of a Retirement Community*
Jacobson, *Itinerant Townsmen: Friendship and Social Order in Urban Uganda*
Jones, *Sanapia: Comanche Medicine Woman*
Jones-Jones, *The Himalayan Woman: A Study of Limbu Women in Marriage and Divorce*
Kaplan-Manners, *Culture Theory*
Kearney, *The Winds of Ixtepeji: World View and Society in a Zapotec Town*
Klima, *The Barabaig: East African Cattle Herders*
Kolenda, *Caste in Contemporary India: Beyond Organic Solidarity*
La Flamme, *Green Turtle Cay: An Island in the Bahamas*
Lamberg-Karlovsky and Sabloff, *Ancient Civilizations: The Near East and Mesoamerica*
Lee, *Freedom and Culture*
Lee, *Valuing the Self: What We Can Learn from Other Cultures*

Lessa, *Ulithi: A Micronesian Design for Living*
Lyon, *Native South Americans: Ethnology of the Least Known Continent*
Malinowski, *Argonauts of the Western Pacific*
McCurdy-Spradley, *Issues in Cultural Anthropology: Selected Readings*
McFee, *Modern Blackfeet: Montanans on a Reservation*
Messenger, *Inis Beag: Isle of Ireland*
Middleton, *The Lugbara of Uganda*
Mitchell, *The Bamboo Fire: An Anthropologist in New Guinea*
Moore, et al., *The Biocultural Basis of Health: Expanding Views of Medical Anthropology*
Nash, *In the Eyes of the Ancestors: Belief and Behavior in a Mayan Community*
Netting, *Cultural Ecology, Second Edition*
Norbeck, *Changing Japan, Second Edition*
Ohnuki-Tierney, *The Ainu of the Northwest Coast of Southern Sakhalin*
Ottenheimer, *Marriage in Domoni: Husbands & Wives in an Indian Ocean Community*
Pandian, *Anthropology and the Western Tradition: Toward an Authentic Anthropology*
Partridge, *The Hippie Ghetto: The Natural History of a Subculture*
Pelto, *The Snowmobile Revolution: Technology and Social Change in the Arctic*
Preston, *Cult of the Goddess: Social and Religious Change in a Hindu Temple*
Quintana-Floyd, *'Que Gitano!: Gypsies of Southern Spain*
Read, *Children of Their Fathers: Growing Up among the Ngoni*
Reck, *In the Shadow of Tlaloc: Life in a Mexican Village*
Richardson, *San Pedro, Colombia: Small Town in a Developing Society*
Rohner-Betrauer, *The Kwakiutl: Indians of British Columbia*
Rosenfeld, *"Shut Those Thick Lips!": A Study of Slum School Failure*
Rosman-Rubel, *Feasting with Mine Enemy: Rank and Exchange among Northwest Coast Societies*
Salzmann-Scheufler, *Komarov: A Czech Farming Village*
Schaffer-Cooper, *Mandinko: The Ethnography of a West African Holy Land*
Spindler, *Being an Anthropologist: Fieldwork in Eleven Cultures*
Spindler, *Culture Change and Modernization: Mini-Models and Case Studies*
Spindler-Spindler, *Dreamers With Power: The Menominee*
Spindler, *Education and Cultural Process: Anthropological Approaches, Second Edition*
Spradley, *Culture and Cognition: Rules, Maps and Plans*
Sutherland, *Gypsies: The Hidden Americans*
Thomas, *Refiguring Anthropology: First Principles of Probability and Statistics*
Tyler, *Cognitive Anthropology*
Tyler, *India: An Anthropological Perspective*
Underhill, *Papago Woman*
van Beek, *The Kapsiki of the Mandara Hills*
Vigil, *From Indians to Chicanos: The Dynamics of Mexican American Culture*
Wagley, *Welcome of Tears: The Tapirape Indians of Central Brazil*
Ward, *Them Children: A Study in Language Learning*
Whitten, *Black Frontiersmen: Afro-Hispanic Culture of Ecuador and Colombia*
Williams, *Community in a Black Pentecostal Church*
Wilson, *Good Company: A Study of Nyakyusa Age-Villages*
Wolcott, *A Kwakiutl Village and School*
Wolcott, *The Man in the Principal's Office: An Ethnography*
Yoors, *The Gypsies*

Waveland Press, Inc.   P.O. Box 400   Prospect Heights, IL 60070   (312) 634-0081